Breakdown

JEFF BINGAMAN | *Foreword by Norman J. Ornstein*

Breakdown

LESSONS FOR A CONGRESS IN CRISIS

High Road Books | Albuquerque

HIGH
ROAD

High Road Books is an imprint
of the University of New Mexico Press

© 2022 by Jeff Bingaman
All rights reserved. Published 2022
Printed in the United States of America

ISBN 978-0-8263-6414-2 (cloth)
ISBN 978-0-8263-6415-9 (electronic)

Library of Congress Control Number: 2022939070

Founded in 1889, the University of New Mexico sits on the traditional home-lands of the Pueblo of Sandia. The original peoples of New Mexico—Pueblo, Navajo, and Apache—since time immemorial have deep connections to the land and have made significant contributions to the broader community statewide. We honor the land itself and those who remain stewards of this land throughout the generations and also acknowledge our committed relationship to Indigenous peoples. We gratefully recognize our history.

Cover illustration: Douglas Rissing | istockphoto.com
Designed by Mindy Basinger Hill
Composed in 10/14pt Parkinson Electra Pro and Mr Eaves Mod OT

Contents

Foreword

I CAME TO WASHINGTON IN THE FALL OF 1969, over thirteen years before Jeff Bingaman arrived in the Senate. When I arrived, the nation and Washington were in turmoil, driven in part by the war in Vietnam and by the growing tension between the parties. Republican Richard Nixon, who had run for president in 1968 on a "law and order" platform—the so-called Southern Strategy to try to outflank George Wallace—won with just over 43 percent of the national popular vote, barely beating Hubert Humphrey with Wallace finishing third, with 13.5 percent of the vote. Humphrey, of course, had been damaged by a bitter convention in Chicago, with a Democratic Party divided by more than the war, and scarred deeply by the assassinations of Martin Luther King Jr. and Robert F. Kennedy.

Nixon came to Washington to face a Democratic Congress, one in which the party had been in the majority in both House and Senate continuously since 1955. But both parties were in flux. In the decades before the sixties, Democrats had a stranglehold on the South, winning at every level there, and the conservative Democrats from the region—called "Boll Weevils," for the insect that infects cotton—provided enough votes to combine with the more liberal lawmakers from other regions to solidify the party's majorities. That hegemony began to crack with the 1964 election—Republican Barry Goldwater carried five deep blue Southern states, buoyed by his opposition to the 1964 Civil Rights Act. For Republicans, the many moderate and liberal lawmakers from the Northeast, mid-Atlantic, and West Coast regions were being supplanted by Democrats as those regions became less red.

A Washington where the center was dominant and there was major overlap between the parties was changing to one where the parties were becoming more homogeneous and separate in their views. But at the same time, major issues dividing the country did not divide neatly along party lines. The strongest supporters of Nixon's policy advancing the war in Vietnam included major Southern Democrats; the strongest opponents included many liberal and moderate Republicans. Nixon, despite a largely antagonistic relationship with the majority in Congress, still worked with Democrats on creating the Environmental Protection Agency, passing the Clean Air and Clean Water Acts, and revenue sharing with the states. And inside Congress, there were partnerships across party lines like the one between George McGovern and Bob Dole to combat hunger in America.

Of course, the relationships deteriorated after the 1972 election, with the impeachment of Nixon, although even that was characterized by a bipartisan investigation in the Senate. And the ascendance of Gerald Ford to the presidency, despite his long tenure in the House and conciliatory manner and approach, did not eliminate either partisan or interbranch divisions. That was true even as Jimmy Carter won the presidency in 1976, uniting party control in Washington, and with the election of Ronald Reagan and the first Republican Senate in a quarter century.

But for all the troubles and tensions, the Congress that Jeff Bingaman joined after the 1982 election still managed to work. The leaders—Speaker of the House Tip O'Neill and House minority leader Bob Michel, Senate majority leader Howard Baker and Senate minority leader Robert Byrd— had strong relationships with each other and managed to avoid gridlock and meltdowns. As deficits rose following major tax cuts in Reagan's first year, the two parties worked together to ameliorate them, with a combination of tax increases and spending restraint. Nineteen eighty-three brought sweeping reform of Social Security, a bipartisan triumph. And, as Bingaman recounts in this book, there were many areas where Congress made progress, including those where he was deeply engaged, even if the progress was halting at times.

But the polarization that had been building since the mid-1960s was already being transformed into something far more insidious and troubling. A key moment came when Newt Gingrich was elected to the House in 1978, four years before Bingaman arrived in the Senate. Gingrich arrived with a full-blown strategy, complete with tactics, to achieve a Republican majority in the House after twenty-four consecutive years of Democratic control. It took him sixteen years, fueled both by a rise in anti-Washington populism in the late 1980s and early 1990s and the election of Bill Clinton, providing the opportunity for a subsequent midterm disaster for Clinton's Democratic Party. Key to that was molding the GOP into a parliamentary-style minority party, uniting in opposition to every presidential initiative.

More broadly, core to Gingrich's strategy was the tribalization of American politics, destruction of the institutional reputation of Congress, and radicalization of policy. The norms of behavior in Congress, what scholars have called the "regular order," were deliberate casualties along the way.

It worked, and not just on the House. The tribalism—moving from vigorous differences in views but a mutual respect between officeholders of different parties to mutual contempt, a belief that the opposition is evil and trying to destroy our way of life, that working with them is like sleeping with the enemy—metastasized down to state legislatures and the public as a whole, and also gravitated to the Senate, especially as House members steeped in Gingrichian approaches moved to the Senate and brought their combative and extreme views with them.

The rise of tribal and social media and the reemergence of sharp populism with the economic collapse in 2008 and 2009 amplified the trends. And with the election of Barack Obama, post-Gingrich Republicans, including especially Senate Republican leader Mitch McConnell, embraced his tactics of obdurate opposition to the new president and distortion of the Senate's rules and norms to create the same kind of midterm backlash that Gingrich had helped create in Clinton's first term. McConnell especially found that he could create a new and potent weapon to help along the way, using the Senate's filibuster in ways it had not been employed previously, as a weapon of mass obstruction on executive and judicial nominations and on legislation.

Through his thirty years in the Senate, Jeff Bingaman was a model senator—fitting the "workhorse, not show horse" description. From defense policy to public lands use, energy to health care, Bingaman worked to craft policy that served New Mexicans and the country at large. But as he recounts in this book—which weaves his own experiences into the path of progress and regress, in these and other key policy areas, with observations about the Senate and broader politics—the ability to find solutions to vexing problems facing the country waned over those decades, and the dysfunction accelerated even more in Barack Obama's first term and after Bingaman left the Senate.

The title expresses the reality—there has been a breakdown in our politics, and especially in the Senate. It is not that there are no more Bingaman-style senators; there are serious-minded, pragmatic, intellectually impressive, and honest lawmakers. But the Republican Party in the Senate is now more focused on obstruction than finding bipartisan solutions to serious national problems, and the rules in the body, which can make the place maddeningly slow but still able to act, have been distorted to serve obstructionist ends. So it is appropriate that Bingaman, an institutionalist with deep respect for the Senate's history and mores, now believes that serious reform, starting with the filibuster, is necessary. His judgments and observations, backed by experience, are important and make this book extraordinarily important and valuable.

Norman J. Ornstein, 2022

Norman J. Ornstein has spent over four decades in Washington studying politics, elections, and the US Congress. He is the author of several highly acclaimed books, including *It's Even Worse Than It Looks: How the American Constitutional System Collided with the New Politics of Extremism*, which he coauthored with Thomas E. Mann.

Acknowledgments

I COULD NOT HAVE COMPLETED THIS BOOK without the generous help of many people.

First, Gail MacQuesten helped immensely at every step of the process, from research to organization to formatting. I thank her for her competence and persistence in getting the book from concept to completion.

John Bingaman, Patrick Von Bargen, Virginia White, and David Pike all made useful suggestions that improved the manuscript. Stephen Hull at UNM Press made many useful suggestions that I have incorporated in the text. Lauren Camp reviewed early drafts of several chapters and helped make them more readable. Bob Simon reviewed and suggested improvements in the chapters on energy and climate change, as did Jorge Silva-Bañuelos in connection with the case study on the Valles Caldera. Don Lamm and Andy Ross were both helpful in reviewing earlier drafts and providing advice on how to find a publisher.

I also thank the Rockefeller Foundation for hosting Anne and me at their Bellagio Center Residency Program, where I wrote early drafts of several chapters.

I thank Norm Ornstein for his excellent foreword. Norm has distinguished himself as an expert on the functioning of Congress. I am honored that he has provided historical context for much of what is discussed in the book.

I thank the people of New Mexico for electing me to represent them in the Senate, and once again thank the dedicated men and women who worked with me on our staff. No public official can accomplish anything without the help of smart, devoted public servants. I was blessed to have many exceptionally capable men and women working on our Senate staff. There are too many for me to mention individually, but as I stated in my farewell speech to the Senate, I am deeply grateful for their exemplary work.

Finally, I thank my wife, Anne, and our son, John, and his wife, Marlene, for their support and encouragement, both during my time in the Senate, and since. Without Anne's encouragement and help I would not have been elected to the Senate, and certainly would not have stayed there for thirty years.

Introduction

THE POLLS CLOSE AT 7:00 P.M. in New Mexico.

At 7:01 p.m. on November 2, 1982, my wife, Anne, our three-year-old son, John, my parents, Jess and Beth Bingaman, and Anne's mother, brother, and sister-in-law were watching the national returns in our room at the AMFAC hotel (now the Sheraton), near the airport in Albuquerque. Dan Rather, the CBS anchor, recognizing the polls had closed in the Rocky Mountain region, announced, "We are now able to project the attorney general of New Mexico, Jeff Bingaman, as the winner in the race for the US Senate in that state." This was before they had counted a single vote.

Once the vote count ended, Dan Rather had been right.

The campaign leading up to election night had been hard-fought. In the primary, my opponent was former New Mexico governor Jerry Apodaca. In the general election I was challenging the incumbent US senator, former astronaut Harrison "Jack" Schmitt. Our campaign was the only successful effort to unseat an incumbent Republican US senator that year.

Two months later, on January 3, 1983, I took the oath of office in the old Senate chamber in the Capitol with Vice President George H. W. Bush officiating.

I remained in the Senate thirty years, until 2013. This provided ample opportunity to experience the Senate and the Congress in action. Occasionally Congress functioned well. At other times, dysfunction was the order of the day. That dysfunction increased beginning in 1995, and since I left the Senate it has increased even more.

In the first few years following my election, as I traveled around New Mexico meeting with constituents, the questions I heard most often were, "Are Washington and the Senate like you expected? What has surprised you about the place?"

Here is a short list of things I had not expected:

- Congress spends much of its time reacting to events outside its control. Some of those events are real, for example, floods, droughts, terrorist attacks, hurricanes, mass shootings, and economic crises. Some events requiring a response are more manufactured, whether by the Congress itself (such as crises to maintain government funding, and debt ceiling increases), by the administration in power, by an interest group, or, sometimes, by the media.
- Congress devotes much time and effort to annual routines, such as attempting to pass a budget resolution, enacting appropriations bills (or more often than not these days, continuing resolutions), and, in the Senate, confirming presidential nominees.
- Members of Congress are under more pressure to toe the party line than I had expected. Pressure comes both from congressional leaders and constituents.
- Ideology, or political philosophy, often wins out over pragmatism in decision-making.
- Special interests, both through their involvement in campaigns and their lobbying activities, have a greater influence on the outcome of legislative efforts than I had expected to be the case. Their undue influence on both the administration and the Congress often frustrates efforts to enact policies to benefit the public.
- And many we describe as the "media" have a well-defined political agenda of their own and are more interested in influencing policy than in reporting the news. That agenda often is dictated by their financial interest, even to the extent of pandering to the misconceptions of their audience and reinforcing false information.

I arrived in the Senate with a naïve view of the world, but the reality quickly became apparent.

During those thirty years, and since, the House of Representatives and the Senate have changed—for the worse. That change has made it more difficult for Congress to do the work of the people. This book identifies major sources of the dysfunction, both in the breakdown of governing norms that, in the past, allowed Congress to function with less conflict, and in the increased outside pressures facing legislators. It also shows how that dysfunction has impacted legislation in eight major policy areas, and continues to do so. And finally, it includes suggestions for Congress and its members. I hope those suggestions can help overcome some of the dysfunction.

PART I

Dysfunction
in the Congress

1   The Breakdown of Congressional Governing Norms

OCTOBER 7, 2021—the morning headlines bring it all back: "Senate Nearing Short-Term Deal over Debt Limit"; "Retreat by McConnell"; "A Temporary Agreement Would Push the Crisis into December."

Ten years ago, in the summer of 2011, I was still in the Senate. We had just averted another crisis. As in the 2021 crisis, the Republican leader, Mitch McConnell, had threatened to block an increase in the debt ceiling.

On August 3, 2011, on a Southwest Airlines flight from Baltimore to Albuquerque, I wrote in my journal:

> Today starts the August break. August is a beautiful month in New Mexico. It will be a relief to be away from the intrigue and conniving that dominate Washington.
>
> Yesterday we had the final vote in the Senate to pass the Budget Control Act of 2011. This was the price Republicans demanded to consent to raising the debt ceiling.
>
> The last few weeks have been characterized by threats to let the government default on its obligations, and tough negotiating, particularly by Boehner and McConnell.
>
> The worst part is that Republican success with these demands will embolden them to make similar demands as the quid pro quo for future debt ceiling increases.
>
> This manufactured crisis adds greatly to the economic uncertainty currently a drag on economic growth. I believe the push by Republicans will continue with the threat now being a refusal to fund the government.

The 2011 debt ceiling crisis prompted my downbeat assessment. It was a manufactured crisis, just like the 2021 debt ceiling crisis was manufactured. Also like the 2021 crisis, it was a dramatic demonstration of the dysfunction in Congress.

Early that summer, Treasury secretary Tim Geithner had advised Congress that to avoid defaulting on its obligations, the government would have to enact an increase in the debt ceiling no later than August 2. In July, Speaker of the House John Boehner told President Barack Obama that, even if it meant the government would default on its obligations, the House would not agree to increase the debt ceiling, unless the president and Senate Democrats agreed to substantial spending cuts. As the August 2 deadline approached, negotiations between the White House and Capitol Hill intensified. Financial markets declined in the face of the increased uncertainty.

The Budget Control Act set up a complex procedure to permit an increase in the debt ceiling and cuts in spending over the next ten years. In a vote of "no confidence" about what had occurred and what Congress had enacted, on August 5 Standard & Poor's downgraded the long-term credit rating of US government bonds for the first time in history.

How did we get to this situation?

In January 1983, four other freshmen and I were sworn in to the US Senate. President Ronald Reagan was in his first term, and Republicans controlled the Senate 54 to 46. Howard Baker (R-TN) was the Republican majority leader. Robert C. Byrd (D-WV) led the Democrats. Tip O'Neill was Speaker of the House. There were no threats to shut down the government. There were no threats to default on the national debt. In fact, we raised the debt ceiling twice that year. Threats to filibuster were rare, and presidential nominations for judicial positions and positions within the administration were either accepted or rejected, without excessive delay. Congressional leaders of both parties shared a sense of responsibility for keeping the government and the Congress functioning. The president and congressional leaders adhered to certain "governing norms," or understandings, about how each institution would function.

Governing norms are not constitutional requirements, or statutes, or even rules, but are understandings and traditions about how officeholders and institutions behave and interact. Steven Levitsky and Daniel Ziblatt refer to these as the "soft guardrails" of American democracy.[1] President Donald Trump's repeated violations of presidential governing norms left many of us mortified, but before Trump, as early as 1995, the breakdown of congressional governing norms was already underway.

In late 1995 and early 1996 Republicans, under the leadership of House Speaker Newt Gingrich, engineered two major government shutdowns.

This demonstrated to me that we were in a new era. The American people could no longer assume both parties would cooperate to maintain a functioning government. Shutting down the government and threatening default on the national debt became an accepted tactic for Congress to increase leverage in negotiations with the president.

How we traveled from the Senate that I joined in 1983 to the gridlock that created the 2011 debt ceiling crisis, and the 2021 debt ceiling crisis, traces back to 1994 when House Republicans elected Gingrich as speaker.

The Constitution sets out the powers and duties of the Congress in Article 1, sections 8 and 9. Although there is a long list of important duties, some are more important than others. I categorize the duties of Congress as either "essential" or as "everything else."

The "essential" duties of Congress involve ensuring that the government can operate. The four most important are:

- raising revenue,
- appropriating money,
- permitting the secretary of the Treasury to borrow, as necessary, to meet government obligations, and,
- in the Senate, providing "advice and consent" on presidential nominations.

The dysfunction we saw in Congress during the 2011 debt ceiling crisis was part of a more general dysfunction that, to a large extent, had resulted from four new tactics that have impeded Congress's ability to perform these "essential" duties. These new tactics are:

- shutting down the government,
- threatening to default on the national debt,

and, in the Senate,

- abusing the right to filibuster, and
- refusing to consider a president's nominee to the Supreme Court.

Each represents a breakdown in a well-established governing norm. Each has contributed substantially to the dysfunction in Congress.

In 1995–1996, congressional Republicans used the first tactic, shutting down the government, to gain leverage in negotiations with President Bill Clinton. They used the same tactic later with President Obama.

Democrats also made the mistake of refusing to fund the government for a three-day period in early 2018. And then in December 2018, President Trump used the tactic, by refusing to sign legislation to fund eight departments of the federal government until Congress would agree to his demand to fund construction of a border wall.

The second of these tactics—threatening to default on the national debt—had its most damaging effects in the 2011 debt ceiling crisis.

The third tactic that has contributed to recent Senate dysfunction is the abuse of the right to filibuster. "Filibuster" is a tactic used in the US Senate to prevent a measure from being brought to a vote. Under Senate rules, proponents of a measure can only end a filibuster by first filing a cloture petition signed by twelve senators, and then getting sixty votes to "invoke cloture." Political scientists usually cite the filibuster as the main problem keeping the Senate from functioning as it should. While the filibuster has for many decades been an obstacle to enacting controversial legislation, only recently have we seen it used by the minority to obstruct the regular business of the Senate.

A fourth tactic contributing to dysfunction in the Senate is refusing to consider a president's nominee for the Supreme Court. In 2016, Senate Republicans denied President Obama the right to a hearing on his nominee for the Supreme Court even though the nomination was made more than ten months before the end of his presidency.

In combination, these breakdowns in congressional governing norms have often left Congress and the government hurtling from crisis to crisis. The public deserves better.

Shutting Down the Government: The Refusal to Appropriate Money

For the government to function, Congress, together with the president, must enact legislation to provide the needed funds. As Article I, section 9, clause 7 of the Constitution states, "No money shall be drawn from the Treasury, but in consequence of Appropriations made by law."

The governing norm during most of our nation's history, and when I arrived in the Senate in 1983, has been for Congress and the president to support maintaining a functioning government. The normal way to maintain a functioning government is to enact appropriations bills once a year, but getting those bills enacted on time is hard to do. It is not easy to get the House and Senate to agree on what to include, and to get the president to sign the legislation. The solution Congress came up with was "continuing resolutions" (i.e., short-term spending bills that maintain current funding levels until all can agree on a more acceptable solution). Enacting continuing resolutions had become a normal part of the appropriations process in most fiscal years.

That was 1983. In 1995, that changed.

THE 1995–1996 GOVERNMENT SHUTDOWNS

In the 1994 election, Republicans won control of both houses of Congress. Eight new Republican senators and fifty-four new Republican members of Congress came to Washington. It was the first time Republicans had won control of the House since 1952, and when the new Congress convened in 1995, Republicans felt emboldened.

Their first act was to elect Newt Gingrich as speaker. His election set the stage for confrontation with President Clinton later that year. The dispute centered on funding levels for education, the environment, public health, Medicaid, and Medicare—all programs important to the president, the Democrats in the Congress, and the American people.

When negotiations between the Congress and President Clinton on those funding levels failed, the House chose *not* to enact a continuing resolution. On November 4, funding for the government ceased. Five days later the House relented and passed a short-term spending bill, but when that bill expired, since the president and congressional Republicans were still at an impasse, and the House was unwilling to pass another spending bill, a second shutdown occurred. It lasted from December 16, 1995, through January 6, 1996.

In speaking on the Senate floor on December 20, 1995, during the second of the two shutdowns, I quoted the following statement Gingrich had made to the *Wall Street Journal*. Gingrich said:

That's the key strategic decision made on election night a year ago.

If you are going to operate with his [the president's] veto being the ultimate trump, you have to operate within a very narrow range of change. . . . You had to find a trump to match his trump. And the *right not to pass money bills* is the only trump that is equally strong.

I then gave my views on Gingrich's so-called "right not to pass money bills":

The Speaker talks about this right, this so-called right. The obvious question is whether this is an appropriate and an acceptable trump for the Presidential veto, as the Speaker seems to believe, or whether, on the contrary, it is an abuse of power. . . . The Founders of the country assumed that the failure of the President to sign legislation or the failure of Congress to enact legislation would be based on specific disagreements on what that legislation should contain, not on the desire of either the Congress or the President to extort concessions from the other on basic policy differences.

Mr. President, I use the word "extort" here because I believe it accurately describes the current situation. The dictionary defines "extort" as "to wrest or wring from a person by violence, intimidation or abuse of authority."

I believe we have an attempt here to wrest or wring concessions from the President by abuse of authority.

This abuse of power or extorting of concessions from the President by refusing to maintain the basic services of Government is not part of the checks and balances that the Framers of the Constitution envisioned. They assumed that the maintenance of government activities which both the Congress and the President deemed to be worthwhile would be supported by mutual consent of the two branches of government. They did not anticipate that one branch would be willing to kill its own children unless the other branch agreed to give ground on policy disputes. . . .

Today we should pass a continuing resolution to bring the Government back to full operation.[2]

That continuing resolution that I and many others were calling for passed January 6, 1996, and the second of these shutdowns ended.

The effects of the shutdowns had been noticeable to many Americans. It resulted in health and welfare services for military veterans being curtailed, national parks being closed, and applications for passports and visas going unprocessed. The US tourism and airline industries incurred substantial losses. The Congressional Budget Office calculated the cost of the shutdowns at $1.4 billion. Most commentators believed the shutdowns had hurt congressional Republicans, and Clinton's strong showing in his 1996 reelection supported that view.

In 2013, eighteen years later, Republican congressional leaders showed they had not learned from the earlier damaging shutdowns.

THE 2013 GOVERNMENT SHUTDOWN

After the 1995 and 1996 shutdowns, Republican threats to force additional shutdowns subsided for the rest of the Clinton presidency. During the presidency of George W. Bush between 2001 and 2009, there were no serious efforts to shut down the government. However, after President Obama took office in 2009, Republicans began making these threats again. The threats became even more strident after they regained control of the House of Representatives in 2011.

On October 1, 2013, after I had left the Senate, Republicans once again shut down the government. The Affordable Care Act (ACA) was the issue in dispute. The ACA had become law three-and-a-half years earlier, in March 2010. Despite this, in 2013 the Republican-led House insisted that any spending bill would have to contain language to delay implementation of the ACA. Such a provision could not have passed the Democratic-controlled Senate. Even if it could have, President Obama would have vetoed it. But because of Republican demands for this delaying and defunding language, Congress could not pass a continuing resolution and the government closed. After sixteen days House Republicans agreed to pass a short-term funding bill proposed by Senators Harry Reid and McConnell, ending the impasse. That bill funded the government for three months, until January 15, 2014. It also suspended the debt limit until February 7, ensuring that, until that date, the federal government could continue to meet its financial obligations.

THE JANUARY 2018 DEMOCRATS' SHUTDOWN

Democrats, myself included, have denounced government shutdowns initiated by Republicans. Unfortunately, Senate Democrats used the same tactic in 2018. It was a mistake, but the pressures that led to it were substantial.

The January 2018 shutdown resulted from the failed negotiation between President Trump and Senate Republicans, on one side, and Senate Democrats on the other, over continuing the legal status of so-called Dreamers. In 2012 President Obama had issued an executive order establishing the Deferred Action for Childhood Arrivals program (DACA). That order protected from deportation undocumented children who were younger than sixteen when their parents brought them to this country, if they arrived here prior to June 2007. On September 5, 2017, Attorney General Jeff Sessions announced that the program was being rescinded, effective March 5, 2018.

In January 2018, negotiations to reinstate the DACA program were taking place as part of efforts to pass another short-term spending bill, the fourth since the start of the 2018 fiscal year. On Friday, January 19, as the midnight deadline for passing a spending bill approached, Democrats in the Senate thought they were within reach of securing an agreement both to fund the government and to protect the legal status of Dreamers. At that point Senate Republican leader McConnell, I assume at President Trump's urging, refused to include the proposed resolution of the Dreamer issue in the spending bill. In effect, he called the Democrats' bluff, and Democrats denied Republicans the votes needed to pass the short-term spending bill.

After a weekend of finger-pointing, on Monday, three days later, Senate Democrats corrected their mistake, and the Senate voted 81 to 18 to pass the short-term spending bill, even without the language protecting Dreamers. As part of the agreement to go forward, Republicans committed to set a time in February for full debate and consideration of proposals to provide continued legal status for Dreamers. After that debate in February, as almost everyone had expected, the issue remained unresolved.

Various commentators and immigrant advocacy groups condemned Senate Democrats for supporting the reopening of the government without some protection for Dreamers. Those criticisms ignored the reality that reopening the government was the only course that made sense. Public sentiment would not support defunding the government until this problem was resolved. Once again, shutting down the government had proved to be an ineffective and damaging way to gain leverage in a policy dispute. In addition to failing to achieve its purpose, it had reinforced the public perception of a dysfunctional government.

THE DECEMBER 2018 TRUMP SHUTDOWN: THE PRESIDENT GETS IN THE ACT

While Congress had shut the government to increase its leverage on the president, during my time in the Senate, presidents did not use this same tactic. Presidents Clinton and Obama, who both faced government shutdowns, stated their desire to maintain a functioning government, and their willingness to sign continuing resolutions to do so. I'm sure both believed the public would blame them for any shutdown they did not at least try to avoid.

That changed with President Trump. He gave early warning of his plans in a tweet issued July 29, 2018: "I would be willing to 'shut down' government if the Democrats do not give us the votes for Border Security, which includes the Wall."[3] On July 31 he tweeted, "a Government Shutdown is a very small price to pay for a safe and Prosperous America . . . I don't care what the political ramifications are . . ."[4]

A number of Republicans took issue with the president's threat, out of concern that it would damage them in the upcoming November election. Representative Tom Cole (R-OK) said, "We're going to have a challenging midterm anyway, and I don't see how putting the attention on shutting down the government when you control the government is going to help you."[5]

The president seemed to agree with Cole's point about not shutting the government prior to the midterm elections, but once the elections had passed, on December 11, he took the occasion of an Oval Office meeting with the Democratic leaders of Congress, Chuck Schumer (D-NY) and Nancy Pelosi (D-CA), to reiterate his willingness to shut down the government unless Congress appropriated the funds he demanded to build a wall along the US-Mexico border. With TV cameras running, Trump stated, "I am proud to shut the government for border security. . . . I will be the one to shut [the government] down. I'm not going to blame you for it . . . I will take the mantle. I will be the one to shut it down."[6]

On December 22 the president made good on his threat. The

continuing resolution providing funds to maintain a functioning government expired that day, and Republican leaders in both the House and Senate, at President Trump's urging, brought to the Senate floor an appropriations bill that included $5.7 billion toward the cost of constructing a wall on the US-Mexico border. Democrats in the Senate opposed the bill, and it failed to receive the necessary votes for passage. At that point Senator McConnell, the Republican leader, refused to bring up a spending bill without the border wall funds included, and eight departments of the federal government saw their funding end.

This partial shutdown lasted thirty-four days, qualifying it as the longest in US history.

On January 24, thirty-four days after the shutdown began, the Republican leader scheduled votes on two proposals to reopen the government. The first was President Trump's proposal to provide the $5.7 billion for border wall construction and also provide legal status for Dreamers for three years. That proposal failed to get the necessary votes for passage. The second vote was on the Democrat's proposal to reopen the government for two weeks, pay back wages to all federal workers, and use the two weeks for serious negotiations with the president on funding for border security. That proposal also failed to pass.

The next day, on January 25, the shutdown ended when the House and Senate unanimously passed, and the president signed, a three-week funding bill that did not include money for a border wall. On the Friday morning prior to the president's announcement that he would sign a new continuing resolution, air traffic control announced that, because of staffing shortages caused by employees calling in sick, planes coming in and out of LaGuardia Airport were being delayed by at least one-and-a-half hours.

In announcing his agreement to reopen the government, President Trump reiterated his demand for the $5.7 billion for border wall construction, and stated that if the funds were not provided within the upcoming three weeks of negotiations, he would have to either shut down the government again or use his authority as president to declare a national emergency and order the wall to be built. When the three weeks ended, President Trump signed the legislation to fund the government, but also issued a Declaration of National Emergency and directed that over $8

FEDERAL FUNDING GAPS LASTING MORE THAN
ONE DAY, 1995–2020

1995	Nov. 13–19	5 days	Clinton
1995–96	Dec. 15–Jan. 6	21 days	Clinton
2013	Sept. 30–Oct. 17	16 days	Obama
2018	Jan. 19–22	2 days	Trump
2018–19	Dec. 21–Jan. 25	34 days	Trump

Source: *History, Art & Archives, United States House of Representatives,*
"Funding Gaps and Shutdowns in the Federal Government," November 18,
2021, https//history.house.gov/Institution/Shutdown/Government
-Shutdowns/.

billion of funds appropriated for other purposes be used to pay for border
wall construction.

In a January 14, 2019, interview with NPR, former Speaker Newt Gingrich defended his own use of shutdowns in 1995–1996. He characterized
shutdowns as "part of the American system."[7] In fact, shutdowns and
threats to shut down the government were not a normal part of the American system before he became Speaker of the House. The table above
shows the frequency and duration of shutdowns from 1995 to the present.

We have come to a point in our politics where the public judges the
seriousness of a politician's commitment on an issue by whether he or she
cares enough about it to shut down the government. If Democrats in the
Senate aren't willing to keep the government shut to gain legal residency
for immigrants covered by DACA, they get criticized for lack of commitment. If President Trump isn't willing to shut down the government and
keep it shut to force Congress to appropriate money for his "wall," many
of his core supporters question his commitment on that issue. And the
more demagoguery on display before the shutdown occurs, and during
the shutdown, the more difficult it is to resolve the dispute.

I will give the last word on this issue to my friend Lamar Alexander
from Tennessee:

Shutting down the government of the United States of America should never, ever be used as a bargaining chip for any issue, period. It should be to governing as chemical warfare is to real warfare. It should be banned. It should be unthinkable.[8]

I agree with Senator Alexander's view.

Threatening Default on the Debt: The Refusal to Permit Borrowing

A second example of a breakdown in governing norms involves the ability of government to borrow what it needs to meet the obligations it has incurred. The tactic, used by Republican congressional leaders in negotiations with President Obama in 2011, was to threaten default on the national debt by refusing to raise the debt ceiling. In 2021, that same tactic was again trotted out by Senate Republicans.

One of the powers of Congress enumerated in Article I, section 8 of the Constitution is the power "to borrow Money on the Credit of the United States." Such a need arises when the revenue raised (through taxes, royalties, tariffs, etc.) is not enough to cover the spending Congress has approved. In fact, revenues fall short of expenditures during most years, and the government has to borrow.

As a matter of arithmetic, when Congress enacts the laws that raise revenue and the laws appropriating money, it also determines how much the secretary of the Treasury will need to borrow. If Congress wants to reduce the need to borrow, it can either raise more revenue or cut spending.

Despite this reality, many decades ago, as part of the Second Liberty Bonds Act of 1917, Congress enacted our first statutory "debt ceiling." Twenty-two years later, in 1939, Congress enacted the first limit on total accumulated debt. That ceiling has never limited the ability of government to incur obligations; instead, it limits the ability of government to pay for obligations already incurred.

For politicians, the debt ceiling has become the impetus for substantial demagoguery. For many voters it is a source of substantial confusion. They interpret a vote to increase the debt ceiling as a vote for more debt. In reality, the votes in Congress that result in more debt are not votes on

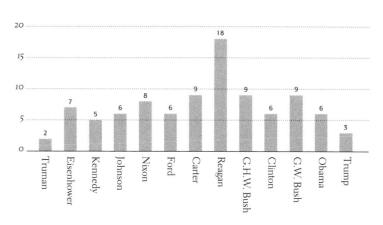

Source: Office of Management and Budget, Historical Tables, Table 7.3—Statutory Limits on Federal Debt: 1940–Current

the debt ceiling, but votes to cut taxes or increase spending. This confusion causes politicians who want to appear conservative to vote against increases in the debt ceiling, even though they may have supported the legislation that resulted in the need for the debt ceiling increase (i.e., the tax cuts or spending increases).

Since the debt ceiling was first enacted, Republican and Democratic Congresses and administrations have raised it many times. From 1978 through 2017, Congress and the president raised or suspended the debt ceiling fifty-seven times. The chart above shows the history of debt ceiling increases during the terms of each president from Harry Truman through Trump. During Trump's term the ceiling was raised three times, but those increases raised the ceiling $3.9 trillion.

The chart does not reflect recent changes in the language Congress uses to discuss the issue. All the time I was in the Senate, we just had votes to "raise the debt ceiling." A few years ago, Congress began enacting provisions to "suspend the debt ceiling." I assume some pollster advised that it sounded less irresponsible to suspend the ceiling than it did to raise the ceiling. There is no substantive difference between the two, since each act to suspend the ceiling contains language that raises the ceiling by the amount the Department of the Treasury will have to borrow by the time the suspension expires.

During my first twenty-eight years in the Senate, both Democratic and Republican leaders followed a well-understood procedure when they needed to raise the debt ceiling. First, the secretary of the Treasury would notify Congress of the need to raise the debt ceiling and the date by which they had to raise it. Next, congressional leaders would settle on the amount of the increase to propose in the two houses of Congress. And then, after various speeches about the need to rein in spending and reduce the deficit, both houses of Congress would muster the majorities needed to enact the increase.

I remember a conversation I had with Jim Exon, a former Nebraska governor and then a Democratic senator, about the debt ceiling. We were at one of the Tuesday lunches of the Democratic Conference in the Mansfield Room in the Senate. We had a vote to increase the debt ceiling coming up, and I asked Jim what he was planning to do. With a twinkle in his eye, Jim said, "My votes on increasing the debt ceiling have been totally consistent. When the president requesting the increase is a Democrat I vote for the increase. When the request comes from a Republican president, I let the Republicans vote for the increase." As I look back at my own votes on debt ceiling increases, I sometimes followed that same pattern.

Implied in Senator Exon's statement was a recognition and understanding that it was not an acceptable option for Congress to just refuse to raise the debt ceiling. That was the governing norm. Both parties recognized that the secretary of the Treasury needed the borrowing authority to meet the obligations of the government. The only real question was which party would have to muster the votes to enact the required increase, and that meant mustering fifty-one votes.

At the time Jim Exon and I were talking, both of us assumed that neither party leader would use the right to filibuster to thwart the other party's effort to raise the ceiling. Any senator can filibuster against an effort to raise the debt ceiling, but until recently it was unheard of for the Senate leader of the minority party to urge his caucus to support such a filibuster. Unfortunately, those days are behind us.

This recognition of a congressional responsibility to allow the secretary of the Treasury to borrow seemed to evaporate after the 2010 election. In 2011 the new Republican majority in the House determined to use the threat of not passing a debt ceiling increase as leverage to force President Obama to agree to substantial long-term cuts in federal spending.

THE 2011 DEBT CEILING CRISIS

In the 2011 debt ceiling crisis, President Obama and most Democrats in Congress—including me—made what I now consider a mistake. The president agreed to negotiate for a resolution of the impasse with Republican congressional leaders. The result was the enactment of the Budget Control Act. Most of the act was misguided, but it included one provision that had merit. Under the act, the debt ceiling increased immediately by $400 billion, and to achieve the additional needed increase of $500 billion, it required the president to make a formal request for the additional borrowing authority. That request would be approved automatically after fifteen calendar days, unless both houses of Congress passed, and the president signed, a resolution of disapproval. Since the president could veto any such resolution, and that veto would prevail unless two-thirds of each house voted to override, everyone could see that the needed increase in the debt ceiling would become law, as it did.

This method of raising the debt ceiling became law, but only applied to that increase. It had the advantage of giving congressional Republicans political cover with their right-wing constituencies. They could continue to denounce the president and the Democrats for increasing the nation's debt (even though it was an increase in the debt ceiling, not the debt), and they could also assure voters that Republicans had not agreed to the increase. Political observers credited Senator McConnell with having devised this procedure, and dubbed it "the McConnell mechanism."

As was clear from the notes I made on that Southwest Airlines flight, congressional Republicans had prevailed in the 2011 crisis. By threatening to filibuster the debt ceiling increase, they had forced Democrats to go along with substantial spending cuts. The cuts in spending were bad for the economy since they came when the economy was still trying to recover from the 2008 recession. Republican success in forcing these cuts would embolden them to engage in similar threats, as they did two years later. In an interview with the *Washington Post*, Senate Republican leader

McConnell confirmed my fears. He said, "I think some of our members may have thought the default issue was a hostage you might take a chance at shooting. Most of us didn't think that. What we did learn is this—it's a hostage that's worth ransoming."[9]

THE 2013 CRISIS: COMBINING THE TWO TACTICS

In early 2013, Republicans once again threatened default by the government if Democrats and the president refused to agree to additional spending cuts and to suspend implementation of the Affordable Care Act. Since Congress had enacted none of the annual appropriations bills, the government was operating on short-term continuing resolutions. And just as the government was depending on short-term spending bills to fund the government, it also was depending on short-term debt ceiling increases to avoid default on its obligations to creditors.

As the end of the fiscal year approached in September, the threat of forcing a government default on its obligations merged with the threat to shut down the government.

The government had ceased many of its operations on October 1 because President Obama had refused the Republican demand that there be a one-year delay in implementing the Affordable Care Act. And while that shutdown continued, financial markets began to reflect concern about the other looming problem (i.e., the approaching October 17 deadline for raising the debt ceiling).

This time, President Obama made the right decision and refused to negotiate with the House about the approaching debt ceiling deadline. He said, "Let's stop the threats. Let's stop the political posturing. Let's keep our government open. Let's pay our bills on time. Let's pass a budget."[10]

Obama's refusal had the effect of backing down Republican congressional leaders. On October 16, they agreed both to raise the debt ceiling and to enact a continuing resolution to fund the government, without the changes in funding levels they had demanded and without their desired language delaying implementation of the ACA.

THE 2021 CRISIS

With a Democrat back in the White House, in the summer of 2021 Mitch McConnell announced that when the deadline arrived for increasing the debt ceiling in October, Democrats should not expect help from Republican senators to raise that ceiling. He urged Senator Schumer and Speaker Pelosi to include whatever debt ceiling increase they desired in the reconciliation bill. Under the Budget Act, if the provision is included in a reconciliation bill, it could not be filibustered.

Janet Yellen, the secretary of the Treasury, announced that the ceiling would have to be raised by October 18 to avoid interrupting the government's ability to meet its obligations. Two weeks prior to that date, Senator McConnell changed his position and agreed to allow Democrats to raise the limit by enough to put off the issue until December. Despite McConnell's statement, Senator Ted Cruz (R-TX) insisted on filibustering to prevent Democrats from voting the debt ceiling increase. It took all fifty Democratic senators, joined by eleven Republicans, including Senator McConnell, to overcome the filibuster. The actual increase in the ceiling, as distinct from the vote to end the filibuster, was achieved by Democrats, with all Republicans voting "no." Following the votes, Senator McConnell stated that when the debt ceiling had to be raised again in December, Republicans would not help.

Senator McConnell's statement that Republicans would not help Democrats raise the debt ceiling requires some interpretation. What he was threatening was that in December Republican senators would vote with Senator Cruz to maintain the filibuster. Senator Schumer, as the Democratic leader in the Senate, did not expect Republicans to vote for a higher debt ceiling, but he was hoping they would refrain from filibustering against the efforts of Democrats to raise the ceiling. For the short-term reprieve on the issue, Senator McConnell evidently wanted to avoid a filibuster, but since Senator Cruz chose to filibuster, Republicans had to supply enough votes to help Democrats achieve the necessary sixty votes.

As in 2011, the debt ceiling crisis of 2021 was finally averted with a negotiated compromise. The "deal" involved passing a provision that allowed a debt ceiling increase to be accomplished with a majority vote in the Senate, but just this one time. The provision required that the dollar amount of the increase be specified, so that attack ads against Democrats who voted for it would be more effective. No longer would Republicans allow Democrats to "suspend" the debt ceiling, as Republicans had done during the Trump administration.

The "deal" worked out between Senators Schumer and McConnell allowed each to achieve his most important objectives. For Senator Schumer, the threat of a default on the nation's debt was averted. Senator McConnell was able to structure the increase so that Republicans could maintain the fiction that they were the party of fiscal responsibility and Democrats were the ones responsible for the increased national debt. Senator John Cornyn (R-TX), the Republican whip, summarized the Republican position, "To have Democrats raise the debt ceiling and be held politically accountable for racking up more debt is my goal, and this helps us accomplish that."[11]

The "deal" also allowed Republicans to maintain the ability to filibuster future debt ceiling increases.

McConnell's position in 2021 differed from his stand ten years earlier. In 2011 he threatened to block the debt ceiling increase to negotiate for constraints on spending (see chapter 4). His motivation in 2021 was to bolster his ability to blame Democrats for the nation's large deficits and debt. He and Senator Cornyn are counting on the fact that most Americans will equate support for a higher debt ceiling with support for more debt.

Abusing the Right to Filibuster—Routine Obstructionism

A third way congressional governing norms have been undermined is by abusing the right to filibuster.

Under the rules and precedents of the Senate, any senator has the right to debate and offer amendments, without limit. During my time in the Senate, this right applied to all executive branch nominations, all federal judges, and all legislation (with the exception of legislation included in a budget reconciliation bill). For all these matters, the only way to end debate and force a vote was to "invoke cloture," which meant getting sixty senators to vote to end debate. This process of invoking cloture not only required sixty votes, but also it required the Senate to use many hours of floor time before reaching a final vote.

In the last decade, the Senate restricted the right to filibuster. In 2013, at the urging of Harry Reid, then the majority leader, the Senate eliminated the right to filibuster presidential nominations for executive branch positions, and for US District Court and Court of Appeals judges. Reid took the step to counter the repeated filibusters employed by the Republican minority to block and delay approval of President Obama's nominees.

Over the long history of the Senate, the filibuster was used by southern senators to block civil rights and voting rights legislation. There is no doubt it has done more harm than good and, if I were still in the Senate and the opportunity arose, I would vote to eliminate it.

There are two distinct ways the right to filibuster can be used, depending on the motives of the senator using it. The first is when a senator or senators feel strongly about an issue and use the filibuster to insist on their position. That is the model most Americans have in mind, based on Jimmy Stewart's performance in *Mr. Smith Goes to Washington*. The other way the filibuster has been used is as a way for the minority to obstruct the ability of the majority to do its normal business—routine obstructionism. By threatening a filibuster to prevent Senate action on almost any matter, the minority can increase its negotiating leverage on any number of issues.

During my final years in the Senate I watched Senator Reid, as majority leader, repeatedly frustrated by Mitch McConnell's use of the threat to filibuster. This obstruction by McConnell is well documented in Adam Jentleson's *Kill Switch: The Rise of the Modern Senate*:

> The unprecedented obstruction McConnell deployed against President Obama's nominees . . . was repeated across everything the Senate did, on every piece of legislation from the major to the routine. McConnell deployed the filibuster at a rate far greater than any minority leader in Senate history.[12]

McConnell repeatedly used the filibuster to delay or prevent the Senate from voting on President Obama's judicial nominees. Senator Reid's frustration with McConnell's obstructionism led Senate Democrats to eliminate the right to filibuster on virtually all presidential nominations, with the exception of Supreme Court nominees. In 2017, once he had become majority leader and Trump had become president, McConnell led the Republicans in eliminating the right to filibuster nominees for the Supreme Court as well.

In the current Congress, Democrats have threatened to eliminate the right to filibuster entirely. In arguing against this, Senator McConnell threatened that such a move would result in Republicans adopting a "scorched-earth Senate" posture. By this he means that since the normal handling of business on the Senate floor is accomplished with "unanimous consent," if the right to filibuster is eliminated, Republicans will retaliate by refusing to grant consent to do even the most mundane of Senate business. Everything will require a roll call vote, and under Senate rules it can take a long time to get to each roll call vote.

Refusing to Consider a Supreme Court Nominee

A fourth abusive tactic that has undermined public confidence in Congress is the refusal of the Senate to perform its duty to provide "advice and consent" on Supreme Court nominations.

On February 13, 2016, Justice Antonin Scalia died. Ten days later, on February 23, and before President Obama had nominated a replacement, Republican members of the Senate Judiciary Committee, with Chuck Grassley (R-IA) as chairman, wrote to Senate majority leader McConnell stating that they would not agree to consider any nomination that President Obama might make and that they would hold no hearing to fill the vacancy until the election of the next president. I have little doubt that Senator McConnell requested that letter.

Despite this threat, on March 16, President Obama nominated Court of Appeals judge Merrick Garland. Senate Republicans held to their position and refused to meet with the nominee or to hold a hearing or otherwise consider Judge Garland's nomination. The nomination was before the Senate for 293 days, the longest period in the history of Supreme Court nominations.

In August 2016, Senator McConnell told a gathering in Kentucky, "One of my proudest moments was when I looked Barack Obama in the eye and I said, 'Mr. President, you will not fill the Supreme Court vacancy.'"[13]

The refusal of Senate Republicans to consider President Obama's nominee was without precedent. It was a refusal of the Senate to carry out one of its core responsibilities under the Constitution. It was also an abuse of power by the Senate Republican majority, and it was a breakdown in the "governing norms" the Senate had adhered to when considering all previous Supreme Court nominees.

As we now know, the tactic worked as intended, and resulted in

President Trump filling that vacancy. It also raised the serious question of what a future Senate, controlled by a different party than the White House, might do when a future Supreme Court vacancy occurs. In 2018, during the political debates swirling around the confirmation process for Justice Brett Kavanaugh, Kavanaugh supporters voiced the fear that if his nomination was delayed until after the 2018 election and if Democrats won control of the Senate in 2018, those Democrats might then follow the precedent established by Republicans in 2016 and refuse to consider Judge Kavanaugh or any other Trump nominee for the Supreme Court. In fact, there was no statement by Democratic Senate leaders to substantiate this fear.

For his part, in 2021 Senator McConnell stated that if a Supreme Court vacancy were to occur in 2024, the last year of President Biden's current term, a GOP-controlled Senate likely would prevent President Biden from getting a hearing on his nominee for the seat.

––––––

In 1789, the Founding Fathers understood they were creating a governmental structure that required negotiation and compromise both between the two houses of Congress, and between the Congress and the president. They did not, however, expect the House, Senate, or president to resort to shutting down the government or defaulting on the debt to increase their leverage in those negotiations. They assumed the majority would prevail on votes held in the Senate. And it is almost certain they also did not expect the Senate to refuse to hold a hearing on a president's nominee to the Supreme Court.

At this stage, how do we reestablish the norms of congressional and presidential behavior in place before 1995? How do we return to the view that both political parties, and both the Congress and the president, have a responsibility to maintain a functioning government? How do we avoid the use of government shutdowns, threats to default on the national debt, and the excessive use of the right to filibuster as ways to increase leverage in negotiations? And how do we get agreement that senators from both parties have a constitutional duty to consider and vote on a president's nominees within a reasonable time, even when a majority of the Senate is of a different party than the president?

My best suggestions for improving the situation are contained in chapters 12 and 13.

The result of these abusive tactics, and this breakdown in governing norms, has been a government and Congress that hurtle from crisis to crisis. The public deserves better.

2   Beware the Five Impediments

PEOPLE RUN FOR CONGRESS out of a desire for recognition, a desire to advocate particular positions, and, in most cases, a desire to serve the public interest. There are disagreements about what that "public interest" entails, and how to promote it, but at some level, most members believe that serving the public interest is their mission.

To achieve that mission, Congress must function as intended, and that includes adherence to governing norms as discussed in chapter 1. But even when those norms are adhered to, each member encounters significant impediments to his or her efforts to pursue the public interest. In Buddhism, the Pali Canon lists five major hindrances a person must overcome to make spiritual progress: sensual desire, ill will, sloth and torpor, restlessness and remorse, and skeptical doubt. I have found that in Congress, there are also five impediments, or hindrances, members must overcome to serve the public interest:

- Pressure to toe the party line;
- Pressure to vote as the polls dictate;
- Ideology (the burden of political philosophy);
- Pressure from special interests; and
- The media.

Pressure to Toe the Party Line

During most of the last few decades, control of the House and Senate has been fairly evenly split between the two parties.

We had divided government in Washington for twenty-three of the thirty years I was there. In the Senate, control shifted from one party to the other six times during those thirty years, and regardless of which party was in control, its majority was small. In the House, although the majorities were larger, they were still not large. The following charts illustrate this point:

TWO-PARTY REPRESENTATION AT THE START OF EACH CONGRESS

■ Democrats   ■ Republicans

President	Date	Senate		House	
BIDEN	2021	48	50	51	49
	2019	45	53	54	46
TRUMP	2017	47	51	45	46
	2015	44	54	43	57
OBAMA	2013	53	45	46	54
	2011	51	47	44	56
	2009	57	41	59	41
	2007	49	49	54	46
G. W. BUSH	2005	44	55	46	54
	2003	48	51	47	53
	2001	50	50	49	51
	1999	45	55	49	51
CLINTON	1997	45	55	48	52
	1995	48	52	47	53
	1993	57	43	59	40
G. H. W. BUSH	1991	56	44	61	38
	1989	55	45	60	40
	1987	55	45	59	41
REAGAN	1985	47	53	58	42
	1983	45	55	62	38

Sources: https://history.house.gov/Institution/Party-Divisions/Party-Divisions/; https://www.cop
.senate.gov/history/partydiv.htm

Note: Although Republicans held 50 seats and Democrats held 48 seats in 2021, the Democrats had
control of the Senate. The two independents caucused with the Democrats, and Vice President
Harris had the tie-breaking vote.

DIVIDED GOVERNMENT: US PRESIDENCY,
THE SENATE, AND THE HOUSE

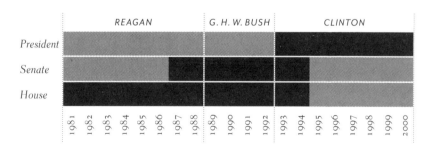

This sharing of power by the two parties leads me to conclude that the proper functioning of Congress depends on the ability of members not only to deliberate together and compromise, but also to act in a bipartisan way. But that willingness to work across party lines is usually in short supply.

I was fortunate to be in the Senate when bipartisan efforts to solve the nation's problems were more common. One example, discussed in chapter 6, is the Low Carbon Economy Act of 2007.[1] That was a good-faith effort to enact a cap-and-trade system to reduce greenhouse gas emissions. I introduced the bill with three Democratic and three Republican cosponsors. Like all other cap-and-trade proposals in the Senate, this bill failed to become law. But the fact that seven senators, from both parties, introduced it was significant. By the time I left the Senate at the end of 2012, such a bipartisan effort to deal with climate change was not possible.

Most people inherit their party identification from their parents. My father used to say he was in college before he learned that "damnRepublican" was two words. Both my parents grew up during the Depression and had no doubt that FDR's activist approach to government made good sense. My uncle, John Bingaman, was the family member most directly involved in politics. He chaired the Democratic Party in our home county for many years, and was appointed by Governor Clyde Tingley as New Mexico's commissioner of revenue. He also managed campaigns for New Mexico senator Clinton Anderson (D-NM). My wife, Anne Bingaman, served as assistant attorney general for antitrust in the first Clinton

■ Democrat Majority   ■ Republican Majority

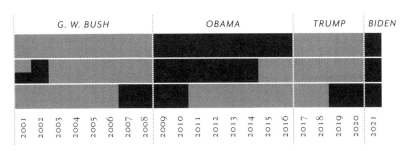

administration, and our son, also John Bingaman, carried on the tradition of public service by working as a chief of staff for New Mexico Democratic governor Michelle Lujan Grisham. He now serves as a member of the New Mexico State Investment Council.

There are people who choose their party affiliation, not because of the politics of their parents, but because of the political views and beliefs they think a party represents. Warren Buffett is such a person. He grew up in a Republican household; in fact, his father was a Republican congressman. In the 1960s, he left the Republican Party because of his belief that they were wrong on civil rights. For Buffett, political beliefs determined party affiliation, but he is more the exception than the rule. Most people come to identify with a party before they have developed strong political beliefs. Once they have identified with a party, many factors conspire to reinforce that identification, although there are examples, like the Reagan Democrats, where voters will abandon their party affiliation to vote for a candidate who appeals to their concerns.

In Congress, in particular, powerful pressures encourage and strengthen a senator's or representative's adherence to a particular party.

First, an election campaign can reinforce the candidate's identification with a party. I recall Republicans who supported me when I ran for New Mexico attorney general, and later for the Senate, but they were few. Once I became an incumbent senator, that situation changed somewhat, but as a general rule, Democrats support Democrats and Republicans support Republicans. Independents are more likely to look at the qualifications, character, and views of the candidate, but the label "independent" does not assure that. A voter may feel a strong affinity for one of the major parties and still register as an "independent."

Once elected, I was struck by the overwhelming importance of party affiliation in the way Congress organizes itself and functions. If your party controls the house of Congress in which you serve, it increases your ability to influence legislation and otherwise exercise authority. That is particularly true in the House of Representatives, where the size of the body (435) and its traditions concentrate more authority in the majority's leadership. House rules are much less concerned than Senate rules about the prerogatives and rights of individual members, especially members in the minority. But the majority party dictates most of what goes on in the Senate, too.

The majority establishes the Senate schedule, determines who chairs committees, and determines which bills and presidential nominations receive a hearing and a vote in committee, and ultimate consideration on the Senate floor.

It is easy to see why members affiliated with the party in control want to keep that control. It is also easy to see why those in the minority are eager to gain the majority. The result is that members of both parties spend considerable time and effort trying to win the next election.

To better understand this, consider the weekly meetings of the two-party caucuses in the Senate. Each Tuesday the two parties meet separately to plan strategy for the week. At these luncheon meetings it is normal for the campaign committee of each party to give an update on the current Senate campaigns. This update includes not only the latest about campaigns for the candidates the party is supporting, but also the latest about efforts to defeat incumbent senators from the other party. On more than one occasion, I recall senators being advised they should remember not to do anything that might improve the chances of reelection of senators from the opposing party, such as joining with such senators to cosponsor legislation.

Another example is the efforts that congressional leaders of each party make to force votes that put members from the other party in a difficult position (i.e., a position contrary to that held by a significant number of their constituents). And those same congressional leaders do their best to shield members of their own party from having to cast "difficult" votes.

For example, when the party controlling the Senate opposes the president, one common practice is to call up the president's proposed budget for a vote. During the presidency of George W. Bush, the budgets proposed by the president always contained many cuts unpopular with most Americans. Early in Senate consideration of a budget, the Democratic leader would call for a vote on the Bush budget proposal. Republicans would want to support the Republican president, but they would not want to vote for cuts to programs their constituents cared about. Such efforts to put the members of the other party in a bind increase as campaigns become heated and elections approach, although I doubt they have much impact on the outcome of elections.

The effort to maintain and increase the number of senators from one's own party is an understood part of the job for each senator, but it also can be an impediment to efforts by members of Congress to serve the public interest.

Pressure to Vote as the Polls Dictate

The public is usually right about what is in their best interest, but not always. Sometimes, to serve the public interest, a member of Congress must take a stand most members of the public do not support.

When President George W. Bush ordered preparation for the invasion of Iraq, polls showed a majority of the public supported his action. The president, Vice President Dick Cheney, and Secretary of Defense Donald Rumsfeld had succeeded in persuading most Americans it was important for the United States to invade. Since the administration wanted members of Congress on record to support the invasion, they pressured Congress to vote on the issue in the weeks leading up to the 2002 election. Although the polls showed most Americans in favor of invasion, the best interests of the public required a "no" vote.

Another example of where the public's view of its own best interest was in error involved the proposed constitutional amendment to permit states to ban flag burning. This came up several times while I was in the Senate. The Supreme Court had struck down laws banning flag burning in two cases as a violation of the first amendment right to political speech: *Texas v. Johnson* and *United States v. Eichman*. Both decisions were 5-4, with the unusual alignment of Justice Scalia voting in the majority both times, and Justice John Paul Stevens voting in the minority.

Once the Supreme Court ruled, veterans' organizations mounted a campaign to amend the Constitution to permit state laws banning flag burning. For several years the leaders of these organizations would come to Washington with their list of legislative priorities, and high on that list would be the anti-flag burning constitutional amendment. When I met with them in my office they pointed out that a large majority of voters supported the amendment, which was true.

Despite its popularity, the amendment struck me as a terrible idea, and I opposed it. On March 29, 2000, in a floor speech I summed up my views:

Mr. President, our Constitution and Nation are strong enough to handle a few miscreants who want to burn a flag. Those who drafted the Constitution envisioned that it would survive speech which the majority finds offensive. I believe that a vote against this amendment is a vote for the Constitution and for the most important principle embedded in that document, the right of every American to free speech.[2]

The vote in the Senate to permit the states to ban flag burning was 63 "ayes" and 37 "nays." But since it was a proposed constitutional amendment, it fell short of the required two-thirds vote and failed.

Ideology: The Burden of Political Philosophy

The burden of political philosophy, or ideology, is another major obstacle to overcome in enacting legislation to serve the public interest. In significant ways, political ideology informs and dovetails with loyalty to one's political party. However, as the Tea Party and Donald Trump have shown, the ideology of either a voter or candidate may diverge from the traditional views of one's party. For example, the Republican Party used to support free trade, but President Trump and his adherents embraced much more protectionist views as part of their effort to "put America first."

During my time in the Senate, the great ideological divide between the two major parties was this: Republicans believed that taxes and the role of government in the domestic economy should be kept to a minimum. They favored a strong military, strict law enforcement, including strict enforcement of immigration laws, and a robust government role in such areas as restricting abortion and banning gay marriage. They opposed the use of governmental power in ways that would redistribute private wealth or strengthen the economic safety net for low-income individuals. Democrats favored a more activist role for government in the domestic economy and in regulating business to improve health and safety, and the environment. They supported government efforts to strengthen the safety net and reduce income inequality. They also supported providing better access for improved education and health care.

Today, the positions espoused by most Democrats are still largely as they were.

On the other hand, Republican political philosophy appears to have changed, and is not as easy to define. Many who supported President Trump adopted an anti-immigrant, anti–free trade, and anti-science posture, and opposed state or federal public health mandates requiring masking and vaccination against Covid. They also have rallied around efforts to restrict voting in many states. The task of defining the Republican political philosophy at this time is made even more difficult by the fact that the party has not agreed on, or issued, a platform since before President Trump was elected in 2016.[3]

As in many areas of our national life, President Abraham Lincoln did a good job of articulating the right balance between these two ideological views: "The legitimate object of government, is to do for a community of people, whatever they need to have done, but can not do, at all, or can not, so well do, for themselves—in their separate, and individual capacities."[4]

There is an argument for the ideological views of both parties. There are many ways government can make a contribution, but there is not a government-based solution to every problem. In many instances markets should be relied upon to get the best result. But markets are not a panacea either. They are often flawed and require regulation.

Since the early 1980s, the anti-government philosophy of the Republican Party has gained prominence in much of our national discourse. Ideological opposition to an activist government has become a major factor in thwarting efforts to pursue practical solutions to our nation's problems. There are several causes for this.

Ronald Reagan's leadership on the issue had a major impact. When he became president on January 20, 1981, the country was facing both high inflation and an anemic economy. In his inaugural address that day he said, "In this present crisis, government is not the solution to our problem; government is the problem."[5]

By 1996, even President Clinton felt the need to use similar rhetoric. In his State of the Union speech that year he declared "the end of big government."[6]

Professors Amy Fried and Douglas Harris make a good case in their recent book, *At War with Government*, that sowing distrust of the government has been a consistent strategy of Republicans from Barry Goldwater to Trump.[7] Grover Norquist, president of Americans for Tax Reform, articulated the more extreme version of this anti-government philosophy in a 2001 interview on National Public Radio. He said, "I don't want to abolish government. I simply want to reduce it to the size where I can drag it into the bathroom and drown it in the bathtub."[8] During Trump's presidency, the rhetoric stayed the same, but he was comfortable with a strong governmental role as long as it was implementing his agenda. One example was his aggressive efforts to "build the wall," even over the objection of many in Congress.

There are two aspects to this anti-government ideology.

One is a concern for the individual: a desire to prevent government from interfering with the right of the individual to live his or her life unimpeded. An example of this concern was the resistance to the government imposing an "individual mandate" for people to get health insurance coverage under the Affordable Care Act (ACA) (see chapter 8). Those opposed to government involvement of this type sometimes call themselves "conservatives," but also sometimes "populists" or "libertarians." There is a huge disconnect between this general ideology and the willingness to ban abortions, and in the case of Texas, to encourage antiabortion activists to take action against anyone who assists a woman to have an abortion.

The other aspect of this anti-government ideology involves a concern for private enterprise: a desire for the government to leave the marketplace and private businesses unimpeded in their efforts to earn profits. Corporate resistance to government-imposed limits on greenhouse gas emissions is an example of this concern. When the government imposes a requirement on business, opponents of that requirement usually label themselves "conservative."

Many adherents to this general anti-government philosophy, particularly those advocating freedom from government involvement in the free enterprise system, have conflated the two concerns into one overarching concern about "liberty" or "freedom." We can see an example of this packaging in the label chosen by right-wing Republican House members: the "Freedom Caucus." We can also go back further for another example. At the time of the Iraq War in 2003, the Republican-controlled House Rules Committee relabeled French fries "freedom fries" in the House cafeteria.

The justification offered was to express dissatisfaction with the French government for being unwilling to support the US-led invasion of Iraq. Since most Americans also came to oppose that invasion, the change of name was short-lived.

This is not a new debate. We have debated for centuries the question of where to restrain government in order to preserve liberty. In his essay "Two Concepts of Liberty" British philosopher Isaiah Berlin reviewed that debate:

> The extent of a man's, or a people's, liberty to choose to live as he or they desire must be weighed against the claims of many other values, of which equality, or justice, or happiness, or security, or public order are perhaps the most obvious examples. For this reason, it cannot be unlimited. We are rightly reminded by R. H. Tawney that the liberty of the strong, whether their strength is physical or economic, must be restrained. This maxim claims respect, not as a consequence of some a priori rule, whereby the respect for the liberty of one man logically entails respect for the liberty of others like him; but simply because respect for the principles of justice, or shame at gross inequality of treatment, is as basic in men as the desire for liberty.[9]

Most major disagreements I observed in the Senate had their roots in ideological views about the proper role of government. On one side were those willing to use the power of government to achieve what they saw as the "common good." On the other side were those who believed that, in domestic affairs, unless there was a threat to law and order, the government should remain uninvolved. There is a caveat to this distinction: "conservatives" often favor government action to prohibit what they consider immoral acts by their fellow citizens, such as abortion or same-sex marriage.

This ideological conflict played out in many contexts. One example occurred at a hearing I chaired in the Energy and Natural Resources Committee on April 12, 2011. The hearing that day was to report legislation to increase energy efficiency standards for various household appliances. As chair of the committee, I had introduced the legislation and was trying to have the bill reported favorably from our committee. In 1975, Congress had enacted the Appliance and Equipment Standards Program, administered by the Department of Energy. At least five times since its enactment (in 1987, 1988, 1992, 2005, and 2007), Congress had added to the law by legislating consensus standards for various types of appliances and machinery. Each time, the purpose was to require greater efficiency in the way we use energy in the economy. Each time, the legislation passed with overwhelming bipartisan support. All experts who had looked at the issue agreed that without these efficiency standards in place, electric utilities would have had to build more power plants.

Before I called for a vote on the proposal bill, I invited any senator on the committee wishing to offer an amendment, to do so. Senator Rand Paul (R-KY), elected from Kentucky in 2010, was the first to speak up. He offered an amendment to make the Appliance and Equipment Standards Program voluntary. The amendment was consistent with the libertarian views he had championed in his election campaign, and if adopted, would have gutted the Department of Energy program.

To explain and argue for his amendment, Senator Paul said:

> On the energy efficiency standards, I think that, you know, to be consistent with a free society, we should make them voluntary.
>
> Ayn Rand wrote a novel, *Anthem*, back in the 50s, and it is a dystopian novel. In that novel, individual choice is banned, and the collective basically runs society.
>
> There is a young man, and his name is Equality 7-2521. He is an intelligent young man, but he is banned from achieving or reaching any sort of occupation that might challenge him. He is a street sweeper.
>
> Over time, he discovers the subway, and he rediscovers the incandescent light bulb. And he thinks naively that electricity and the brilliance of light would be an advantage for society, and that it would bring great new things as far as being able to see at night and to read, and the advancement of civilization.
>
> Well, he takes it before the collective of elders, and they take the light bulb, and basically it is crushed beneath the boot heel of the collective.[10]

Prior to the vote on his amendment, Senator Paul added:

You know, there still seems to be a little bit of discussion, and maybe misunderstanding, about whether or not the collective boot heel is going to smash the light bulb or not. So, I wanted to really point out that, yes, the collective boot heel will smash the light bulb because it will be illegal to make the light bulbs. You will be fined. If you do not pay the fine, you will go to jail. If you keep making the light bulb, they will come with armed agents to your business and shut you down.[11]

I made my best case against the amendment, pointing out that efficiency standards had enjoyed bipartisan support under Republican and Democratic administrations for many years. The vote tally on the Paul amendment was 6 "ayes" and 16 "nays," allowing the committee to report the legislation improving appliance efficiency standards to the full Senate. To my regret, the bill containing that legislation was a casualty of the general dysfunction afflicting the Senate by that time, and the Senate did not consider it during the rest of that two-year Congress.

I concede this may be an extreme example of anti-government ideology, but Senator Paul was reflecting a sentiment expressed in many other debates taking place on Capitol Hill. This adherence to an anti-government ideology made it much more difficult to reach consensus.

As I discuss in chapter 8, that same anti-government ideology made it impossible to get Republican support for including an individual mandate in the Affordable Care Act. After I left Congress, it was also at the core of the resistance to efforts to encourage mask-wearing and vaccinations in response to the Covid pandemic. Although some refused to be vaccinated because of false information they had received, others refused out of ideological opposition to anything akin to a government mandate.

Pressure from Special Interests

Special interests are another factor that make it difficult for members to act in the public interest.

The first amendment to the Constitution prohibits Congress from passing laws to interfere with the right to petition the government for redress of grievances. This constitutional provision is both wise and important.

But recognizing that we need to protect the rights of all to petition for the redress of grievances does not mean we must be blind to the adverse effects that special interest lobbying has on the ability of Congress to act in the nation's best interest.

The term "special interest" is difficult to define. When the interest being advocated is one that benefits the nation, that advocacy is an essential part of our democracy. For example, if a group of citizens worried about the effects of climate change on the planet and future generations wants to lobby Congress, such lobbying should be encouraged. But what about instances where the individual or group is lobbying for a policy to benefit themselves at the expense of the populace as a whole? What if the tobacco industry is trying to protect its profits by avoiding Food and Drug Administration (FDA) regulation of tobacco products? What if the National Rifle Association (NRA) is trying to keep Congress from banning the use of cop-killer bullets? Efforts to pursue the public interest can conflict with such "special interest" lobbying.

Even if their arguments on the merits of an issue are not persuasive, there are two other ways a special interest can still hope to influence a member of Congress.

The first is to rally opposition among the politician's constituents at the time of the next election. In states with large rural populations, the threat this poses is one reason many members of Congress will vote for positions advocated by the NRA. During the time I was in the Senate, I was well aware that a decision to oppose the NRA could engender opposition at the next election. That was not because a majority of the public supported the positions advocated by the NRA; on most issues, they did not. However, the public considers many factors in deciding whom to support or oppose in the next election. Many NRA members, in contrast, consider only a narrow set of issues, and work to defeat any candidate who disagrees with them on those issues.

In 1994, the NRA announced its opposition to my reelection. Charlton Heston, the national president of the NRA, traveled to Albuquerque and Roswell to endorse my opponent, Colin McMillan. Heston was best known for his portrayal of Moses in *The Ten Commandments*. At a press conference in Albuquerque, he made the usual NRA argument for electing my opponent: it was necessary if people wanted to avoid government confiscation of their guns. The argument did not persuade most New Mexico voters.

The second way special interests attempt to influence votes in Congress is through political contributions.

In 1982, the year before I was sworn in to the Senate, I was at a Washington reception hosted by the Democratic Senate Campaign Committee (DSCC). The reception, at a restaurant near the Capitol, offered a chance for nonincumbent Democratic Senate candidates to meet Washington lobbyists and gain their support. Each of us running for a Senate seat had three minutes to make our sales pitch. After the speeches, an attractive woman lobbying for the insurance industry approached me. She said, "We can't contribute to your campaign at this time because you are running against Senator Schmitt and he's on the committee [Commerce] with jurisdiction over our industry. But if you win, please call, and we'll be glad to help you pay off your debt." Following my election, we had a large campaign debt. To pay it off we had a series of fund-raisers. I don't recall any specific contribution from the insurance industry, but I have little doubt they contributed to the effort.

The influence campaign contributions can have on public officials increases as campaigns become more expensive. Also, the increased costs of campaigns require each candidate to spend more time and effort fundraising. In the *Citizens United* case the Supreme Court made the problem worse by holding that Congress lacks the authority to restrict large contributions to independent expenditure groups.

Special interests have particular influence on issues involving foreign policy since members realize that most of their constituents are not focused on such issues. The Cuban American lobby has been very successful in maintaining restrictions on trade with Cuba to put pressure on the Castro regime. Also, the pro-Israel lobby has played a large role in determining US policy in the Middle East.

The Media

For our system of government to function, we must have freedom of speech and freedom of the press. The Founding Fathers wisely enshrined those freedoms in the Constitution, just as they enshrined the right to petition the government. Nonetheless, in our present political and technological environment, the "media" can make it difficult for members of Congress to serve the public interest. There are several reasons for this.

One problem is that the number and variety of people and organizations that claim to be the "media" has grown substantially during recent decades. When I was first elected to the Senate in 1982, the "media" comprised the print media (newspapers, magazines, etc.), radio, and broadcast TV. Since that time cable TV, talk radio, internet webcasts and blogs, and social media of many types have become major parts of the "media." Even some of those arrested for invading the Capitol on January 6, 2021, defended themselves with the claim they were there as part of the media.

Another problem is that much of the media, and particularly those parts that have recently emerged, are more interested in advocating a point of view than in reporting either the facts or the views of others. Many times, they blatantly advocate for a position. In other cases, they try to disguise that advocacy as reporting. One unfortunate side effect is that as the media become more interested in advocating a point of view, they abandon the job of educating the public about the complexity of issues. Everything is presented as a policy the public should favor or oppose. Everything is seen as black or white.

The media, when they were still the print media plus radio and television, used to "broadcast" news and commentary to the general population. Today, that news and commentary are "narrow-cast" to those who agree with the viewpoint being presented. Technology, and the internet in particular, allows people to choose which sources of news and commentary to access, and most of the time they choose those with which they agree. This creates a business opportunity for companies catering to the biases and prejudices of particular segments of society. It also provides a financial incentive for media outlets to embrace the role of advocate rather than reporter. Companies with that kind of business model provide a steady diet of biased news coverage and commentary.

A particularly troublesome development is the increase in media outlets devoted to spreading false information. Much of this "disinformation" originates in social media, but then is picked up and amplified by larger media outlets. So far, efforts to control, or even monitor, the spread of false information have been largely unsuccessful.

These features of the current media environment make deliberation and compromise more difficult. Media that cater to people with a right-wing bias see their job as sounding the alarm about members of Congress who might stray from that orthodoxy. The same goes for the media catering to people from the left wing of the political spectrum. Once a member has stated his position on an issue, he will be attacked if he considers changing that position to achieve a compromise.

PART II

The People's Business— Eight Worthy Efforts

Despite the growing dysfunction that first alarmed me in 1995, Congress still worked to address the country's major challenges. Here are eight of those challenges:

1. Support a strong economy
2. Control deficits and debt
3. Lead in science and technology
4. Meet our energy and climate-change challenges
5. Improve health care
6. Improve elementary and secondary education
7. Manage and preserve public lands
8. Avoid unnecessary wars

Some of Congress's efforts were successful, at least for a time. Others failed. Each remains a worthy purpose that requires our nation's continued commitment.

3   Support a Strong Economy

A PRIMARY FUNCTION of the federal government is to stabilize the economy and reduce the length and severity of economic downturns. The most dramatic examples of government action of this type that occurred during my time in the Senate were in response to the 2008–2009 economic crisis: the Great Recession. That response involved multiple actions taken by the Federal Reserve, the Bush administration, the Obama administration, and the Congress. The timeline below shows the most important of these actions.

On January 20, 2009, when President Obama took office, the economy was in free fall. That month payrolls dropped by 741,000 jobs. In February, we lost an additional 651,000 jobs, and in March, 663,000 more.

The Great Recession of 2008–2009 resulted from the subprime mortgage crisis brought on by mismanagement in the financial sector. Subprime mortgages had been securitized and then purchased by financial institutions. With the realization that many of these securities represented nonperforming loans, markets lost confidence in financial institutions. That loss of confidence quickly spread to the entire economy.

The Federal Reserve is the federal government's first line of defense

TIMELINE OF ACTIONS IN RESPONSE TO FINANCIAL CRISIS

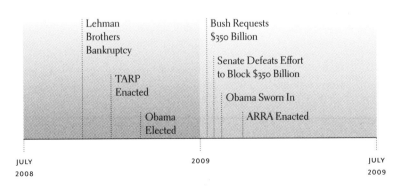

Lehman Brothers Bankruptcy	Bush Requests $350 Billion
TARP Enacted	Senate Defeats Effort to Block $350 Billion
Obama Elected	Obama Sworn In
	ARRA Enacted

JULY 2008   2009   JULY 2009

in maintaining and growing the economy. That was never more true than in the Great Recession, since the crisis developed in the financial system. Yet earlier actions by the Fed had not helped the situation. In fact, the Angelides Commission, appointed to determine the causes of the Great Recession, concluded in its report that one factor in causing the crisis was the failure of the Fed to adequately regulate the banks.[1]

But once the problem came into view, Chairman Ben Bernanke responded with bold, unprecedented actions. Beginning in September 2007, the Fed lowered the federal funds rate and the discount rate that banks have to pay on loans they receive from regional Fed lending facilities. In what he described as "expanding the Fed's balance sheet," Chairman Bernanke also began to increase the money supply. The Fed established several broad-based programs to provide financial support for banks and even provided specific help to some of the nation's major financial institutions. Bernanke, Secretary of the Treasury Hank Paulson, and Tim Geithner, the head of the Federal Reserve Bank of New York, worked together to confront the crisis. They all shared the view that markets are not always self-correcting.

Congress also acted. Its first major step was to pass the Emergency Stabilization Act of 2008, which included funding for TARP, the Troubled Asset Relief Program.

The Troubled Asset Relief Program (TARP)

When Lehman Brothers filed for Chapter 11 bankruptcy in September 2008, the severity of the financial crisis became apparent. This was the largest bankruptcy filing in US history. Economic historians disagree about whether the Department of the Treasury and the Fed should have done more to avoid Lehman's collapse, but once that collapse occurred, the crisis spread quickly.

That same month, with the presidential election only weeks away, President Bush's secretary of the Treasury, the former chairman and chief executive officer of Goldman Sachs, Hank Paulson, came to Congress accompanied by Federal Reserve chairman Ben Bernanke. They came to plead the administration's case for passing the Troubled Asset Relief

Program (TARP). At the time, speculation was rife in Congress and in the media about the administration's proposed response to the financial crisis. No one was sure either about what would be proposed or how large the proposal would be.

On September 24, Majority Leader Harry Reid convened a special meeting of Democratic senators in the LBJ Room, just off the Senate floor, to hear the administration's request, and the reasons they believed it was needed. Both Paulson and Bernanke spoke, and their message was clear. They explained the severe economic problems facing the nation's large banks, and the damage that could result to the economy if we allowed the nation's financial system to collapse. They then outlined their proposal to head off this economic disaster: the federal government would buy $500 to $700 billion of so-called troubled assets from the nation's largest banks. These were the subprime mortgages, now considered almost worthless. Paulson needed Congress to appropriate the funds and grant him the needed authority.

A few days later, when they presented the written proposal for authority to spend $700 billion, critics attacked it for exempting Paulson and his successors from any effective oversight by Congress or the courts. Once they had corrected these problems in subsequent drafts of the legislation, the bill came to the House floor for a vote on the evening of September 29. To the surprise of many, including President Bush, the Republican-controlled House defeated the bill: 205 votes for and 218 against. The next day the stock market registered its concern with the House action: the Dow dropped 778 points and Standard and Poor's 500 Index dropped 9 percent. Two days later, on October 1, a much-improved bill came before the Senate. It appropriated the needed funds and provided broad authority to the secretary of the Treasury to either buy assets from banks, or to provide loans. It passed by a vote of 74 to 25. On October 3, the House followed the Senate's lead and passed the legislation 263 to 171. Within hours President Bush signed the bill. As it turned out, Paulson used his authority to make investments in new preferred stock in the large banks, rather than to buy "troubled assets." He credited Warren Buffett for suggesting this as a simpler and more convincing way to respond to the crisis.[2]

In mid-January 2009, another problem presented itself. In order for the incoming Obama administration to have access to the second half of the $700 billion, the Bush administration had to send Congress a formal request for authority to spend the money. Congress then had fifteen days to disapprove the request; otherwise, the president could go ahead.

At President-elect Obama's urging, President Bush sent Congress the required formal request to use the funds. Senator David Vitter (R-LA) proposed a resolution to block it. On January 15, the Senate rejected the resolution 52 to 42. That vote cleared the way for Obama to continue with the economic rescue effort. The 52 votes came from 46 Democrats and 6 Republicans.

The politics involved in the enactment of TARP were fascinating. This was a proposal by a Republican administration to use taxpayer dollars to bail out the nation's largest banks, but most of those in Congress supporting the Bush administration proposal were Democrats. Most Americans did not support the bailout. Ben Bernanke told a reporter, "A senator during the heat of the crisis told me his calls from constituents on TARP were running 50/50; 50% said 'no,' 50% said 'hell no.'" The senator was Jon Kyl of Arizona.[3]

Despite the fast-approaching election day, both candidates for president, Senators Barack Obama and John McCain, publicly endorsed and voted to pass the bill. Alan Greenspan, the former chair of the Federal Reserve, who many, including me, thought deserved significant blame for failing to prevent the crisis by adequately regulating the banks, also urged Congress to enact the legislation. Some on the liberal end of the political spectrum, such as Bernie Sanders, opposed the bill as a giveaway to the very institutions that had caused the crisis. Others who were well-known conservatives, such as Sam Brownback from Kansas, opposed the bill because it involved the federal government intervening in the private sector in unprecedented ways, and doing so with borrowed funds.

Paulson and Bernanke had made a strong case in that meeting in the LBJ Room. They had argued that a collapse of our major banks would catapult the US economy into a deep recession, or even depression. In their view, action by Congress was essential. Most of us attending the meeting recognized this would not be a popular vote, but also believed the threats to the economy were great enough that the only responsible course was to vote "aye."

For some senators, the political consequences of an "aye" vote proved significant. Among Republicans, an early casualty was Senator Bob Bennett of Utah. Bob was a three-term incumbent, planning to run for reelection in 2010. He had a well-deserved reputation as a conservative Republican, in the tradition of his father, who had earlier served as a senator from Utah. In deciding how to vote, Bob made the same basic calculation that I had: it was the only responsible course available. Many of his Republican constituents in Utah disagreed.

In the lead-up to the 2010 election, the rules of the Utah Republican Party required all candidates wanting to run in the Republican primary to present themselves at the party's nominating convention. Only the top two vote-getters for each office at the convention would be allowed on the ballot. In his bid for the party nomination for another term in the Senate, Bob came in third.

Following the convention vote denying him a place on the ballot, I watched on television as Bob was being interviewed from the convention floor. As he tried to explain what happened, I could hear delegates chanting in the background, "TARP, TARP, TARP, TARP."

Senator Bennett's defeat was an early show of force in the 2010 election campaign by the antiestablishment elements in the Republican Party. Right-wing outrage about the approval of TARP, together with strong opposition to Obamacare, would show themselves to be potent issues for activating Republicans. It was an early show of strength for the Tea Party and also a harbinger of the rising populism that helped elect Trump in 2016.

The Bailout of General Motors and Chrysler

In the early months of 2009, it became clear that the second half of the TARP funds would be needed to rescue the auto sector.

At the time of the financial crisis, US auto manufacturers produced larger, less fuel-efficient vehicles than their foreign competitors. The rising price of gasoline together with the slowdown in economic activity was causing a dramatic drop in vehicle sales for the "Big Three:" General Motors (GM), Ford, and Chrysler.

In the Energy Independence & Security Act of 2007 (EISA), we in Congress had tried to encourage the use of more fuel-efficient vehicles by raising Corporate Average Fuel Economy (CAFE) standards and allowing the administration to raise them even more in future years. We considered this good energy policy because it would reduce future US demand for oil, most of which was being imported. It would also reduce greenhouse gas emissions.

The "Big Three" argued these higher standards would put them at a significant disadvantage compared to foreign manufacturers. If they were to compete in this new environment, they would need government help to modernize their plants.

To address the problem, at the urging of the auto industry, Congress had enacted the Advanced Technology Vehicles Manufacturing (ATVM) Loan Program as part of EISA. As chair of the Energy Committee, I was glad to include it in the larger energy bill. The program authorized the Department of Energy (DOE) to provide direct loans to automakers and their parts suppliers to retrofit their factories to produce more fuel-efficient vehicles. In 2008, Congress began implementing the program by appropriating $25 billion for such loans.

I considered the ATVM Loan Program to have been a success, but by the fall of 2008, with the financial crisis well under way, the auto industry needed even stronger medicine. In early December 2008, the CEOs of General Motors, Ford, and Chrysler testified to Congress that GM needed additional financial help from the government. Getting the votes to provide that help was made more difficult when the news came out that Rick Wagoner, GM's CEO, had flown to DC to give testimony to Congress the previous month, in GM's corporate jet.

Congressman Ron Paul (R-TX) expressed the opposition of many to providing additional government help:

> In bailing out failing companies, they are confiscating money from productive members of the economy and giving it to failing ones. By sustaining companies with obsolete or unsustainable business models, the government prevents their resources from being liquidated and made available to other companies that can put them to better, more productive use. An essential element of a healthy free market is that both success and failure be permitted to happen when they are earned. But instead with a bailout, the rewards are reversed—the

proceeds from successful entities are given to failing ones. How this is supposed to be good for our economy is beyond me. . . . It won't work. It can't work. . . . It is obvious to most Americans that we need to reject corporate cronyism, and allow the natural regulations and incentives of the free market to pick the winners and losers in our economy, not the whims of bureaucrats and politicians.[4]

Mitt Romney, the future Republican nominee for president in 2012, wrote an op-ed in the *New York Times*, also arguing against government intervention to help the US auto industry.[5] Romney's position was of special interest considering his family's history with the industry. His father, George Romney, had been chair and president of American Motors Corporation from 1954 to 1962.

In the last weeks of the Bush administration, GM and Chrysler requested the government to provide them with emergency loans, and the Department of the Treasury did so with TARP funds. However, early in the Obama administration, corporate leaders made the case that these short-term loans provided by the Bush administration would not be enough to protect GM and Chrysler from bankruptcy and liquidation. President Obama, with the advice of Larry Summers and Tim Geithner, made the wise decision to ask Steven Rattner[6] to oversee their administration's efforts to rescue the US auto industry. Using $80 billion of TARP funds, and under Rattner's direction, the government restructured the threatened companies. Fortunately for the taxpayer, the Treasury recovered the lion's share of that amount by selling its interest once the economy had stabilized.

The American Recovery and Reinvestment Act (ARRA)

Despite the bold actions taken by the Fed and the congressional enactment of TARP, most leading economists believed more help was needed from the government if we were to avoid a full-blown depression. Their recommendation was for a "stimulus package" (i.e., a combination of tax cuts and new spending to provide more economic demand). And while there was little doubt about the economic justification for strong government action of this type, the political resistance proved to be substantial.

After President Obama took the oath of office in early 2009, Democratic senators gathered as they did each Tuesday for lunch in the Mansfield Room on the second floor of the Capitol. Most Tuesday lunches involve routine business—talking about the Senate schedule for the rest of the week, hearing announcements about upcoming events and meetings, and hearing whatever words of wisdom the majority leader and his leadership team choose to impart. This particular Tuesday all of us realized this would not be a routine lunch.

After Harry Reid made a few announcements, he turned the meeting over to the president's economic advisors, Larry Summers and Gene Sperling. Each made the case for enacting a "stimulus package" and discussed the size of the package they wanted, and its makeup.

With TARP, the Fed and the Department of the Treasury had been breaking new ground. The idea of the government buying "troubled assets" and making large cash infusions into the nation's largest financial institutions was without precedent. The American Recovery and Reinvestment Act (ARRA) was different: it was a straightforward effort by the federal government to stimulate demand in the economy. Legislation to stimulate the economy during times of economic downturn was neither new nor innovative. It seemed clear to me that Congress needed to pass a stimulus package. The only proper questions related to the size of the package, the particular tax cuts, and what new spending to include.

Since the ARRA was an effort to stimulate demand in the face of a severe economic downturn, I initially thought the bipartisan coalition that had supported the passage of TARP would similarly support a significant stimulus bill. But as we quickly found out, the political ground had shifted. We now had a Democratic president.

President Bush had proposed TARP, and it had passed with bipartisan support. The ARRA was being put forward by the just-inaugurated Democratic president, Barack Obama. While many Republicans in Congress had been willing to incur the wrath of conservative constituents and support TARP when asked to do so by a Republican president, they were not willing to do the same for the stimulus package put forward by President Obama.

Stimulus packages contain proposals to spend more and cut taxes.

Obama's proposal was to provide $787 billion of stimulus to the economy by cutting taxes by $288 billion and increasing spending by $499 billion. The spending portion of the bill added $224 billion for extended unemployment benefits, education, and health care, and $275 billion for federal contracts, grants, and loans. The proposal was to spend all these sums within a ten-year period. In fact, over 90 percent of the stimulus occurred during the first three years.

As we later discovered, the tax cut portion of the bill was structured in a way that made it difficult to explain to the public. The tax cuts involved reducing the withholding from employees' payroll checks. When they were paid each month, most taxpayers did not see the tangible benefits they were receiving. It also allowed opponents of the ARRA to characterize the bill as nothing more than an enormous increase in government spending. If the public had understood that a third of the cost of the bill represented cuts in their taxes, it might have been possible to pick up some Republican support.

In the lead-up to the vote in the Senate, most Republicans who spoke against the measure began with a familiar complaint. Senator Orrin Hatch stated it well: "I am outraged by the amount of government expansion that is contained in this bill . . . [and I] do not know what you call it other than socialism."[7] The other major argument raised against the ARRA was that it would balloon the federal deficit. In the short term, the deficit would rise. However, to my mind, the need to stimulate demand in the economy far outweighed concern about short-term additions to the deficit. The sooner we could get the economy growing again, the sooner we could see deficits come down.

During my years of hearing political debates in the Senate, I had developed considerable skepticism about speeches bemoaning the size of the deficit. In most cases, members trotted out their arguments about the deficit as a justification for votes they were casting for other reasons. I remember thinking that many of those same senators lamenting how the ARRA would increase the deficit had also been advocates for the Bush tax cuts of 2001 and 2003, which had in fact added more to the national deficit and debt than was being added by the ARRA.

On February 12, 2009, the ARRA passed the House 246 to 183, without a single Republican voting "aye." The next day it passed the Senate 60 to 38 with all Democrats voting "aye," and all but three Republicans voting "no."[8] President Obama signed it on February 17, 2009.

———

Three times in 2008–2009 Congress acted to respond to the financial crisis: approving $700 billion in TARP rescue funds, refusing to block the use of the second $350 billion of those funds, and enacting a stimulus package (the ARRA). In each case the primary impediments Congress faced were pressure to toe the party line, pressure to do what the polls dictated, and ideology. Fortunately, Presidents Bush and Obama and a majority in both houses overcame those impediments and took the necessary actions.

4   Control Deficits and Debt

JUST BEFORE NOON one hot Wednesday in July 1993, the director of my state Senate offices, Vince Murphy, and I drove into the parking lot of the Holiday Inn Pyramid on the north side of Albuquerque. About thirty protesters met us. They were carrying homemade signs: "No More Taxes." The Omnibus Budget Reconciliation Act of 1993 had passed in the Senate a few days earlier.

Congress was taking its usual one-week recess for Fourth of July celebrations, so members could be in their home states. President Bill Clinton had been in office less than six months. During that time, he and Democratic leaders of the House and Senate had made it a priority to pass a budget to rein in the federal deficit. The Senate had passed such a budget the previous week, but without a single Republican voting "aye." With fifty Democrats and fifty Republicans, Vice President Al Gore had cast the deciding vote.

The Albuquerque Chamber of Commerce had invited me to the Holiday Inn that morning to update them on the latest developments in Washington. I knew that many in the audience disagreed with the "aye" vote I had cast at 3:15 the previous Friday morning. But I had not expected protesters to meet me outside the hotel.

The protesters did not represent a broad cross-section of the citizenry of New Mexico. In fact, I recognized several as prominent figures in the state Republican Party. My second term in the Senate would end the next year—in 1994—and I had not yet announced whether I would seek a third term. That hot, sunny July morning it flashed through my mind that the election campaign was starting a little early.

I see this as an example of how politics, rather than economics, dominates our national debate on deficits and debt.

The Basics

A crucial role of Congress in trying to support a robust economy comes under the heading of "setting fiscal policy" (i.e., determining how much revenue the government will raise, how much it will spend, and how much it will have to borrow). That taxing, spending, and borrowing activity affects the economy both in the short and the long term. In the short term, spending cuts and tax increases reduce economic activity, while increased spending and tax cuts stimulate the economy. In the longer term, it is Congress's job to keep deficits and the overall debt of the government at reasonable levels in relation to the size of the economy.

During most years, the federal government runs a deficit (i.e., federal spending exceeds revenues collected). Only rarely in the last century have revenues exceeded spending. The simple explanation for why deficits are the norm is that most people prefer to pay as little as possible in taxes and still enjoy the benefits provided by government. This creates pressure on Congress to support tax cuts and spending increases, which are popular, and to oppose tax increases and spending cuts, which are not.

The net sum of annual deficits, minus the occasional surplus, makes up the national debt.

Neither running deficits nor having a national debt is necessarily a problem. In fact, sometimes the government should borrow. One example was in 2009 when Congress enacted the American Recovery and Reinvestment Act (ARRA) (see chapter 3). That legislation added to the deficit in the short term, but it was essential in helping the economy recover from recession.

Problems develop when the government runs too large a deficit, or runs large deficits even in periods of high employment and strong growth in the gross domestic product (GDP). That can lead to the national debt becoming too large relative to the nation's GDP. By that measure, our annual deficits add up to a larger national debt today than we have had since World War II, and projections are for it to continue growing as a percentage of GDP.

One way to see the problem today is to look at our gross federal debt as a percentage of GDP:

GROSS FEDERAL DEBT AS A PERCENTAGE OF GDP

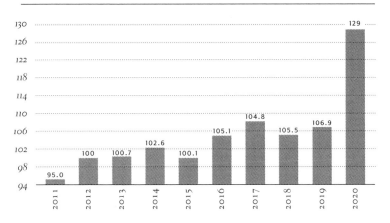

Source: Trading Economics, US Bureau of Public Debt.

SURPLUSES AND DEFICITS AS PERCENTAGE OF GDP

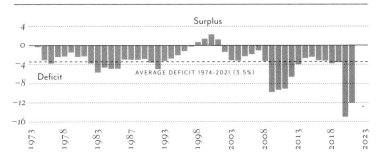

Source: Congressional Budget Office.

One other point worth noting is that the fastest-growing part of the federal budget is projected to be interest on the national debt.

Many economists believe that, over the long term, the nation should try to keep annual deficits near the rate of growth in the economy. As the chart above shows, since 1974, on average, government expenditures have exceeded revenues by over 3 percent.

A Short History of Deficits since 1980

When I arrived in the Senate, Ronald Reagan was president. At his urging, Congress had cut taxes and increased defense spending; deficits were growing. Some members of Congress worried about this, but reducing the deficit was not a top priority either for Congress or for President Reagan. Large deficits remained the norm throughout the 1980s and into the 1990s. In the late 1990s we were able—for the first time in a generation—to achieve a balanced budget and even a surplus. That unusual circumstance continued for four fiscal years (1998, 1999, 2000, and 2001), but by the time I left the Senate at the end of 2012, the deficit had grown dramatically, and deficits and debt were once again a major concern. During the Trump presidency, tax cuts and spending to respond to the pandemic raised deficits and debt to record levels. Increased spending in the first year of the Biden administration continued that trend. That roller-coaster ride from significant deficits, to budget surpluses, and back to significant deficits, should teach us something about the deficit and debt challenges faced by Congress.

GROWTH OF DEFICITS DURING THE REAGAN PRESIDENCY

In 1979, the year before Ronald Reagan became president, the federal deficit was $74 billion, or 2.6 percent of the country's GDP. The deficit rose to $128 billion, or 3.8 percent of GDP, in 1982. The next year, it rose again to $208 billion, or 5.6 percent of GDP. Several factors explain this increase: increased defense spending, reduced revenue to the Treasury because of tax cuts, and growth in the costs of government-provided health care. During the rest of the 1980s, deficits remained high by historical standards but decreased as a percent of GDP.

BEGINNINGS OF DEFICIT REDUCTION DURING THE G. H. W. BUSH PRESIDENCY

The 1990 Budget Enforcement Act (BEA), part of the Omnibus Budget Reconciliation Act of 1990, was the first serious effort to rein in the growth in deficits that had occurred since the beginning of the 1980s. This act created caps on discretionary spending and also established pay-as-you-go (PAYGO) rules for tax cuts and future increases in certain entitlement programs. In other words, future tax cuts that reduced the revenue coming to the government would have to be matched with comparable cuts in future spending. From my vantage point, the impetus for this 1990 deficit reduction effort appeared to come both from the president and from the leaders of Congress. The negotiated compromise contained both limits on spending and increased taxes. I credit Senate majority leader George Mitchell (D-ME) for his role in helping bring those negotiations with the Bush administration to a successful conclusion.

Although he agreed to the compromise and signed the legislation, President Bush later expressed regrets for his actions. In his campaign for reelection in 1992, critics in his own party attacked him for signing the bill. The charge was that he had broken the pledge he made at the 1988 Republican National Convention: "Read my lips: no new taxes."

President Bush should not have regretted signing the bill. His regret should have been about making such an irresponsible "no new taxes" pledge. He and all of us in the 101st Congress who supported the legislation should be proud that we enacted a bill to begin reducing the deficit.

GETTING TO SURPLUS IN THE CLINTON PRESIDENCY

In his first year in office, President Clinton urged Congress to pass the Omnibus Budget Reconciliation Act of 1993, referred to as the Deficit Reduction Act. This act resulted in deficit reduction of $433 billion over five years, with $241 billion of that coming from tax increases. By constraining the growth in spending and increasing the revenue coming to the government, it was a significant factor in helping us achieve budget surpluses beginning in 1998.

Bob Rubin, then assistant to the president for economic policy and the coordinator of the National Economic Council, and soon to be secretary of the Treasury, articulated the need for the legislation. He argued that reducing the federal deficit would reduce interest rates, which would increase economic growth, and through expanded private investments, result in a more productive economy. Now, with the advantage of hindsight, the correlation between large deficits and high interest rates is not so clear, but in the early 1990s, that argument seemed persuasive.

The Deficit Reduction Act raised taxes and constrained most areas of spending. It also added to the progressivity of the tax code (i.e., more of the tax burden would fall on those with higher incomes). The bill contained new top income tax rates of 36 percent for incomes above $150,000 per couple, and 39.6 percent for incomes above $250,000 per couple.

One provision in the bill singled out for condemnation by critics raised the federal gas tax by 4.3 cents per gallon from 14.1 cents to 18.4 cents.

It took substantial debate for Democratic senators to agree on the increase in the gas tax. I recall attending a meeting of Democratic senators in the LBJ Room on the second floor of the Capitol. One senator suggested that, to have a more rounded number, we should increase the tax by 4.5 cents per gallon, rather than 4.3 cents. At that point, another senator spoke up and stated that if we expected his vote on the final legislation, we needed to keep the increase to the lower number. Since all Democratic senators were needed to pass the bill, we kept the increase at 4.3 cents per gallon.

Going through this experience of voting to raise the gas tax helped me to understand why it happens so rarely.

Prior to the final vote on the entire bill, we had a heated debate in the Senate. Opponents of the bill voiced dire predictions of economic disaster if the bill became law. On April 5 the Republican leader, Senator Bob Dole, sounded the alarm, "The Clinton plan does not solve the debt problem. It will not keep the economy moving. And it will not create jobs."[1] As the vote approached, Dole's rhetoric became even more strident:

> We are bogged down because this thing is just killing us with taxes, taxes, taxes, taxes. There will not be any 1996 if this bill passes, probably. There may be a few politicians left, but there will not be any small business men and women left.[2]

The legislation passed, and the dire economic predictions proved unfounded. During the rest of the Clinton presidency, the United States enjoyed one of its strongest periods of economic growth.

At the same time that deficits were beginning to come under control, Newt Gingrich developed the Contract with America as the Republican platform for the 1994 midterm election. A central part of that "contract" was the promise to enact a constitutional amendment requiring a balanced budget. Early in 1995, Gingrich used his newly acquired Republican majority in the House to pass the amendment. When it came to the Senate on March 2, 1995, it got 65 votes, including 14 from Democrats. Since a constitutional amendment requires a two-thirds vote in both houses to pass, it failed. I voted with most Democrats against the proposal, believing that we needed to maintain the flexibility to deal with future economic downturns. Virtually all serious economists agreed with that position.

The other major deficit reduction effort during the Clinton presidency was the 1997 Balanced Budget Act. This act differed from the 1993 legislation in that it had the support of both Democrats and Republicans. The 1997 act was also important legislation, but without the 1993 Deficit Reduction Act we would not have achieved a balanced budget.

The strong economy of the 1990s—and the policy actions in 1990, 1993, and 1997 to raise taxes and to constrain growth in spending—brought the federal budget into surplus beginning in 1998. The four fiscal years from 1998 through 2001 were the first time the federal budget had been in surplus since 1969. No Congress has enacted a balanced budget or achieved a surplus since 2001.

RETURN TO LARGE DEFICITS
IN THE GEORGE W. BUSH PRESIDENCY

Four factors explain why the country's fiscal situation deteriorated again after 2001: the economy weakened, defense spending grew (because of the Afghanistan and Iraq wars), mandatory spending for health care (Medicaid and Medicare) increased because of increased enrollments plus growth in health care costs, and Congress enacted major tax cuts. The tax cuts and the increased defense spending were both large factors, directly resulting from policy decisions of the Bush administration and Congress.

For an excellent case study to show that Congress is eager to embrace almost any proposal to cut taxes regardless of its effect on the budget deficit, look no further than the Bush tax cuts in 2001 and 2003.

In making the case for his tax cuts, President Bush argued they would impose a constraint on the growth in government spending. It seemed very much as though fiscal policy had become a multistage strategic game in which Republicans, when they are in power, try to lock in large tax cuts to limit what future Democratic Congresses and presidents can do. Democrats, when they are in power, try to establish permanent new entitlement programs that will be difficult for Republicans to undo. This back-and-forth dodgeball game that determines fiscal policy adds to the uncertainty about our economic future.

The chair of the Federal Reserve, Alan Greenspan, provided cover for supporters of the Bush tax cuts during his testimony before the Senate Budget Committee leading up to the votes on the 2001 tax cut bill. He said that recent projections "make clear that the highly desirable goal of paying off the federal debt is in reach before the end of the decade,"[3] but he then raised the concern that if the government runs surpluses after we pay off the debt, it might undermine the ability of government to implement monetary policy, and might even lead the federal government to use the excess funds to buy "private assets." Greenspan thus gave members of Congress cover to vote for huge tax cuts and worry not at all about budget deficits.

Unsurprisingly, the federal budget was back in deficit by 2002. Those deficits continued to grow during the rest of that decade. The 2001 and 2003 Bush tax cuts reduced the revenue available to the government by cutting the estate tax, and lowering tax rates on income, capital gains, and dividend income.

THE GREAT RECESSION AND DEFICITS DURING THE OBAMA PRESIDENCY

Although deficits were large when the Great Recession began in 2008–2009, the recession caused them to balloon. As the economy slowed, the ranks of the unemployed grew, and tax revenues dropped precipitously. At the same time, government spending on entitlements grew to meet the increased needs of those without work. The tax cuts and new spending in the ARRA also added to the deficit.

Following the 2010 election, President Obama and Speaker John Boehner talked about their desire to reach a "grand bargain" to resolve differences concerning the budget and to reduce future-year deficits. Boehner would insist on future-year spending cuts, accomplished through changes in entitlements (Medicare, Medicaid, and Social Security), and Obama would insist on increased revenue, to keep spending cuts as modest as possible. To show his willingness to make difficult political decisions to reach an agreement, President Obama stated his willingness to put cuts in Social Security, Medicare, and Medicaid on the table. He also stated that in return for $100 billion in increased revenue each year for ten years, he would agree to cut government spending by three times that amount. He made clear that any "grand bargain" must include tax increases and well as spending cuts.

But Speaker Boehner soon discovered he could not get support from House Republicans for anything that increased taxes. House Republicans even opposed closing "tax loopholes" because they considered it a violation of the "Pledge."

The "Pledge" was the brainchild of Grover Norquist, the founder of Americans for Tax Reform. The Americans for Tax Reform began promoting the "Pledge" in 1986, to institutionalize resistance to efforts to increase revenue for the government. It states that the candidate will oppose any increase in income tax rates and will oppose "any net reduction or elimination of deductions or credits, unless matched dollar for dollar by further reducing tax rates."[4] To my mind, the terms of the "Pledge" added substantially to the difficulty of controlling budget deficits.

In the last Congress in which I served (the 112th Congress), 238 members of the House and 41 members of the Senate signed the "Pledge." Of the signers, all but two in the House and all but one in the Senate were Republicans. In many Republican-leaning districts and states, Republicans considered it difficult to win their party's nomination unless they had signed the "Pledge."

The failure of President Obama and Speaker Boehner to achieve a "grand bargain" had significant adverse consequences for the country. One consequence was that it assured large deficits for the foreseeable future. Another consequence was that during most of the 112th Congress, the government operated on a series of continuing resolutions (i.e., short-term appropriations bills that kept funding at a flat level). It also set the stage for enactment of the Budget Control Act of 2011, discussed in the context of the debt ceiling crisis, in chapter 1.

In law school they taught us that "hard cases make bad law." Usually this is cited regarding judicial rulings, but it could also apply to the Budget Control Act of 2011. It was a case where a terrible set of circumstances resulted in a bad law. The act had the effect of reducing the deficit in the short term. But it did so by imposing unnecessary and arbitrary ceilings on discretionary spending and did nothing to deal with the larger factors causing the deficit: the shortage of revenues and the growth in the cost of health care entitlements.

THE TRUMP PRESIDENCY

Regardless of the health of the economy, the government's fiscal situation, or the extent of the national security threats we face, newly elected Republican presidents almost always have two priorities: cutting taxes and increasing defense spending. That had been the case with President Reagan and President George W. Bush, and it was also the case with President Trump. In his first year as president he proposed both tax cuts and increased defense spending. Enacted by Congress, these policies returned the federal budget to a trillion-dollar deficit in 2019. By the end of Trump's term, the economic crisis caused by the pandemic and the mishandling of the US response resulted in even more dramatic increases in both deficits and the national debt. By the time President Biden took office in the midst of the pandemic-related economic crisis, most economists agreed with his view that Congress should appropriate whatever was required to return us to a robust economy.

THE BIDEN PRESIDENCY

Joe Biden's election as president and the urgent need to rebuild the economy after the pandemic set the stage for another debate about how much borrowing Congress should approve. In March 2021 Congress passed, and the president signed, the American Rescue Plan Act. Much like the ARRA enacted in response to the 2008–2009 recession, most of the bill was intended to stimulate economic growth, and it did not propose to raise revenue to pay for the spending. Also, much like with the ARRA, Republicans in Congress uniformly opposed the bill.

Lessons for the Future

A STRONG SCENT OF HYPOCRISY

Most people who run for and get elected to Congress support the idea of reducing the deficit. There is no magic required to accomplish this; Congress can either raise taxes or cut spending. When I first came to the

Senate, I assumed that members concerned about the deficit would be willing to do some of each—raise taxes and cut spending. I soon learned I was wrong.

Reducing the deficit is a priority for both conservatives and liberals, and for both Republicans and Democrats. The problem is that it is seldom, if ever, their first priority. The first priority for conservatives is reducing the size of government. They profess their concern about deficits and will vote for deficit reduction when they want to resist spending increases (in areas of the budget other than the military) or to argue for reductions in entitlement programs. They will not vote for deficit reduction if it involves increased taxes. For liberals or progressives, the first priority is to ensure that government raises and spends the amounts necessary to achieve what they believe is needed for the common good. They will vote for deficit reduction so long as they can reduce the deficit consistent with that goal.

THE FALSE PROMISE TO ELIMINATE THE DEBT

One of the great myths that remains alive in US political dialogue is the notion that some future administration and Congress will achieve a balanced budget, and then pay down, or even pay off, the national debt. Many candidates for public office have made this the centerpiece of their campaigns.

It is possible for a future Congress to pass a balanced budget, or even a budget with a surplus, such as we had in 1998–2001, but it is not realistic to think it will pay off the national debt, or even reduce it significantly. Each party has higher priorities that will thwart any such effort. That happened early in the George W. Bush presidency. If any future Congress can forecast budget surpluses, neither party will choose to sacrifice its chief priority simply to eliminate the debt. They have not done so in the past, and they will not do so in the future.

One of Benjamin Franklin's most quoted statements is, " . . . nothing can be said to be certain except death and taxes."[5] I would amend his statement by adding: " . . . and the national debt."

THE LONGER TERM

When the US economy is once again at full employment, some tax increases and spending restraint would make excellent sense. Some argue

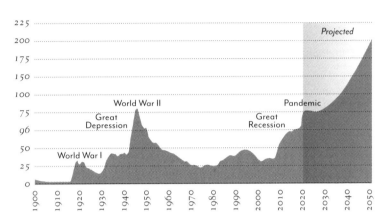

Source: The Congressional Budget Office, the 2021 Long-Term Budget Outlook, issued March 4, 2021, www.cbo.gov/publication/56977#data.

that since interest rates are low, the interest burden imposed by a large federal debt is not a problem to worry about. My concern is that if history is any guide, it is folly to assume low interest rates from now on. In December 2020 Paul Krugman wrote a column in the *New York Times*, "Learn to Stop Worrying and Love Debt,"[6] an obvious reference to *Dr. Strangelove, or: How I Learned to Stop Worrying and Love the Bomb.* In that film, Peter Sellers did not persuade me to love the bomb. I also have difficulty believing we should love debt.

Above is a recent Congressional Budget Office projection of where we are headed unless better judgment prevails.

In dealing with deficits and debt, most members of Congress do what the polls dictate. Much of what passes for policy discussion is thinly disguised political posturing. Ideology can be a factor with some members, but in most cases the ideological attachment is to smaller government, rather than a smaller deficit.

5   Lead in Science and Technology

OF THE FIVE IMPEDIMENTS discussed in chapter 2, ideology is the primary one we need to overcome to remain the world leader in science and technology. Where the federal government has taken an activist approach (i.e., in defense-related science and technology and in the health sciences), we have a record of leading the world. But in non-defense related areas, our position of leadership is less secure.

In 1983, during my first year in the Senate, I traveled to Palo Alto, the heart of Silicon Valley, to educate myself on what was happening with the semiconductor industry. Intel had established a semiconductor manufacturing facility (a "fab") in Rio Rancho, next to Albuquerque, and I felt I should know more about the industry. The evening I arrived, Intel had arranged a dinner for me with some industry leaders at an Italian restaurant in downtown Palo Alto. Bob Noyce and Gordon Moore, the founders of Intel, hosted the event.

After dinner, when my chance to speak came, I thanked Intel for building its newest fab in New Mexico, and asked what I, as a newly elected senator, could do to help the semiconductor industry prosper and continue creating jobs in the United States. The answer was unequivocal: the best thing the government could do was to not get involved. They felt comfortable about their ability to compete in world markets. Any involvement by the US government would only be counterproductive.

Two years later, Noyce and several others who had been at the dinner in Palo Alto scheduled an appointment to see me in my office in the Hart Building on Capitol Hill. Their opinion about the value of government involvement had changed dramatically. Japanese chipmakers were gaining market share. Japanese companies were dumping chips in the US market at below cost, and the Japanese government was denying US chipmakers access to the Japanese market.

Noyce and his colleagues had developed a strategy to respond: first, they wanted the US trade representative to insist on Japan granting them access to the Japanese market, and second, they wanted US government help to establish a consortium for US-based manufacturers to pursue improvements in the technology for making semiconductors. They wanted Congress to pay half the cost of the effort for the first five years.

Sematech, established in 1987, was the name given to the consortium. I was on the Armed Services Committee at the time of Noyce's visit, and we were developing the annual defense authorization bill, as we did each spring. That annual bill contains the authority for the Department of Defense to carry out its missions, and provides for military personnel pay. Every year it was, and still is, considered "must-pass legislation." Working with industry, we drafted language to include in the bill, authorizing the Department of Defense to provide the government portion of the required funds. Since the effort had the support of Secretary of Defense Casper Weinberger, it passed without opposition.

I see Sematech as a good example of how government can and should assist US businesses to remain competitive in world markets. From the beginning, industry conceived of the initiative and took responsibility for managing it. The government's role was to help underwrite the cost during its early years. Today, thirty-five years after its establishment, the US semiconductor industry continues to enjoy a leadership position in the world. Industry leaders involved at the time deserve credit for recognizing both that the US government could help ensure they received fair treatment in trade relations with Japan, and that by establishing Sematech they could remain on the forefront of new developments in technology.

Science and Technology: The Proper Role of Government

US economic strength depends on our ability to maintain a world-class science and technology enterprise. In its report "Rising above the Gathering Storm," the National Academies of Science and Engineering spoke of the "science and technological building blocks critical to our economic leadership."[1] During my time in the Senate, and since, our country has failed to pursue consistent and effective policies to support these building blocks. What explains this?

Much of the explanation derives from the general bias many in official Washington have against the federal government taking action that might interfere with the free market. Another factor is that we have never had a national consensus about when the federal government should act to support science and technology. If we can justify government involvement by citing national security, everyone supports the effort. But where the issue relates to economic well-being rather than national security, many in Washington oppose federal government involvement.

The history of how the United States became a world leader in science and technology explains much of this bias. Until late in the nineteenth century, Great Britain and then Germany led the world in science and technology. By the beginning of the twentieth century, that was changing. The United States gained its leadership role largely because of the two World Wars and the Cold War. These military challenges provided the stimulus and rationale for substantial federal government investment in science and technology.

Throughout our history, when our national leaders perceived a security threat, federal government support for science and technology has increased. When the national security threat appeared to diminish, support has shrunk.

The Essential Building Blocks

If science and technology are important for a robust economy, what are the building blocks for world leadership in science and technology? Four of the most important are:

1. Math and science education
2. Support for research and development (in addition to the life sciences and military research and development)
3. Commitment to nurture and assist strategic industries that emerge from new scientific and technological developments
4. Commitment to support US companies competing in international markets

MATH AND SCIENCE EDUCATION

US schools do a poor job in math and science instruction. This is not a recent problem. In 1957, when the Soviet Union launched Sputnik I, President Dwight D. Eisenhower and the Congress woke up to the fact that the USSR was ahead in the science and technology needed to compete in outer space. To address the perceived threat, Congress passed the National Defense Education Act in 1958. That act provided funds to upgrade science and math education in the nation's public schools and in colleges and universities. Part of the funding went to summer programs to improve the teaching skills of high school math and science teachers. The act also committed a billion dollars over four years to loans, scholarships, and graduate fellowships for students pursuing careers in math and science.

In July 1969, the United States landed the first manned mission on the moon. In the eyes of most, just as Sputnik had shown our inferior position relative to the USSR in space-related science and technology, the moon landing showed US leadership. Ironically, since the United States was again leading in the space race, the perceived threat to national security diminished. In turn, concern about the adequacy of science and math education also waned.

Today the prevailing view in official Washington is that elementary and secondary education, including education in math and the sciences, is primarily a state and local responsibility and not a priority concern for the federal government (see chapter 9). The Trump administration stated its commitment to local control of schools, and with enactment of the Every Student Succeeds Act, Congress also backed away from any major effort to improve the performance of US students in math and the sciences. That may change with the Biden administration. I hope so.

RESEARCH AND DEVELOPMENT

Federal government support for research and development in universities and national laboratories has also waxed and waned depending on the nation's perceived national security threats. At the height of the Cold War, federal support was substantial. Since the fall of the Berlin Wall and the collapse of the Soviet Union, support for nondefense research and development has declined relative to the nation's gross domestic product (GDP).[2]

One exception has been support for research in the health sciences, funded primarily through the National Institutes of Health (NIH). There are several reasons, including concern about the ailments afflicting our aging population and the effective lobbying of the pharmaceutical and medical device industries.

However, in other areas of research, the primary justification for federal government support has been national security. Congress funds most of the non-health related research and development supported by the federal government through the Departments of Defense and Energy. These two departments, based on their historical missions, favor research and development proposals that can show a clear connection to national security. With a new technology, such as artificial intelligence, that connection may not be sufficiently appreciated to spur these two departments to make the needed effort.

NURTURING SUNRISE INDUSTRIES

For the United States to remain the world leader in science and technology, it is not enough for the federal government to support math and science education in our schools, and research and development in our universities and laboratories. It is also essential that the new industries that emerge from this research receive the support they need to remain in the United States and to create jobs here at home. If entrepreneurs who build companies in these newly emerging industries locate their activities abroad, not only do we lose the opportunities for job creation, but also at some point we will lose our world leadership in the scientific and technological fields those industries depend on.

In recent decades, developments in the sciences and technology have spawned several new industries. Examples include LED lighting, robotics, photovoltaic solar cells, fuel cells, advanced batteries, and electric vehicles. In each case, much of the research to develop these new products and industries has occurred in US universities and laboratories. However, in the competition to commercialize the advances in technology and produce products and capture jobs in these emerging industries, there is little effort by the federal government to ensure that the United States succeeds.

Opponents of government action of this type argue that government involvement constitutes "industrial policy." The generally used definition of "industrial policy" is "government intervention in a specific sector which is designed to boost the growth prospects of that sector and to promote development of the wider economy."[3]

The arguments raised against "industrial policy" are: government needs to maintain a level playing field, government should not "pick winners and losers," and government should not try to behave like a venture capitalist. The claim is that questions about which of these emerging industries are important to our economic future, and where they locate production and create jobs, should be decided by market forces; unless national security is involved, the government should keep "hands off."

I first observed this ideological opposition to government support for emerging industries during a debate about the Advanced Technology Program in the National Institute of Science and Technology (NIST). Congress established that program in 1991 to help start-up firms commercialize new technology. With the Republican takeover of the House in 1995, the program encountered substantial opposition and saw its funding cut. Nineteen ninety-five was also the year Congress eliminated funding for the Congressional Office of Technology Assessment. It is worth noting that the hobgoblin of "industrial policy" had not been a problem in the previous decade when Congress funded Sematech. Any potential ideological opposition was avoided in that case by labeling it a national security concern and funding it through the Department of Defense.

A second instance where this ideology had an adverse impact involved the Department of Energy (DOE) program to provide loans and loan guarantees, established in Title XVII of the 2005 Energy Act. Although Congress had agreed to establish the program, when it got to implementation, the loan guarantee program encountered the same type of resistance the Advanced Technology Program had met. I had hoped that through the loan program the government could provide much-needed help to small companies trying to commercialize energy-related technologies, particularly those that would both help us meet our energy needs and reduce greenhouse gas emissions. During the George W. Bush administration, there was no concerted effort to implement the law. Early in the Obama administration's efforts to make the program a reality, Republicans seized on a Department of Energy loan guarantee to Solyndra, a California solar panel manufacturer, as a basis for denouncing government efforts to provide loan guarantees to businesses trying to commercialize new technologies (see chapter 7).

One success of the program was the loan provided to Tesla during the early years when Tesla needed an infusion of cash. In June 2009, when car companies could not get financing from other sources, Tesla applied for a $465 million loan to help reopen the shuttered auto plant it purchased in Fremont, California. That plant has been the main location for production of Tesla cars for sale in the United States. In May 2013 Tesla paid off the last of the loan.

The reality of the modern world persuades me that the federal government should do all it can to nurture emerging industries and encourage them to locate and succeed in the United States. Only in that way can we continue to create the high-wage jobs that result from technological innovation. In some cases that requires helping individual companies to survive and succeed.

During most of our history as a nation, and today, the federal government has had a major role in supporting particular industrial sectors. We have always had, and continue to have, various "industrial policies" in place.

One obvious example is agriculture. Beginning with the Morrill Act of 1862 and continuing today, the federal government has helped the agricultural sector by establishing and subsidizing land-grant colleges, providing county extension agents, offering loans for farmers, and establishing price supports for crops. Another example is the pharmaceutical industry. Here the government has underwritten much of the biomedical research that has led to the production and sale of new drugs. The NIH had a budget exceeding $42 billion in fiscal year 2020. Most of that funding supports research that the pharmaceutical industry depends on. By granting patents and exclusive licenses to the discoveries that result from this research, government provides an additional major assist to this sector of the economy. This heavy government support has been a prerequisite for the development of vaccines to counter Covid-19.

A third example is the open patenting system enjoyed by the hard-rock mining industry for mineral discoveries on public lands. This government subsidy to support the mining industry has remained in place since enactment of the 1872 Mining Act.

It is hard to reconcile this history of government support for particular industries with the entrenched resistance to efforts to think through an appropriate set of policies to help emerging industries succeed within our borders.

US government action in this area is particularly important because our economic competitors (China, Japan, Korea, Germany, etc.) have adopted aggressive strategies to compete for these industries. A prime example of such a strategy is China's blueprint for future technology development: "Made in China 2025." This is a strategic plan to position China to dominate advanced manufacturing industries such as robotics, advanced information technology, aviation, and clean energy vehicles. Much of the plan focuses on gaining both advanced technologies and the foreign companies that lead in developing and applying these technologies. The Chinese government supplements these investment and acquisition efforts with policies to force foreign companies wishing to do business in China to transfer technological know-how to Chinese firms.

The United States and other developed countries have complained about many elements in China's strategic plan. However, the primary response in the United States has not been to develop our own plan for encouraging companies in these high-tech fields to maintain and grow their operations in the United States. Instead, it has been to impose tariffs on a broad range of Chinese-made products. The ultimate effect of these across-the-board tariffs is unknown, but it seems like a case of using a truncheon where a scalpel would make more sense.

Not only do foreign nations pursue job creation based on emerging technologies, but also many US states and cities have well-funded and aggressive efforts to do so. Members of Congress who resist federal government efforts to develop these strategies on the theory that the free market should prevail, have no problem with similar efforts being pursued in the states and cities they represent. This might make sense if states and cities could compete against foreign national governments. But the reality is that Albuquerque, Atlanta, and Denver simply cannot provide businesses with the subsidies and tax incentives that are provided by the governments of China, Korea, and Ireland.

Francis Fukuyama argues that while other countries have succeeded in their efforts to attract and build emerging industries, any effort in the United States to plan and develop national strategies to promote such job creation is destined to fail, because of lobbying by special interests:

> An industrial policy worked in Taiwan only because the state was
> able to shield its planning technocrats from political pressures so

that they could reinforce the market and make decisions according to criteria of efficiency—in other words, [it] worked because Taiwan was not governed democratically. An American industrial policy is much less likely to improve its economic competitiveness, precisely because America is more democratic than Taiwan or the Asian NIEs (Newly Industrialized Economies). The planning process would quickly fall prey to pressures from Congress either to protect ineffi-cient industries or to promote ones favored by special interests.[4]

Fukuyama seems to assume that if we refuse to have a conscious policy to support strategic industries, special interests will have less opportunity to protect inefficient industries.

The sad fact is that ideological opposition to anything characterized as industrial policy leaves the field open for each special interest to advo-cate for its own pet subsidy or preference. It also results in the president and Congress taking actions based on ignorance, or politics, or simply on whim.

President Trump imposed tariffs on imported steel and aluminum and justified it with the argument that without steel and aluminum, "you almost don't have much of a country."[5] He also proclaimed that our national inter-est requires that we maintain jobs in the coal industry, and the administra-tion scrambled to cobble together proposals to promote more use of coal.

Many in Congress who oppose government efforts to help emerging industries have no hesitation in supporting the coal industry, even though the pernicious environmental impact of burning coal is well understood. This support continues also despite the fact that the economic importance of coal production in our economy has been declining for years, and will continue to decline.

A particularly egregious example of a Trump administration proposal to help the coal industry was the Department of Energy's effort to have the Federal Energy Regulatory Commission (FERC) issue requirements to utilities to maintain stockpiles of coal. The implausible theory advanced to support this was that we needed stockpiles of coal to increase the resil-iency of the electric grid. To their credit, FERC rejected the argument.

There is an obvious conflict between opposing "industrial policy" and at the same time supporting government help to those industries that contribute the most to your campaign, or that have the most effective lobbyists, or that have a large presence in your home state or congressional district. The ideological bias against government involvement prevents us from being proactive in identifying and assisting new industries that will be vital to our economic future. At the same time, the undue influence of special interests ensures that government will be involved in favoring certain already established and aging industries. Thus, ideology does not prevent us from adopting industrial policies, but in most cases it prevents us from making wise choices about which industries to help.

If we could overcome the ideological bias against the government trying to assist emerging and strategic industries, the logical first priority would be to strengthen the ability of policy makers to understand which industries are most important for our economic future. This is not a simple question to answer, and we will make mistakes, but that does not mean we should refuse to try.

We are long overdue for a meaningful national dialogue about which industries are important to our economic future, and when the government should act to help those industries create and maintain jobs. These decisions are too important to cede to the lobbying efforts of special interests.

HELPING US COMPANIES COMPETE
IN INTERNATIONAL MARKETS

Today, US firms involved with developing and manufacturing products, and providing high-skill services, are operating in a global marketplace. The nations with which we trade and compete have adopted policies to ensure that companies that create jobs and generate revenue within their borders can produce and export their products and services. In the United States we have no consensus about what role our own government should play.

The recent struggle to reauthorize the Export-Import Bank (the Ex-Im Bank) shows the problem. It is an example of how ideological bias against government involvement can retard efforts to create and maintain jobs in the United States.

In 1934, President Franklin D. Roosevelt urged Congress to establish the Export-Import Bank to assist companies selling US-produced goods and services in international markets. Since its founding, Congress has reauthorized the bank sixteen times with support from both Republicans and Democrats. The agency performs its mission by providing working capital guarantees, export credit insurance, direct loans, and loan guarantees, all to facilitate purchases of US-produced products by foreign buyers. Today, all industrialized countries with which we compete have similar governmental programs engaged in export financing.

During the period of Republican control of the Senate beginning in 2015, the Ex-Im Bank could not function. The law requires the bank to have a quorum of at least three members to conduct business, and the Senate refused to confirm enough members to make a quorum until May 2019. The Senate's inaction was prompted by the anti-government views of constituents. A 2018 article in *The New American* summed up the argument against maintaining the Ex-Im Bank and criticized President Trump for nominating a new president for the bank:

> The Ex-Im Bank is a creature of FDR's New Deal-era swamp, intended to subsidize U.S. exports during the Great Depression and World War II. Unfortunately, the Ex-Im Bank remained after World War II and has since become synonymous with crony capitalism and corporate welfare. . . . The Ex-Im Bank does anything but put "America First" or "Make America Great Again," which makes it rather surprising that President Trump would nominate a new president and board members in order to give the Ex-Im the necessary quorum to undermine the American taxpayer and free market.[6]

Anyone who believes US firms selling abroad are operating in a "free market" is mistaken. With the aggressive support provided to foreign firms by their governments, it is imperative that the US government be able to counter the actions of our economic competitors. The "free market" that some fear the Ex-Im Bank will "undermine" does not exist.

⎯⎯⎯⎯

The success of the US economy in the last century owes much to our world leadership in science and technology. The consensus to build and maintain that leadership resulted from twentieth-century wars and other threats to national security. Today, it is essential that we maintain US scientific and technological leadership to secure both our national security and our economic future. That will require that we adopt a more serious and consistent effort to support the building blocks for a sustainable world-class science and technology enterprise. It will also require us to overcome the impediment of an ideological aversion to government support for policies to help us remain the world's science and technology leader.

6   Meet Our Energy and Climate-Change Challenges (through 2008)

Supply and Price Concerns Meet the Reality of Climate Change

One of my first committee assignments was to the Senate Energy and Natural Resources Committee. For a newly elected senator from New Mexico, that made sense. New Mexico is a major oil- and gas-producing state and the home to two Department of Energy national laboratories (Los Alamos National Laboratory and Sandia National Laboratory). The federal government also owns over one-third of the land in New Mexico. The committee had jurisdiction over all of that.

During my thirty years on the committee, I saw the country's energy challenges change. In 1983, the major energy problems related to supply and the price of energy. By 2013, when I left the Senate, the nation's energy problems had become more complex. Climate change was the new and complicating factor. It demanded changes in policy to pursue two somewhat contradictory goals: ensuring an abundant and affordable supply of energy, while also reducing greenhouse gas (GHG) emissions. Since the reality of climate change has become apparent, we have adopted policies to meet our goals regarding the supply of energy. So far, though, we have failed to effectively confront climate change.

During most of the twentieth century, the United States enjoyed the luxury of cheap energy. Coal was the dominant fuel during much of our history. In recent decades, natural gas has become plentiful and cheap, and to a great extent has replaced coal for heating and power generation. For transportation, oil refined into gasoline has been plentiful. As a result, for many decades the subject of energy was not a regular priority on the national agenda, or the agenda of Congress. In the transportation sector, that changed with the 1973 and 1979 oil crises when we found we could no longer count on plentiful supplies of oil at a reasonable price.

THE 1973 OIL CRISIS

By the early 1970s, the United States had become dependent on foreign sources of oil. In October 1973, the Organization of Arab Petroleum Exporting Countries (OPEC) began an oil embargo against the United States, prompted by US support for Israel in the Yom Kippur War. The embargo curtailed US supplies of gasoline and increased prices for consumers.

To respond, the United States took several important steps, some related to oil and some related to other energy challenges. During the Ford administration (1974–1977) Congress established the Strategic Petroleum Reserve. It also enacted Corporate Average Fuel Economy (CAFE) standards (requiring vehicle manufacturers to improve vehicle fuel efficiency), and it established the National Renewable Energy Laboratory (NREL) in Golden, Colorado.

PRESIDENT CARTER'S ENERGY AGENDA AND THE 1979 OIL CRISIS

Jimmy Carter became president in June 1977, with ambitious goals for dealing with the nation's energy problems. The 1973 energy crisis had persuaded him that the United States needed to reduce imports of oil; increase domestic production of energy, particularly from nuclear power and renewable resources; and reduce the growth in our demand for energy.

His first legislative success to carry out his agenda was in 1977 in the Department of Energy Organization Act, which established the Department of Energy. The next year Congress passed the National Energy Act that continued much of what Carter's plan had called for, including the beginnings of deregulation of natural gas, and tax incentives for energy conservation and increased use of renewable energy.

In 1979, the United States faced another oil crisis. This time it was not an embargo, but a dramatic increase in the price of gasoline that shocked the world economy. The actions the United States and other oil-importing nations had taken to reduce dependence on foreign oil had not been adequate. In response, President Carter proposed and Congress passed the Energy Security Act, establishing the US Synthetic Fuels Corporation as well as important programs to promote production of biofuels.

Although some of the initiatives that began during the Carter administration did not bear fruit, President Carter's policies put the nation on a new path for meeting its energy needs.

THE 1980S

After Carter left the White House, energy issues took a back seat to other concerns on the national agenda.

By the early 1980s, when I joined the Energy Committee, the energy crises had passed. President Carter had installed solar panels on the White House roof; President Reagan had them removed. Members of Congress still complained about our growing dependence on foreign sources of oil, but usually only when the price of oil spiked on world markets. Whenever such a spike occurred, this would be the normal pattern in Congress: the price of oil would rise, which would cause the price of gasoline to go up at the pump, and constituents would complain to their senator or representative. Those senators and representatives would interrupt other work to give speeches, clarifying that they shared the outrage of their constituents. But most members understood Congress could not legislate a solution to the problem of high gas prices over the short term, since world oil prices largely determined the price of gas at the pump.

When oil prices returned to a more acceptable level, Congress and the country would once again return to other issues.

EARLY WARNINGS ON CLIMATE CHANGE

With the benefit of hindsight, we can see that the problem of climate change was being discussed by climate scientists long before the 1980s. But in my experience on the Energy Committee, 1988 was an important milestone. That year, Dr. James Hansen, the director of NASA's Goddard Institute for Space Studies, testified to our committee on climate change. He predicted continued global warming because of human-produced GHGs:

> I would like to draw three main conclusions. Number one, the earth is warmer in 1988 than at any time in the history of instrumental measurements. Number two, the global warming is now large enough that we can ascribe with a high degree of confidence a cause and effect relationship to the greenhouse effect. And number three, our

computer climate simulations indicate that the greenhouse effect is already large enough to begin to effect the probability of extreme events such as summer heat waves.[1]

His conclusion was, "The greenhouse effect has been detected, and it is changing our climate now."[2]

Hansen's testimony did not result in any immediate action by Congress, but calls for attention to the problem continued to grow. In that same year, the United Nations (UN) established the Intergovernmental Panel on Climate Change (IPCC), made up of many of the world's leading climate scientists. The IPCC developed a major report reflecting the scientific consensus that the buildup of GHG emissions in the atmosphere was causing the climate to warm. The report concluded that the primary cause of the warming was human production and use of fossil fuels.

In 1992, in response to the work of the IPCC, the UN convened the Earth Summit in Rio de Janeiro, which resulted in the United Nations Framework Convention on Climate Change (UNFCCC). That treaty recognized the adverse effects of GHG emissions and pledged the 165 countries that signed it to adopt policies to confront the problem.

The United States was forthright in its support of the treaty. To underscore that support, President George H. W. Bush traveled to the Rio

THE EVOLUTION OF US POLICY ON ENERGY
AND THE ENVIRONMENT

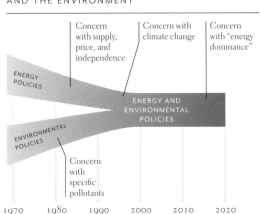

conference. In a statement in Rio on June 13, he explained the US position: "Let me be clear on one fundamental point. The United States fully intends to be the world's preeminent leader in protecting the global environment. We have been that for many years. We will remain so."[3]

Four months later, on October 7, the US Senate adopted a Resolution of Ratification for the treaty.

Before climate change became a major issue, Congress had considered energy policy and environmental policy as two separate sets of policies. Now, the scientific community was sounding the alarm about the growth in GHG emissions in the atmosphere. With this increased awareness of climate change and its causes, energy and environmental policies began to merge (see the chart on the previous page).

POLICY OPTIONS

Many types of policies can help reduce GHG emissions resulting from energy production and use. Some are carrots. Some are sticks. Some focus on reducing the demand for energy. Others try to discourage the continued use of fossil fuels and inefficient, polluting technologies.

In the power-generation sector, policies can seek to reduce GHGs from electric power plants, as the Environmental Protection Agency (EPA) tried to do with the Clean Power Plan in the second Obama administration, or reduce consumer demand for electric power by encouraging increased efficiency in using energy. Some policies require manufacturers of machinery and appliances to sell products that are more energy efficient. Examples of these policies are energy-efficient refrigerators, and LED lighting to replace low-efficiency incandescent bulbs.

In transportation, our most effective national policy has been Corporate Average Fuel Efficiency (CAFE) standards: increasing the requirements on vehicle manufacturers to improve the fuel efficiency of the vehicles they sell. Congress has also adopted policies to affect consumer behavior. An example is the tax credit for those who purchase a zero or low-emission vehicle.

In both power generation and transportation, Congress has enacted some version of most of these policies. The executive branch has also found ways to use its rulemaking authority to reduce GHG emissions. Although each of these policies makes some contribution to reducing the growth in GHGs, most economists argued that the most effective action government can take is to "put a price on carbon." By this they meant imposing a financial penalty on the use of energy from GHG-emitting sources. Congress has made efforts to accomplish this, but so far those efforts have not succeeded.

Early Efforts to Address the New Reality, 2000–2010

THE 2000 PRESIDENTIAL CAMPAIGN

In 2000, climate change and how to respond to it became an issue for the first time in a US presidential campaign. Vice President Gore advocated reducing GHG emissions and made that a significant part of his campaign. His opponent, then-governor George W. Bush, also endorsed mandatory emission limits, and pledged to cap carbon dioxide fumes and require power plants to reduce GHG emissions "within a reasonable period of time."[4] After being elected, Bush largely abandoned those earlier commitments.

By the time President Bush took the oath of office, a majority in Congress recognized that energy policy had to reflect concern about climate change, and not just concern about the supply and price of energy. Despite pushback from the George W. Bush administration, members in both houses of Congress, and from both parties, launched efforts to enact energy legislation to address this larger set of issues. The two parties had different priorities represented in their policy proposals, but if they could overcome the obstacles, Republicans and Democrats might agree on enough to enact constructive legislation. But first Congress spent several years pursuing various time-consuming false starts.

THE BUSH-CHENEY ENERGY PLAN

In his second week in office, President Bush established his Energy Task Force and named Vice President Cheney as its chair. The task force quickly moved to develop recommendations, but its meetings were closed to the public. Industry representatives and lobbyists were providing most of the advice, and leaders of the environmental community denounced the process.

The task force report, dated May 17, 2001, focused on how the United

States could ensure an abundant supply of energy in the future. It called for a redoubling of United States efforts to produce energy from the traditional sources of oil, gas, coal, and nuclear. The report also contained a halfhearted endorsement of continuing efforts to diversify sources of energy by developing renewable energy technologies. The rationale offered was not concern about climate change; it was the need to diversify supply. In fact, the report was notable for its lack of discussion of climate change and its implications.

JIM JEFFORDS'S SWITCH

On May 24, 2001, a week after Vice President Cheney issued the Bush-Cheney energy plan, Senator Jim Jeffords of Vermont held a press conference in Burlington, Vermont, to announce he was leaving the Republican Party to become an independent. In the future, he would caucus with Democrats in the Senate. I'm sure there were many reasons for Jim's decision, but based on my visits with him, I believe one factor was his strong disagreement with the Bush administration positions on energy and the environment.

The Jeffords announcement had major consequences in the closely divided Senate. It shifted control from Republicans to Democrats. This was the first time in the history of the Senate that a single senator's actions had had that effect. Before Jim's announcement, the Senate was divided 50-50. On strict party-line votes, Vice President Cheney could break the tie in favor of Republicans. After Jeffords' switch, Democrats could count on 51 votes, so there was no longer a tie for the vice president to break.

THE 2002 EFFORT

To get an early start on the Cheney task force recommendations, chairman of the Energy Committee Frank Murkowski (R-AK) prepared an energy bill in the spring of 2001. I, and most Democrats on the committee, objected to many of the provisions he included. One sticking point was his insistence on opening the Arctic National Wildlife Refuge (ANWR) for exploration and drilling. With Jim Jeffords's switch, I became the chair of the committee and Murkowski became the ranking member. A comprehensive energy bill had passed in the House in 2001, and as chair, I could prevent the committee from reporting Frank's objectionable proposals, including the plan to open ANWR, as part of a Senate bill. But getting agreement on a bipartisan bill was going to be difficult.

At that point, Senator Tom Daschle asked me to hold off on efforts to report an energy bill to the full Senate. Instead, he put together energy-related provisions from our committee and several others and brought that larger package of provisions to the Senate floor for consideration. Republicans did not like the procedure, but Daschle's promise that he would allow an open amendment process on the Senate floor assuaged their concerns. He was true to his word, and in the Senate we devoted seven weeks of floor time to debate and amendment on the bill. On April 25, 2002, the Senate voted for its version of an energy bill, 88 to 11. The eleven votes in opposition split almost evenly between Republicans and Democrats. We set up a conference committee with the House to see if we could agree on a final bill, but with the 2002 midterm elections approaching, and with Republicans likely to regain control of the Senate, the efforts to get a conference agreement went nowhere.

THE 2003 REPUBLICAN BILL

As expected, in the 2002 election Republicans regained control of the Senate and kept control of the House. Frank Murkowski left the Senate in December 2002, after winning his campaign for governor of Alaska. He took office as governor on December 2, 2002, resigned his Senate seat, and appointed as his successor his daughter, Lisa Murkowski, who was then the majority leader designate in the Alaska House of Representatives. Upon Frank's resignation from the Senate, my colleague from New Mexico, Senator Pete Domenici, became the new chair of the Energy Committee. With Republicans controlling the Senate, I was once again the committee's ranking Democrat.

The first instinct of Republicans in 2003 was to get back to where they had been before Jim Jeffords's switch (i.e., to take the Bush-Cheney task force report and enact energy legislation based on its recommendations). Under Pete's leadership, the committee did just that. It reported a bill to the Senate that I could not support. Because of opposition from Democratic senators, that bill stalled on the Senate floor.

In order to move ahead with the process, Majority Leader Bill Frist took the suggestion of Harry Reid, the minority leader, to bring up the energy

This cartoon by John Trever of the *Albuquerque Journal* was his depiction of our successful effort to defeat the 2003 Republican bill. © 2003 by John Trever, *Albuquerque Journal*.

bill the Senate had passed in 2002 by an 88 to 11 vote, and the Senate passed it again. Senate Republicans then set up a conference committee with the House, but they took the unusual step of banning Democrats from the meetings of the conference. In short order, the Republican-controlled House and Senate conference committee reported a bill. As the ranking Democrat on the relevant committee, who had been excluded from conference committee deliberations, I urged all senators to oppose it.

Besides objecting to the procedure Republicans had followed, I also objected to many of the bill's provisions. It contained large subsidies for the coal industry, provided for the elimination of royalty payments for oil wells on public lands, rolled back certain environmental regulations, opened new areas (including ANWR) for oil and gas exploration, and shielded the industry from lawsuits over MTBE—a cancer-causing gasoline additive that had leached into groundwater. The bill also was loaded with special interest provisions. The House-passed version of the bill even included a subsidy for a Hooters restaurant in Louisiana.

On the Senate floor, I joined other Democrats and some Republicans in a filibuster of the bill. To end the filibuster, Senator Frist filed a cloture petition, and on November 21, 2003, the effort to move the legislation forward came to an abrupt end when he and Senator Domenici, the manager of the bill, failed to get the necessary sixty votes to end debate.

In addition to the Democrats, several Republican senators also voted "no." The most outspoken Republican to oppose the bill was Senator McCain. He dubbed the bill the "Leave No Lobbyist Behind Act of 2003."[5] In his statement on the Senate floor, he described the process by which the bill was developed: "A secretive, exclusive process has led to a 1,200-page monstrosity that is chock full of special interest giveaways and exemptions from environmental and other laws that, frankly, cannot withstand the light of scrutiny."[6]

We made no further progress on enacting energy legislation during the rest of that two-year Congress.

THE ENERGY POLICY ACT OF 2005

In January 2005, Republicans again controlled both the Senate and the House. In the Senate Energy Committee, Senator Domenici was chair, and I was the ranking Democrat. Recognizing that partisan efforts to enact energy policy in the previous Congress had accomplished nothing, we agreed the time had come to try a bipartisan approach.

In Senate committees, there are separate staffs for Democrats and Republicans. Our first challenge was to see if our respective staffs could work together to produce a comprehensive bill that both of us could support.

The procedure we followed was straightforward: Pete and I agreed that we would present to the committee the bill our respective staff directors had put together. We did that with a full understanding that each of us had provisions we would like to add to the bill. During the markup, we and the other committee members offered amendments to add, delete, or change provisions. That markup process took several weeks, but once we finished considering all amendments, we reported the revised bill to the full Senate.

To say the bill we developed was multifaceted is an understatement. It encompassed most of the energy-related issues the committee had jurisdiction to consider: provisions intended to increase energy production from most sources (i.e., oil and gas, coal, nuclear, solar, wind energy, geothermal, energy from tidal waves, etc.). We also included provisions to encourage more energy efficiency and conservation.

The next hurdle was the Senate floor. But before floor consideration was possible, we needed to incorporate energy-related bills developed by other committees. The Environment and Public Works Committee, the Commerce Committee, and the Finance Committee each had proposals with a legitimate claim to being included in "comprehensive energy legislation."

The Republican and Democratic leaders, and their staffs, had the final say on what provisions from other committees they would add to the bill. When the merged bill came to the Senate floor in June 2005, we followed the same basic procedure we had followed in committee (i.e., we gave all senators a chance to offer their amendments).

An important amendment, adding energy-related tax provisions, was adopted late in the process. Max Baucus, who chaired the Finance Committee, offered it toward the end of the floor debate to reduce the opportunity for opponents to mount a major lobbying effort. It included tax incentives for three broad purposes: to encourage more domestic production of fossil fuels, to encourage more production and use of energy from renewables, and to encourage more conservation and attention to improved energy efficiency.

Once the Senate had disposed of all amendments, we proceeded to a final vote. The bill passed the Senate 85 to 12. At any stage, any senator who objected to the bill could have filibustered. The bipartisan process we followed in developing and managing the bill helped avoid that result. By the time the vote on final passage was called, many senators had been able to add amendments on issues that mattered to them. Even some senators whose amendments had failed were willing to support the bill, in part because they appreciated the open amendment process the Senate had followed.

Before the full Senate began consideration of an energy bill, the House had already passed its bill. The House did not follow the same type of genuine bipartisan effort that took place in the Senate. The vote to pass the House bill was 249 to 183. Many of the votes in opposition reflected the fact that Democratic House members saw the bill as too weighted with Republican priorities.

The House had passed its proposed bill in April 2005, and the Senate passed its bill right before leaving for the Fourth of July break. We were now ready for a conference committee between the House and Senate. In July, Joe Barton, the chair of the House Energy and Commerce Committee, and John Dingell, the ranking Democrat, met with Pete and me in a series of sessions. Together, we negotiated a final package we could present to the full conference committee.

After substantial compromise on all sides, the conference committee issued its report. That final bill—The Energy Policy Act of 2005 (EPACT)—passed the House 275 to 156 and passed the Senate 74 to 26. I was glad the final votes for the bill in the Senate included a majority of Republican senators, and a majority of Democrats.

Partly in recognition of the role Pete and I had played in getting the bill passed, President Bush chose Sandia National Laboratory in Albuquerque as the location for signing the bill on August 8, 2005.

The reason we could get bipartisan support for the bill was that it contained provisions to address the energy priorities of both parties. Republicans focused on the adequacy of supply; Democrats focused more on speeding up the transition to less polluting sources of energy and improving energy efficiency.

NUCLEAR ENERGY   Nuclear power is a substantial source of energy for power generation in the United States. In the 2005 bill, we tried to include provisions that would help support continued use of nuclear energy. One-fifth of our electricity comes from nuclear power plants. Both Pete and I supported taking action to encourage more use of nuclear energy. My motivation was to provide a source of "base load" power that utilities could rely on, and that would not contribute to the global warming problem. Increased use of nuclear power was far preferable to continued reliance on energy from pulverized coal plants.

The pro-nuclear provisions in the bill included increased research and development funding for advanced nuclear designs, a production tax credit for energy produced from nuclear plants for an eight-year period, and an extension of the provisions in the Price-Anderson Nuclear Industries Indemnity Act through 2025. That act, first passed in 1957, provided partial compensation for the civilian nuclear industry against liability claims that might arise from nuclear incidents.

Despite these provisions in the 2005 act, economic factors have not proved favorable for nuclear energy. Low-cost and plentiful natural gas, plus wind and solar resources, have made it difficult for most utility executives to consider constructing new nuclear-generating capacity. The high upfront capital costs of constructing a nuclear power plant, and the frequent cost overruns, have made it uncompetitive. For the time being, at least, these cost considerations have dimmed the prospects for increased use of nuclear power in the United States. The most recent reactor to enter service in the United States is the Tennessee Watts Bar Unit 2, which began operations in June 2016. Prior to that, it had been twenty years since a reactor had entered service: the Watts Bar Unit 1 in 1996, also in Tennessee.

Cost is not the only problem faced by nuclear power. There is also deep-seated concern by many about safety and health, and as a nation we have failed to find and implement an acceptable method for disposing of nuclear waste. I remain convinced that nuclear power can be produced safely without posing undue risk to human health. I also believe we can deal effectively with the waste disposal problem. The Blue Ribbon Commission Report issued in 2012 describes how that can be accomplished.[7]

THE ENERGY INDEPENDENCE & SECURITY ACT OF 2007

The 2006 election was good for Democratic candidates running for the House and Senate. I saw that in New Mexico, where I succeeded in my campaign for a fifth term. When the 107th Congress began in January 2007, President George W. Bush was entering the final two years of his second term. For the first time, he faced both a House and Senate controlled by Democrats.

One consequence of the election was that in January 2007 Pete and I traded positions in the Energy Committee; he became the ranking Republican and I became the chair. As chair, I went about trying to determine if we could build on our success in the previous Congress and enact significant energy legislation in this 107th Congress to deal with issues left unaddressed in the 2005 bill. I concluded that another bipartisan effort at energy legislation might well succeed.

As with the 2005 bill, we began the process by having committee staff (both Democratic and Republican) develop a proposed bill that Pete and I could support. That bill then went through a period of consideration and amendment in committee. Senator Reid, now as majority leader, followed the same process that was used with the 2005 bill; he merged energy-related bills reported from other committees with our Energy Committee bill, in order to bring a comprehensive energy bill to the Senate floor.

Very early in the new Congress, the now Democratically controlled House passed its own version of energy legislation. Given the procedure we had set out for trying to get a bipartisan bill, the Senate did not vote on a bill until late June. At that point, the House and Senate leadership had to decide whether to follow the traditional route and appoint a conference committee to work out the differences in the two bills, or have the chairs and ranking members of the committees negotiate the differences. Senator Reid chose the less formal path of negotiating about differences. Those negotiations consumed much of the fall of 2007. The bill resulting from these negotiations—the Energy Independence & Security Act of 2007 (EISA)—then passed both houses of Congress, and President Bush signed it on December 19, 2007. As with the 2005 energy bill, a majority of senators from each party supported final passage.

The 2007 bill contained provisions dealing with both power generation and transportation, the two sectors that account for most of the energy used in our economy. Now, with a Congress under Democratic control, the clear priority of the legislation was to reduce demand for energy, and to support alternative sources of energy. In the power-generation sector the bill encouraged more efficiency in the use of electricity and more use of power from non-emitting sources (wind, solar, nuclear, et al.). In the transportation sector, the bill sought to reduce the growth in demand for gasoline.

ENERGY EFFICIENCY IN THE USE OF ELECTRICITY In the case of electricity, the most effective policies enacted to date have been policies to improve energy efficiency. Higher efficiency standards for appliances, machinery, and lighting have reduced the demand for new power plants. In 1975, Congress had enacted the Energy Policy and Conservation Act. In 1987, 1992, and 2005, Congress strengthened and added to that legislation. These statutes established efficiency standards for several types of appliances and allowed the DOE to update those standards in future years. Congress set standards for a long list of appliances, including refrigerator-freezers, room air conditioners, washing machines and dryers, kitchen ranges and ovens, pool heaters, and water heaters. Consistent with this general effort to promote more efficiency in appliances, we had included provisions in the 2007 bill to require greater efficiency in lighting.

As the twenty-first century began, the world was still reliant on inefficient incandescent light bulbs to meet its lighting needs. The incandescent bulb had improved only marginally since Thomas Edison invented it in 1879. While an impressive invention at the time, only 10 percent of the electricity used in the bulb gets converted into light. The rest becomes heat. Since lighting accounts for a significant portion of the electricity used in the US economy, I saw improving efficiency in lighting as having great potential for reducing electricity demand. That potential was the impetus for enacting lighting efficiency standards and for establishing the "L Prize," both of which we did in the 2007 energy act.

The L Prize was a competition run by the DOE to encourage manufacturers to develop high-quality, high-efficiency, solid-state lighting. The DOE announced the prize in May 2008 with the goal of finding a more efficient replacement for the common incandescent light bulb. A $10 million prize was offered. Phillips won with a bulb that produced the same amount of light as a 60-watt incandescent bulb, but used less than 10 watts: an 83 percent energy savings. This L Prize helped stimulate technology innovations, resulting in much more efficient lighting products.

ENERGY EFFICIENCY IN TRANSPORTATION (CAFE STANDARDS) All members of Congress agreed on the need to reduce oil imports. But some of us believed that reducing oil imports was not an adequate solution; we also needed to reduce the demand for oil in the US economy. Reducing US dependence on oil, whether from domestic or foreign sources, would lessen the impact of volatile world oil prices on the US economy. It would also reduce GHG emissions from tail pipes of cars and trucks.

Most economists argue that if Congress wants to increase vehicle fuel efficiency, it should simply raise the tax on gasoline. Their arguments are valid, but given the difficulty of getting the votes to raise the gas tax, we needed to adopt an alternative policy to achieve the same result. Since 1975, that alternative policy has been Corporate Average Fuel Economy (CAFE) standards. CAFE standards require all manufacturers selling in the US market to meet certain miles-per-gallon targets for different types of vehicles.

The most significant action taken in the 2007 bill was to increase CAFE standards and to allow the administration to raise those standards even higher in the future. CAFE standards had been implemented in 1978, setting fuel efficiency requirements for cars at 27.5 mpg by 1990. During my first twenty-five years in the Senate, there were several efforts made on the Senate floor to raise CAFE standards. I supported those efforts, including an unsuccessful effort to enact this policy change as part of the 2005 energy bill. Until 2007, each time the issue came up, a combination of US auto manufacturers, the US Chamber of Commerce, and the auto unions defeated the proposal. They argued that increased CAFE standards would put US manufacturers at a disadvantage compared to foreign competitors who were selling smaller, more fuel-efficient vehicles. Based on this argument, you could count on a large majority of Republicans and a few Democrats from auto manufacturing states to vote "no."

In 2007, the effort to increase CAFE standards finally succeeded. Senator Dianne Feinstein and several cosponsors had persuaded the Senate Commerce Committee, which had jurisdiction on the issue, to report a bill to increase standards. That provision raised fuel economy standards for cars, light trucks, and SUVs, and called on the EPA to adjust standards through 2030 to the maximum feasible levels.

California's aggressive action to raise its state CAFE standards proved important in getting the federal standards raised. The automobile industry had resisted increased federal standards for many years. Faced with the 2007 legislation, they finally concluded that it was in their interest to agree to higher standards at the federal level if those standards would preempt even higher standards in California. In 2009, they agreed with the federal government and state regulators to increase CAFE standards dramatically in future years.

For many decades, the problem of inadequate battery technology had impeded manufacturers from developing electric cars and trucks. To promote the use of electricity in the transportation sector, the 2007 bill increased government support for research and development for advanced batteries.

COMPARISON OF CAFE STANDARDS AND COMPLIANCE.

This chart shows the nearly 30 years during which opponents stalled efforts to raise CAFE standards.

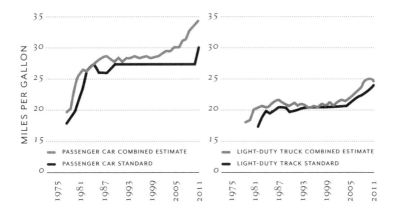

Source: US Energy Information Administration, August 3, 2012.

TAX PREFERENCES FOR CLEAN ENERGY   The 2007 act included various tax provisions to promote renewable energy and energy efficiency. In fact, most of the "expenditures" by the federal government to support increased energy efficiency and deployment of renewable energy have been "tax expenditures." By that I mean tax credits, deductions, or exemptions offered to encourage greater energy efficiency or more use of alternative, non-emitting sources of energy. Beginning in 1992, Congress enacted a production tax credit of 30 percent of the value of power produced from renewable energy projects. In 2005, as part of the Energy Policy Act, Congress enacted an investment tax credit to promote the installation of solar panels.

These tax provisions created substantial financial incentives for investments in wind and solar facilities. The problem with the incentives was that Congress enacted them for short periods of one or a few years. As the date would approach for the provisions to expire, investors would be reluctant to invest. In most cases, Congress extended the provisions, but sometimes not until after they had expired.

The tax code contains many tax preferences that are permanent law and therefore do not expire. Included among those are several preferences enjoyed by producers of fossil fuels, such as the depletion allowance for oil and gas producers. Those are provisions enacted before Congress passed the 1974 Budget Act. That act, plus the "pay-go" rules adopted by the House and Senate budget committees, put requirements on Congress to offset cuts in taxes with cuts in spending or with increased taxes elsewhere. In response to the Budget Act, Congress began the practice of enacting short-term, temporary tax provisions. Since the tax provisions to encourage renewable energy and energy efficiency were all adopted after enactment of the Budget Act, they were short term and temporary.

━━━

I would cite four reasons we were able to pass the 2005 and 2007 bills. First, we followed a bipartisan process in developing, amending, and reporting the bills from committee. Second, the bills that came to the Senate floor included energy-related provisions reported from several committees. This gave more senators a reason to support enactment. Third was the balanced nature of the two bills. Each bill contained provisions to maintain our traditional sources of energy and increase energy supplies (which appealed to Republican senators), and each also contained provisions to speed up the transition of the economy to greater energy efficiency and greater reliance on non-emitting sources of energy (which appealed to Democrats). A final reason the bills enjoyed bipartisan support was that the Republican Party had not yet enshrined opposition to dealing with climate change as the party's position.

Following the 2008 election, it soon became clear that it would be difficult to find common ground on energy issues in the new Congress. The various special interests that were determined to oppose any significant climate-change legislation had worked hard to enlist congressional Republicans as allies in that effort. In addition, many Republicans in Congress had determined to follow the lead of Senator McConnell and opposed the new president on virtually all his major policy objectives, including his efforts to deal with climate change.

7   Meet Our Energy and Climate-Change Challenges (2009 and After)

AT THE BEGINNING OF PRESIDENT OBAMA'S FIRST TERM, I hoped Congress would join the president in taking bold action to deal with climate change. The president did take bold action, but most of Congress's legislative efforts failed. The American Recovery and Reinvestment Act (ARRA) was the most important energy and climate-change related legislation enacted during his two terms in office. That bill became law during his first month as president.

The American Recovery and Reinvestment Act (ARRA)

To stimulate demand in the economy—even before the President Obama was sworn in—a version of the American Recovery and Reinvestment Act (ARRA) was introduced in the Senate. The total cost of the ARRA was $831 billion. The new administration proposed to spend over 10 percent of those funds to moving the country to a clean energy economy. Besides outright expenditures for renewable energy research and deployment, the act extended tax provisions to reward private-sector investment in renewable energy projects. One useful provision extended the investment tax credit for solar energy at the 30 percent level for eight years.

In the ARRA, the amount of funding made available for renewable energy and efficiency efforts far exceeded the amounts Congress usually appropriated for these purposes. This large, additional source of funds also provided first-time funding for some important agencies and programs Congress had previously authorized, but had not yet funded.

ARPA-E

The Advanced Research Projects Agency-Energy (ARPA-E) was the most significant of these agencies that benefited from first-time funding provided in the ARRA.

In 2005, Senator Lamar Alexander of Tennessee and I had written to the National Academy of Sciences (NAS), asking them to make recommendations on actions Congress could take to keep our economy competitive in world markets. The NAS appointed a blue-ribbon commission to develop its recommendations. That commission, headed by Norm Augustine, the former CEO of Lockheed Martin, issued its report entitled "Rising above the Gathering Storm" in 2005, and one of its recommendations was the establishment of ARPA-E. Statutory language to do so was then enacted as part of the America COMPETES Act (America Creating Opportunities to Meaningfully Promote Excellence in Technology, Education, and Science Act of 2007).

The commission believed the country should have an agency as part of the Department of Energy, modeled on the very successful Defense Advanced Research Projects Agency (DARPA)[1] in the Department of Defense. In the bill establishing ARPA-E, we specified that it would make grants and provide technical assistance to American energy researchers to advance high-potential, high-impact energy technologies that were too early for private-sector investment. I'm persuaded that it was not objected to as part of the America COMPETES Act partly because Congress was just being asked to authorize the establishment of the agency, not fund it. Some in Congress who might have objected were willing to withhold their criticism of the idea since no funding was being provided.

When the administration decided to propose the ARRA, White House staff contacted those involved in energy issues in the Congress, including me and our staff on the Senate Energy and Natural Resources Committee. They requested advice on how to use funding in the ARRA to promote a "clean energy agenda." Since ARPA-E had been authorized but was not yet operating, it was a natural place to use the available funds. The ARRA provided $400 million for the startup of ARPA-E and for its operation during its first two years of existence. Secretary Steven Chu wisely chose Arun Majumdar as the first ARPA-E director, and he was able to take the ARRA funding, and get the new agency up and running very effectively. Since being established, ARPA-E has gained support from both Democrats and Republicans in Congress.

FINANCING CLEAN ENERGY: THE LOAN GUARANTEE PROGRAM

The most controversial energy issue that arose because of ARRA funding related to loan guarantees to firms engaged in renewable energy development and deployment. Congress had established the loan guarantee program as Title XVII of the 2005 energy bill with strong bipartisan support. It was an effort to use the financial strength of the federal government to guarantee private-sector loans to developers of clean energy projects. The idea was to charge fees to recipients of loans, in return for these guarantees. The government would set the fees at a level to keep the program solvent, even if there were defaults on some loans.

We enacted the loan guarantee program while President Bush's energy secretary, Sam Bodman, was in office. He was less than enthusiastic about the program and did little to implement it. In 2009, President Obama appointed Steven Chu as the new secretary of energy. During Secretary Chu's early visits to Capitol Hill, I and other senators from both parties urged him to make this loan guarantee program a priority. I believed the loan guarantees would allow the federal government to assist the private sector in completing many more clean energy projects than would otherwise be possible.

Secretary Chu chose Jonathan Silver to direct the program. Silver was an experienced expert, and put together a team of professionals to insure the proper management of the program. As expected, the projects applying for government support were, in most cases, too risky for the private sector to fund, absent the government guarantee. This meant the government would have to incur losses on some of its loan guarantees, as happens with any portfolio of investments involving risk.

The highest-profile loss for the government was with a solar panel manufacturer in Fremont, California, named Solyndra. It had raised $198 million from private investors, but to construct a new plant, it applied for a $535 million loan guarantee from the DOE. The Loan Project Office determined that the project had promise and that the risk to the government was acceptable. After the DOE issued the guarantee and the funds were borrowed, Solyndra found itself unable to compete with other, cheaper manufacturers, primarily in China. The company declared bankruptcy on September 1, 2011, and the government had to honor its guarantee.

The 2012 campaign season had begun. Republicans in Congress seized upon this loss of taxpayer dollars as an example of crony capitalism and political favoritism. They cited it as evidence that government should stay out of the private market. To focus as much attention on this failure as possible, the Republican-controlled House had many hearings on the issue in the lead-up to the 2012 election.

Despite the loss in the loan guarantee for Solyndra, DOE's Loan Project Office had a successful record in its management of the loan program.[2] In fact, the LPO has maintained a very low project failure rate, well below the failure rate of many commercial loan portfolios.[3]

Trying to Use the Market: Efforts to Put a Price on Carbon

While the 2005 and 2007 energy bills and the ARRA contained provisions intended to reduce energy consumption and encourage more use of renewable energy, they were not bold attempts to confront the problem of climate change. The conventional wisdom was that Congress would still have to adopt policies to "put a price on carbon." The three main policy options were: adopting a cap-and-trade system, adopting a clean energy standard, or adopting a carbon tax. Along with others in Congress, I made efforts to move forward with each of these options, but to date, all such efforts have failed.

CAP AND TRADE

Many economists argued for a cap-and-trade system; they saw it as the most economically efficient way to reduce GHG emissions. In a cap-and-trade system, government puts a firm cap on the level of carbon pollution from a company or organization. That cap is then reduced each year. Firms desiring to emit more than they are allowed must buy allowances from others who will emit less. The ultimate effect is to impose a cost on those firms with the greatest emissions, thereby incentivizing everyone to emit less.

In 2003, Senators John McCain and Joe Lieberman introduced the first bill in the Senate proposing to address climate change. It was a type of cap-and-trade bill, and called for capping emissions by major emitters and setting up a system for trading permits to emit. The Environment Committee never reported the bill, but the sponsors offered it as a floor amendment to the Climate Stewardship Act of 2003. I supported the amendment, but it failed 43 to 55.

In the next Congress McCain and Lieberman introduced a variation on that initial bill. That proposal, like its predecessor, was not reported from a Senate committee, so they offered it as an amendment to the 2005 energy bill. Again, I voted "aye." This time the amendment failed by a larger margin: 38 to 60. In 2007, they introduced yet another version of the proposal, but it never came to a vote in the Senate.

Besides the McCain-Lieberman efforts, several others of us in the Senate wrote proposals. Together with six other senators (three Democrats and three Republicans), I introduced the Low Carbon Economy Act of 2007. Arlen Specter (R-PA) agreed to be the lead Republican cosponsor on the bill. It proposed to set up a cap-and-trade system, but without all the complexity included in the other proposals. It encouraged me that three Republicans—Specter, Ted Stevens (R-AK), and Lisa Murkowski (R-AK)—agreed to cosponsor the bill. This was before opposition to dealing with climate change became such a litmus-test issue for Republicans in Congress.

Recognized leaders in the business community also threw their support behind these efforts to deal with climate change. Several forward-thinking corporate CEOs formed a group called the United States Climate Action Partnership (USCAP). Founding corporate members of USCAP included Alcoa, BP America, Caterpillar, Duke Energy, Dupont, FPL Group, General Electric, Lehman Brothers, PG&E, and PNM Resources. Four nongovernmental environmental organizations joined the group as well: The Environmental Defense Fund, the Natural Resources Defense Council, Pew Center on Global Climate Change, and the World Resources Institute. In January 2007, USCAP issued a report urging the federal government to put in place a cap-and-trade system. By May, many more companies and organizations had joined as well.

In the 2008 campaign, Barack Obama pledged that, if elected, he would make it a top priority to confront the challenge of climate change. Early in 2009, in his first State of the Union speech to a joint session of Congress, he said:

> But to truly transform our economy, protect our security, and save our planet from the ravages of climate change, we need to ultimately make clean, renewable energy the profitable kind of energy. So I ask this Congress to send me legislation that places a market-based cap on carbon pollution and drives the production of more renewable

energy in America. And to support that innovation, we will invest fifteen billion dollars a year to develop technologies like wind power and solar power; advanced biofuels, clean coal, and more fuel-efficient cars and trucks built right here in America.[4]

At the beginning of Obama's presidency, Democrats controlled both the House and the Senate, and the Democratic congressional leaders supported the president's effort. Most political commentators believed the prospects for taking bold action to deal with climate change looked good. The obstacles turned out to be greater than expected.

By this time (early 2009), our national debate about energy policy had changed substantially. Two innovations in the oil and gas sector had dramatically increased projections for the supply of those fuels: horizontal drilling and fracking. These technologies made it possible to produce both oil and gas from shale formations previously considered inaccessible. The projected increase in the supply of these fuels had mixed effects on policy efforts to reduce GHG emissions. On the one hand, the low expected prices for oil and gas reduced incentives to increase energy efficiency and to develop alternative non-emitting sources of energy. On the other hand, the abundant supply of low-cost natural gas sped up efforts by utilities to substitute natural gas for coal in electricity production. Since the GHG emissions from natural gas are about half as great as from coal, this was a positive development.

In the House, Henry Waxman, the chair of the House Energy and Commerce Committee, and his colleague Ed Markey developed an ambitious proposal to cap and then reduce GHG emissions in all sectors of the US economy. That bill, called Waxman-Markey, passed the House at the end of June 2009, 219 to 212. Two hundred and eleven Democrats and eight Republicans voted in favor of the bill; 44 Democrats and 168 Republicans voted "no."

In the Senate, it seemed clear to me we did not have the votes to enact economy-wide cap-and-trade legislation. So, as chair of the Energy Committee, I went to work to put together an energy bill that could enjoy enough bipartisan support to pass the Senate. Although my colleague Pete Domenici had retired, the new ranking Republican on the committee, Lisa Murkowski, was willing to work with me to have the committee report a bipartisan bill. I hoped and believed that we could pass legislation in the Senate to move the United States toward a clean energy economy, even though it would be far less ambitious than what the House was considering. The bill would eventually include not only a "renewable electricity standard," but also the creation of a Clean Energy Development Administration (CEDA) to help finance breakthrough clean energy and energy efficiency technologies, the creation of an "interstate highway system" for electricity by creating a new bottom-up planning system for a national transmission grid, and robust support for the deployment of new energy-efficient products across the economy. If a bipartisan bill of that type could pass the Senate, I believed we might then go to a conference committee with the House and negotiate for a bill that could pass both houses of Congress.

The "renewable electricity standard" was the most controversial item in the legislation we were working on in committee. This "standard" was an attempt to do at the national level something similar to what many states had already done with adoption of "renewable portfolio standards." These state laws required electric utilities to produce or get a certain portion of the power they sell from non-emitting sources of energy. Thirty states had adopted requirements of this type. The remaining states, primarily in the Southeast, had not. I hoped that adopting a "renewable electricity standard" at the federal level would help make alternative energy a priority in all states.

After extensive discussions with both Democratic and Republican members, I was confident we had enough votes for the committee to include a "weak" renewable electricity standard in the bill. The markup process in committee took much longer than I had expected. We began the last day of March, and finally finished, after eleven markup sessions, in early June. The final vote for reporting the bill out of committee was 15 to 8, with two Democrats voting against the bill and four Republicans voting for it.[5]

The support of Senator Murkowski as the ranking Republican on the committee, and the 2 to 1 vote in committee, gave me hope that we could pass a bipartisan bill in the Senate.

Separate from the work we were doing in the Energy Committee, the momentum behind the Waxman-Markey proposal in the House prompted several senators to attempt similar legislation. As chair of the Environment Committee and a longtime advocate of curbing GHG emissions, Barbara Boxer took the lead. She and John Kerry, who had been an outspoken supporter of cap-and-trade legislation, developed an ambitious cap-and-trade proposal: the Kerry-Boxer bill. It was like Waxman-Markey in that it attempted to establish an economy-wide cap-and-trade system. It contained a mandate to reduce the nation's GHG emissions 20 percent by 2020 from their 2005 levels. The sponsors described the GHG trading provisions in the bill as a "pollution reduction and investment" program, avoiding the use of the term "cap and trade." Later, Senator Kerry joined with Senators Joe Lieberman and Lindsey Graham in trying to promote a variation of the Kerry-Boxer bill.

After we completed work on our bipartisan bill in the Energy Committee, I went to see the majority leader, Harry Reid. We discussed the roster of senators, and I gave my best estimate for how each senator was likely to vote on a major cap-and-trade proposal. In my view the Senate could not pass such a proposal, and I urged that instead we should proceed to consider an energy bill. Such a bill could include the bill we had reported from the Energy Committee, and Harry could add whatever other provisions from other committees he felt should be included. At that point, senators could offer floor amendments and once all amendments were accepted or rejected, each senator could decide whether to support the final bill. This was the procedure that had succeeded with energy proposals in the two previous Congresses.

After the House passed Waxman-Markey, and while this legislative activity was going on in the Senate, President Obama invited those of us most involved in these Senate discussions to meet with him and his advisors at the White House. Once we were seated around the table in the Cabinet Room, the president welcomed us all and then asked each of us to give our opinion on how we should proceed in the Senate. I stated what I had told Senator Reid and urged that we consider an energy bill. Senator Murkowski spoke in favor of that same course of action. Senator Boxer, Senator Kerry, and others argued that this approach would weaken our chances of passing cap-and-trade legislation in the Senate. They favored continuing to build support for a stand-alone cap-and-trade bill, similar to what had passed in the House.

Jeff Bingaman
U.S. SENATE

P.O. Box 5775, Santa Fe, New Mexico 87502-5775

Hand card for Jeff's 1982 campaign for the Senate.

Anne and Jeff celebrating election victory, November 2, 1982.

Jess Bingaman, Senator Dan Inouye (D-HW), and Jeff at reception in the Senate Dirksen Building following Jeff's swearing in on January 3, 1983. US Senate Photographic Services.

Jeff outside the Russell Building on Capitol Hill.

Jeff and John Bingaman walking
in the Silver City Fourth
of July parade, ca. 1984.

Jeff with President Clinton at the Albuquerque International Airport
during a Clinton visit to New Mexico.

Jeff at Senate hearing.
US Senate Photographic Services.

Senator Chuck Schumer (D-NY)
and Jeff at Senate Finance
Committee hearing. US Senate
Photographic Services.

Senate HELP Committee,
after passage of the Affordable
Care Act. US Senate
Photographic Services.

above Senator Joe Manchin
(D-WV) and Jeff before
a hearing of the Senate
Energy Committee. US
Senate Photographic
Services.

left Jeff meeting with
the press after Senate
Energy Committee
hearing. US Senate
Photographic Services.

Jeff and Senator Lamar Alexander (R-TN) before a HELP
Committee hearing. US Senate Photographic Services.

Jeff and Senator Bob Corker (R-TN) having lunch in the
Dirksen Building cafeteria. US Senate Photographic Services.

Jeff with Rudy Chavez, owner/creator of Chavez New Mexican Foods, at the Albuquerque Balloon Fiesta.

Jeff campaigning in Albuquerque in 2006.

Jeff campaigning in Silver City at the
Fourth of July parade, 2006.

Jeff speaking at Sandia National Laboratory's Computer Science
Research Institute event in Albuquerque, August, 2005.

Jeff, Senator Byron Dorgan (D-ND), Senator Harry Reid (D-NV), and Senator Pat Leahy (D-VT) with the Dalai Lama in the LBJ Room of the US Capitol, 2005.

President Obama and Jeff visiting near the Rose Garden after a bill signing, June 22, 2009. AP Photo/Ron Edmonds.

Toward the end of the meeting, President Obama indicated he would like to see any energy legislation that came to the floor also include a cap-and-trade proposal. He and others at the meeting seemed to believe that Republicans would welcome the chance to vote for an energy bill such as the one we had reported from the Energy Committee, and that we should deny them that chance unless they would also agree to include cap-and-trade legislation. I did not agree. Since we had included a renewable electricity standard in the Energy Committee bill, I believed many Republican senators, and some Democrats, would oppose the bill. And that was even without a cap-and-trade provision included. In short, I thought we should move forward with what the Senate could enact, even if a cap-and-trade provision could not be included. If we had done so, it is possible that we could have included some useful steps toward dealing with climate change.

The conclusion coming out of the meeting was that the majority leader would not bring an energy bill to the Senate floor unless and until he could combine it with an economy-wide cap-and-trade proposal. In the end, all the lobbying and maneuvering about cap-and-trade legislation in the Senate came to very little. In July 2010, a full year after the House passed Waxman-Markey, Senator Reid announced that there was not enough support in the Senate to enact legislation putting a cap on GHG emissions. He was correct. Opponents of cap-and-trade legislation could have kept anything like Waxman-Markey from passing in the Senate. That was the end of efforts during the Obama presidency to legislate an economy-wide cap-and-trade system. Now, more than a decade after the House passed Waxman-Markey, the fascination with market-based mechanisms, and particularly cap-and-trade proposals, has begun to wane. The political obstacles to enacting this type of broad legislation are too great, and even where such market-based mechanisms have been adopted, the excessive use of offsets has lessened their effectiveness in reducing emissions.

Some who have written about the first two years of the Obama presidency argue that legislation to establish a cap-and-trade system could have passed if President Obama had chosen this as his top priority, instead of health care reform. I disagree. By the time the House passed Waxman-Markey, opponents of cap-and-trade legislation in the Senate were adamant in their opposition; and that was the case regardless of what either the president or Congress did on health care reform.

A CLEAN ENERGY STANDARD

A second way to put a price on carbon is to enact a clean energy standard. Following the 2010 election, Republicans controlled the House. Since Congress would not enact cap-and-trade legislation such as Waxman-Markey soon, President Obama called on Congress in both his 2011 and his 2012 State of the Union speeches to enact a clean energy standard (CES) instead.

A CES (now referred to as a clean electricity standard) differed from the cap-and-trade proposals that Congress had considered in two ways: first, any source of energy was eligible to receive credit based on its success in producing energy with reduced GHGs, and second, the proposal only applied to the power-generation sector of the economy (i.e., it was not economy-wide). It would impose a requirement on electric utilities to get more of their power from non-emitting or less-emitting sources, but it would recognize and give credit to all types of energy generation in determining whether the requirement was being met. This was intended to meet one criticism leveled against Waxman-Markey.

With the failure of Waxman-Markey in the Congress, climate change began to take a back seat to other issues. Although I could not detect any great enthusiasm for a clean energy standard in either the House or the Senate, I thought the proposal advocated by President Obama deserved serious consideration. This was to be my last year in the Senate, and even though there was no chance of enacting the bill in that Congress, I thought introducing it might make it easier for someone in a future Congress to revive the proposal. I asked the able staff of the Senate Energy Committee to draft a bill, and on March 1, thirteen Democratic cosponsors and I introduced the Clean Energy Standard Act of 2012.

On May 17, we held a hearing in the Energy Committee to take testimony on the CES proposal. Had we been able to enact the legislation, I am persuaded the policy would have been effective in speeding up emission reductions from the nation's utilities. Now, more than ten years later, I am glad to see a new and updated version of the proposal being considered in Congress.[6]

A CARBON TAX

A third way to "put a price on carbon," and the most direct way, is to impose a carbon tax. Taxes are easier to understand than a cap-and-trade regime. But a carbon tax has the great disadvantage of being a tax. To deal with that problem, it needs to be combined with a dividend or rebate large enough to return to most taxpayers an amount equal to or greater than they would pay in carbon taxes. Proponents of enacting a carbon tax have called for it to be revenue neutral, with a guarantee that consumers overall receive back all revenues raised from the tax. Proponents argue that allowing use of revenue from a carbon tax for purposes other than the dividend would undermine public support. To have the desired effect of lowering emissions, the tax would have to be substantial, and to increase each year.

Although enacting a carbon tax might well be an effective economy-wide policy to reduce GHG emissions, I see little prospect for the Congress taking such action.

WHY CONGRESS FAILED TO ACT

To date, Congress has failed to adopt any of the three policy actions I've discussed: cap and trade, a clean energy standard, or a carbon tax. The obvious question is, "Why?"

In my view, opponents of climate-change legislation had been well-organized, well-funded, and very effective. Americans for Prosperity, a creation of the Koch brothers, had led the opposition, but many others in the right-wing media joined in. For several years, proponents of continued and increased use of fossil fuels had sown doubt about the scientific evidence of human-caused global warming. This generalized doubt about the science was the backdrop for opposing any cap on GHG emissions. The strategy was to persuade right-wing activists, loosely organized as the Tea Party, that efforts to deal with climate change were an overreach by the federal government.

Most Republicans in Congress who opposed efforts to deal with climate change did so, not because of any disagreement about the science, but because the special interests opposing action on the issue had been skillful and effective in their lobbying. They undermined concern about the problem among Republican voters and spent heavily on campaigns and lobbying aimed at Republican candidates and members of Congress. Ignoring the issue of climate change was easier for Republican members of Congress because they believed there would be no political price to pay. In fact, their chances of drawing a challenger in their next primary election would increase if they were to break with the general party consensus and support effort to deal with the problem.

Obama's Actions

Following the 2010 election, President Obama—and anyone else who was paying attention—could see that the next Congress was not likely to enact legislation to deal with global warming. While the president continued to urge Congress to enact a clean energy standard, the administration turned to the question of what they could do administratively. That meant taking action both in the United States and with other nations.

On the domestic front in the transportation sector, the administration took the authority Congress had given it in the 2007 energy bill regarding CAFE standards, and raised those standards substantially. In the power-generation sector it adopted the Clean Power Plan, requiring states to reduce GHG emissions from coal-burning power plants by 32 percent by 2030.

President Obama's greatest climate-change successes were in the international arena. In 2009 he attended the UN Climate Change Conference in Copenhagen and is credited with playing a central part in making that conference successful. In 2014 he and his administration reached an agreement with China in which the United States pledged to cut emissions substantially and China pledged to reach peak emission levels by 2030. In 2015, Obama was credited for his leadership in getting agreement among 193 nations for the Paris Climate Accords.

Reversing Course: The Trump Administration

It is an understatement to say Hillary Clinton and Donald Trump disagreed on climate change in the 2016 campaign. Clinton supported President Obama's efforts to reduce US GHG emissions. Trump characterized

Obama's actions as a "war on coal." Clinton promised to carry through on the US commitments in the Paris Climate Accords and to build on those efforts. Trump promised to withdraw the United States from the agreement.

Once elected, Trump acted quickly to carry out his campaign promises on the issue. He began by filling key administration positions with people known for their unwillingness to confront climate change. A prominent example was Trump's choice for EPA director, former Oklahoma attorney general Scott Pruitt. After his confirmation by the Senate, he said, "I think that measuring with precision human activity on the climate is something very challenging to do and there's tremendous disagreement about the degree of impact, so no, I would not agree that it's a primary contributor to the global warming that we see."[7]

On March 15, 2017, President Trump announced his interest in relaxing the CAFE standards the Obama administration and the auto manufacturers had agreed to in 2011.

On June 1, 2017, he announced that the United States would withdraw from the Paris Climate Accords.

On June 29, 2017, he announced his administration would pursue a policy of "energy dominance." By this he appeared to mean that his administration would pursue the goal of ensuring that the United States was the world's largest producer of fossil fuels. In fact, we reached that goal in 2018. There was no sign that the Trump administration supported increasing US energy production from alternative energy sources.

On October 9, 2017, the EPA administrator announced that the EPA withdrew the regulations establishing the Clean Power Plan.

The general strategy of President Trump and the Republican-controlled Congress was to delete climate change from the national agenda as a problem requiring attention. In his 2018 State of the Union speech, it was no accident that Trump never mentioned the issue. Unfortunately, Democrats failed to counter this strategy effectively. In the Democratic response to the president, Congressman Joe Kennedy (D-MA) also failed to mention climate change.

GLOBAL CARBON EMISSIONS FROM FOSSIL FUELS, 1900–2014

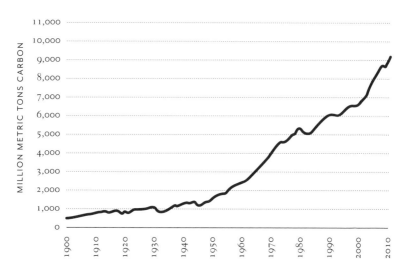

Source: Boden, T. A., Marland, G., and Andres, R. J. (2017). Global, Regional, and National Fossil-Fuel CO2Emissions. Carbon Dioxide Information Analysis Center, Oak Ridge National Laboratory, US Department of Energy, Oak Ridge, Tenn., USA. doi 10 .3334/CDIAC/00001_V2017.

ANNUAL GLOBAL SURFACE TEMPERATURE, RELATIVE TO AVERAGE IN THE LATE 1900S

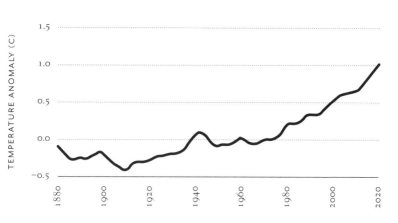

Source: climate.nasa.gov

Source: U.S. Energy Information Administration, "International Energy Outlook 2017," https://www.eia.gov/outlooks/ieo/exec_summ.php.

The Uncertain Path Forward

The magnitude of the challenge of reducing GHG emissions is enormous. While world leaders continue to profess their commitment to eliminating most GHGs by 2050, the charts on the preceding page show that is unlikely. Greenhouse gas emissions continue to increase and global temperatures continue to rise.

Also, forecasts for the next few decades show projected increases in the amount of fossil fuels used as demonstrated in the chart above.

At the time I am writing this, the gap has grown between what the scientific community says nations must do to reduce GHG emissions and what those nations are committed to do. Most climate scientists saw the commitments President Obama and the other world leaders agreed to as part of the Paris Climate Accords as actually falling short of what our nation would have to do as part of a worldwide effort to limit global temperature increases to 2 degrees Celsius. But President Trump disavowed even those commitments, and his administration did its best to reverse the actions taken in Obama's presidency.

To enact significant energy and climate-change legislation in the future, we will have to once again find consensus on a goal. To date, policy makers have failed to recognize the extent of the risks posed by climate change, and special interests have been largely successful in resisting bold changes in policy.

President Biden has recommitted the United States to a leadership role in confronting climate change. His most notable action to date has been rejoining the Paris Climate Accords. Under his direction the EPA has also issued strong regulations to limit methane emissions.

Time will tell whether he is able to get the support he needs in Congress to enact significant legislation on the issue.

8 Improve Health Care

Efforts at Reform

THE FIRST EIGHTY YEARS OF EFFORT

In the United States we have a long history of efforts to improve and reform the health care delivery system. We also have a long history of resistance to those efforts. Three impediments have caused most of that resistance: ideological bias against a more activist governmental role, the substantial influence of special interests, and pressure to toe the party line.

During the twentieth century and now in the twenty-first century, most presidents and many members of Congress tried to move the country toward some form of universal health care.

In 1912, Teddy Roosevelt advocated for national health insurance in his campaign for a third term. As the candidate of the Progressive or "Bull Moose" Party, he had leeway to propose bold solutions to our nation's problems, and he did.

In 1945, President Truman sent Congress a message proposing a major federal effort to improve health care. His proposal addressed the lack of medical professionals and hospitals in rural and lower-income areas. It called for creating medical standards for hospitals and establishing a board to ensure they met those standards. It proposed more federal funding for medical research, and it would have established a national insurance plan run by the federal government, open to all, but voluntary. Critics attacked Truman's plan as "socialized medicine."[1]

During and after the Second World War, many large employers began providing health care coverage. Since the government had frozen wages during the war years, these health care benefits were used to attract and keep workers. Federal tax policy supported this by allowing employers to claim the cost of providing health care to their workers as a business expense. The tax code also allowed the value of the benefit to go untaxed to the employee. Most experts believe this favorable tax treatment of health care benefits has reduced incentives for both employers and employees to concern themselves with the cost of care, and has contributed to the rapid growth in health care costs in the United States. This tax treatment of health care benefits also contributed to entrenching the health insurance system that we have, preventing the adoption of a different structure, such as a single-payer system.

Since the 1940s, most Americans working for larger companies have had health care coverage through their employment. In 2009, 58 percent of non-elderly Americans had health care coverage this way. Those working for small firms often had no coverage. Until the enactment of the Affordable Care Act (ACA), there had never been a requirement that employers provide health care coverage, and many employers chose not to do so.

The United States' greatest progress in expanding access to health care services occurred during Lyndon Baines Johnson's presidency. After the 1964 election, Democrats used their large majorities in both the House and Senate to enact Medicare and Medicaid. Medicare, signed into law in 1965, extended health care coverage to people aged sixty-five and older. Medicaid, signed later that same year, provided access to health care for pregnant women and children in low-income families, and nursing-home care for poor seniors.

Congress structured both Medicare and Medicaid as "entitlement programs," which means that individuals who meet certain criteria become entitled to the benefits. With Medicare, the federal government determines the criteria for coverage and provides the funding. Congress structured Medicaid as a program administered by the states, where the states contribute a substantial portion of the funds, and have broad discretion about whom to cover. The federal government contributes more than half of Medicaid's total funding, with the exact amount depending on the economics and demographics of each state. Given the significant differences in circumstances and politics among the states, health care coverage under Medicaid has been good in some states but inadequate in others. Unfortunately, during most decades, my state of New Mexico has been in this latter category.

By 1990, 32.1 million Americans lacked health care coverage, and that number was growing. Health care in the United States consisted of employer-sponsored coverage for some, and for others, a patchwork of government-supported programs, including Medicare, Medicaid, the Indian Health Service, and the Veterans Affairs network of hospitals and clinics. But many people did not qualify for any of these programs. Our laws left them without secure access to affordable health care.

THE CLINTON REFORM EFFORT

Bill Clinton made reform of the health care system a priority in his 1992 campaign. In his speech accepting the Democratic nomination, he spoke about his mother's struggle with breast cancer and his commitment to see that all Americans have access to quality health care. He attacked the incumbent, George H. W. Bush, saying, "He won't take on the big insurance companies and the bureaucracies to control health costs and give us affordable health care for all Americans, but I will."

When Clinton took office in 1993, the prospects for reforming the health care system seemed good. He asked his wife, Hillary, to head up the effort, and she prepared a comprehensive reform proposal. That effort failed. It is hard to avoid the conclusion that it failed because Republicans in the Senate determined that it would damage their political prospects in the 1994 election if they allowed the reform effort to succeed.

The decision by congressional Republicans to oppose the Clinton plan came after a series of strong indications that they would support major reform. In 1993, twenty-three Republican senators, including then-minority leader Bob Dole, cosponsored a bill, proposed by Senator John Chafee (R-RI), which followed the basic outline of a proposal from the Heritage Foundation, a conservative think tank. In 1989, the foundation had issued a paper entitled, "Assuring Affordable Health Care for All Americans." That paper endorsed a market-based health care system as an alternative to a single-payer system. Part of the proposal included an "individual mandate" for all Americans to purchase insurance. Another part included a mandate for employers to provide coverage to their workers. The US Chamber of Commerce stated its support for the general idea of health care reform, including an employer mandate.

In an address to a joint session of Congress on September 22, 1993, President Clinton outlined the plan Hillary had developed. He presented the details on November 20. By that time, the political ground had shifted. Republican opposition to the president had hardened during the partisan fight over Clinton's budget proposal. Congress enacted the Clinton budget, including tax increases on the wealthy, but without a single Republican vote in either house. Republicans were bearing down on the president over the so-called Whitewater scandal. And to add to the difficulty of gaining bipartisan support for health care reform, Republican leaders in Congress were seeing the 1994 midterm election as an opportunity to gain control of one or both houses of Congress.

Many congressional Republicans concluded it made no political sense for them to line up and support a "Clinton health care plan." Senator Dole and other Republican senators withdrew their support from the Chafee bill and from the idea of an "individual mandate." The US Chamber of Commerce, in a show of support for congressional Republicans, also reversed its position and announced it would oppose an "employer mandate."

In September 1994, a few weeks before the midterm election, Senate majority leader George Mitchell acknowledged that efforts to reform the health care system in the 103rd Congress had failed. Part of the explanation for that failure became clear to me in a phone call I received in the early '90s, while health care reform still seemed a real possibility. The call was from a friend and political supporter, who owned an insurance agency in southern New Mexico. "Jeff, I can't believe you are thinking of supporting this health care reform bill. Most of my business is selling health insurance policies, and this proposal would drastically reduce what I and other brokers could earn. I want you to know if you vote for this proposal, you have lost my support."

In fact, my friend and former supporter was right: a substantial portion of each dollar paid for individual and small group health insurance policies was going to brokers as commissions. This explained at least some of the political opposition to reform. It also helped explain the high cost being paid by many Americans for health care.

STATE CHILDREN'S HEALTH INSURANCE PROGRAM (SCHIP)

After Clinton's comprehensive reform proposal failed, the question was whether Congress could enact something more modest. In March 1997, Ted Kennedy and his cosponsor, Orrin Hatch, proposed the State Children's Health Insurance Program (SCHIP). This was a proposal to provide matching funds to states to cover uninsured children from low-income families with incomes too high to allow them to qualify for Medicaid. Republicans who had opposed more comprehensive reform were willing to support the proposal, since the benefits went to children, and because each state would have discretion in what they would provide. The legislation gave states three basic options for how they could use the funds. They could expand Medicaid coverage, design a program separate from Medicaid, or do some combination of the two.

Congress enacted the law in 1997 as part of the Balanced Budget Act of that year and has reauthorized it several times since then. In 2009 we expanded it by adding coverage for about 4 million more children, including legal immigrants.

MEDICARE PART D

During the George W. Bush administration, the major improvement in the nation's health care laws was enactment of Part D of Medicare, to provide prescription drug coverage to seniors. This proposal had the vigorous support of the AARP (American Association of Retired Persons) and other groups representing seniors.

The Bush administration proposed adding this benefit to Medicare while providing no revenue to pay for it. This was not an "unfunded mandate" since no one was being required to take part in Medicare Part D. It was an easy vote for most members since it was a promise of "all gain" to Medicare beneficiaries and "no pain," either to them or to the taxpayers. At the time of enactment in 2003, the Congressional Budget Office (CBO) projected that the change in law would add $550 billion to the federal debt during the first ten years. The CBO later determined that the actual cost was closer to $350 billion.

The Affordable Care Act (ACA)

By the time President Obama came to office in 2009 and despite enacting SCHIP and adding Part D to Medicare, the need to reform the health care system was becoming more urgent. Americans were paying much more for health care than people in other industrialized countries. According to the CBO, health care was consuming 17 percent of the US economy, and health care costs had been growing much faster than the costs of other goods and services in the economy. The number of Americans without coverage had increased to 45.7 million.

With these problems in mind, Obama campaigned for president—much as Bill Clinton had a decade before—on a platform of reforming the health care system. But by the time he took the oath of office, the collapsing economy was the most urgent problem facing the new president. In September 2008, Lehman Brothers had failed, and by January 20, 2009, the economy was well into recession (see chapter 3).

Despite the economic meltdown, both the administration and the Congress were proceeding with efforts to develop health care reform proposals. These efforts were despite the stated opposition of many congressional Republicans, including Mitch McConnell, the Senate Republican leader.

Even before the first committee drafted a bill, opponents of the reform effort labeled it "Obamacare." I am sure pollsters advised them that the public would be much less receptive to something labeled "Obamacare" than to a bill called "The Affordable Care Act." It was an excellent tactic for those wanting to undermine public support for the effort. Now, years

TIMELINE ON THE ACA

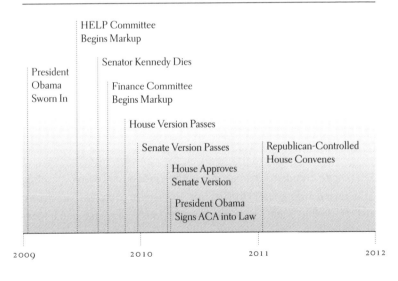

after the bill's enactment, many still don't know the two labels refer to the same law.

In the Senate, two committees have jurisdiction over health care: the HELP (Health, Education, Labor and Pensions) Committee and the Finance Committee. I served on both, so during many weeks in 2009 it seemed like I did nothing but attend meetings on the subject. A timeline for events leading up to and shortly after the ACA became law appears on the previous page.

The two committees settled on at least four goals. First, reform the health care insurance market to deal with insurance practices harming those who had insurance or attempted to purchase insurance. Second, improve the quality of health care. Third, deal with the relentless increase in the cost. And fourth, provide access to care for the approximately 46 million Americans who lacked coverage. With these objectives in mind, we began developing legislative proposals.

To improve the chances of enacting major reforms, we made three threshold decisions: first, maintain the existing employer-based health care delivery system; second, permit insurance companies to continue playing a central role; and third, do not extend health care coverage to undocumented immigrants.

In the United States, most Americans get their health care services through their employer, and most employers provide health care by contracting with an insurance company, which then contracts with the hospital, the physician, or other health care provider. This structure contrasts with the way most advanced countries deliver health care. The alternative single-payer system, where the government pays providers directly for health care services, would have had the advantage of reducing costs, but enacting such a far-reaching change was not a viable political option at the time. Republican lawmakers opposed a single-payer system, and some congressional Democrats were also unwilling to support such a drastic change.

Even in 2022 a national debate continues among Democrats about whether the country should scrap the current system of paying for health care and replace it with a "single payer" or "Medicare for all" system. In my view, the political obstacles to making such a change remain insurmountable. Many Americans resist the idea of giving up the health insurance they receive through their employment.

Early in developing legislation, we decided not to cover undocumented immigrants. There were four primary reasons: (1) adding coverage for undocumented immigrants would have made it difficult, if not impossible, to keep Democrats united in favor of the overall reform proposal; (2) it would have added to the cost; (3) some feared it could increase illegal immigration, by providing an additional incentive for immigrants to seek unauthorized entry into the country; and (4) it would have given opponents of the reform effort an issue around which to rally.

The fact that undocumented immigrants were not covered did not dissuade opponents from claiming the proposed law provided such coverage. The most dramatic example of this occurred on September 9, 2009, during a speech by President Obama to a joint session of Congress. In his statements about the ACA, the president said, "There are those who claim that our reform effort will include illegal immigrants. This, too, is false—the reforms I'm proposing would not apply to those who are here illegally." At that point, Congressman Joe Wilson (R-SC) interrupted the president and stunned the joint session with the shout, "You lie." In a statement issued later, Wilson apologized to the president for his outburst, but reiterated his disagreement with what the president had said. I saw Wilson's outburst as more evidence of the coarsening of our national politics.

The other threshold decision Democratic congressional leaders and the administration agreed to was that the legislation needed to raise the revenue to pay for the reforms. It was the responsible thing to do, but it undoubtedly increased opposition to the reform.

ELEMENTS OF REFORM IN THE ACA

As enacted, the ACA contained a long list of reforms. The Congressional Research Service (CRS) summarized the act:

> Among its many provisions, the ACA restructures the private health insurance market, sets minimum standards for health coverage, creates a mandate for most U.S. residents to obtain health insurance coverage, and provides for the establishment by 2014 of state-based insurance exchanges for the purchase of private health insurance. Certain individuals and families will be able to receive federal subsidies to reduce the cost of purchasing coverage through the exchanges.

The new law also expands eligibility for Medicaid; amends the Medicare program in ways that are intended to reduce the growth in Medicare spending; imposes an excise tax on insurance plans found to have high premiums; and makes numerous other changes to the tax code, Medicare, Medicaid, the State Children's Health Insurance Program (CHIP), and many other federal programs.[2]

At the heart of the debate was the proper role of the federal government. With health care, that larger issue required Congress to answer many more specific questions. To my mind, the most significant of those were the following seven:

1. What new requirements should we impose to deal with abuses by insurance companies?
2 Should we enact a requirement on insurance companies that some minimum percentage of health insurance premiums go directly to health care providers, called a "medical loss ratio requirement"?
3. What incentives or penalties should we include to encourage health care providers (hospitals, clinics and physicians) to improve the quality of care?
4. What requirements should we include for states to expand Medicaid coverage?
5. What requirements and incentives should employers have to maintain or add coverage for their employees?
6. What obligation, if any, should individuals have to get coverage?
7. Would the legislation include a "public option"?

REGULATION OF HEALTH INSURANCE PRACTICES Much of the impetus for health care reform arose from the objectionable practices of health insurance companies. In 1945, the McCarran-Ferguson Act became law. Its purpose and effect was to grant states authority and responsibility to regulate the sale of insurance. With health care, most states exercised broad authority to prevent fraud in the sale of policies, but they did little else in the way of effective regulation.

The ACA contained several provisions to curb abusive health insurance practices that states had failed to address. It prohibited insurers from denying coverage based on a patient's preexisting condition (the "must carry" requirement). It also prohibited both canceling coverage once the insured became ill or injured, and the capping of coverage at a certain level. The law also included a requirement that insurers allow parents to continue coverage of their children up to age twenty-six.

After Congress enacted the ACA, it was clear that these provisions to regulate insurance practices were popular with the general public. Consequently, many members who advocated repeal of the ACA were quick to assert they would keep these provisions even if they repealed the rest of the law.

MEDICAL LOSS RATIO The "medical loss ratio" required insurers to spend 80 percent of the funds they collected in premiums each year on payments to health care providers. The purpose was to ensure that premiums paid for health care insurance would go to reimburse providers of medical care, and not for administrative overhead, or executive compensation, or insurance company dividends to their shareholders. This is similar to the way we regulate utilities. In both cases, the policy tries to ensure that when rates go up, the increased payments help consumers and are not going for corporate overhead or profits.

The health insurance industry opposed this provision of the ACA. They saw it as an unwarranted government mandate. To my surprise, we got the votes to include it in the bills reported from both the HELP Committee and the Finance Committee.

INCENTIVES FOR IMPROVEMENTS IN CARE One of the most widespread criticisms of the US health care system is that we have structured it to compensate providers for the number of procedures performed rather than for the quality of the services provided. In the ACA, we began an effort to change those incentives.

The provisions intended to improve the quality of care included:

- Directions to the secretary of Health and Human Services (HHS) to strengthen the mechanisms that measure quality of care for those on Medicare and Medicaid.
- Requirements for greater transparency in reporting health care outcomes. (One example was the Hospital Readmissions Reduction

Program, under which we required hospitals to report and make public their readmission rates. If a hospital had an excessive re-admission rate for certain high-cost conditions, we authorized HHS to penalize the hospital until it corrected the situation.)

• Financial incentives for hospitals showing improvements in the quality of care.

THE REQUIREMENT FOR STATES TO EXPAND MEDICAID COVERAGE
If states wished to continue in the Medicaid program, the ACA required them to expand coverage under Medicaid to all individuals with incomes of 138 percent of the poverty level or less.

The Supreme Court ruled in *NFIB v. Sebelius* that the requirement for states to expand Medicaid violated the Constitution. That court decision allowed each state to decide whether to expand Medicaid coverage. (See discussion below.) At the time I am writing this, thirty-six states and the District of Columbia have expanded Medicaid, and twelve states continue to oppose expansion.

THE REQUIREMENT FOR EMPLOYERS TO PROVIDE COVERAGE The ACA required employers with over fifty employees either to provide coverage to their employees, or pay a penalty of $2,000 each year for each employee over the fifty who lacked coverage. We saw an employer mandate as necessary to lessen the incentive for firms providing coverage to drop that coverage once the ACA took effect. We had extensive debates in both the HELP and Finance Committees on the size of the firm that should be subject to the mandate, and the size penalty for failing to provide coverage. It was an arbitrary decision to make the employer mandate only applicable to employers with over fifty employees, but it seemed reasonable to most of us. Imposing a $2,000 penalty per employee also seemed reasonable.

THE INDIVIDUAL MANDATE The "individual mandate" was the most controversial provision in the ACA. This was a requirement on each individual to get coverage or pay a penalty as part of their tax bill the next year. This idea dated back to the Clinton administration and to the Heritage Foundation proposal that twenty-three Republican senators supported in 1993. Massachusetts also had adopted a similar provision as part of their health care reform while Mitt Romney was governor.

Opponents of an "individual mandate" argued not only that it was bad policy, but also that it violated the Constitution. They argued it was bad policy because it interfered with each person's individual liberty. The counterargument for the mandate was that government should not require insurance companies to provide coverage to all who wanted it, unless it also required people to get coverage, if they could afford it. Otherwise, the cost of coverage would be excessive because the only people getting coverage would be those patients with serious health needs.

The constitutional issue came before the Supreme Court in *NFIB v. Sebelius*. In oral argument, Justice Scalia asked whether, if the government could require a person to buy health insurance, the government could not also require a person to "buy broccoli." Various commentators tried to respond to Justice Scalia's question (i.e., make the case that health care coverage was not the same as broccoli). Justice Ruth Bader Ginsburg also did so in her dissenting opinion. She pointed out that the market for health care services differs from the market for broccoli, both because of the "inevitable yet unpredictable need for medical care" and also by the "guarantee that emergency care will be provided when required. . . ."[3] She argued those factors establish a societal interest in providing health care coverage, which justified Congress's decision to impose the requirement.

In its decision, the majority of the court rejected Justice Scalia's argument and upheld the individual mandate. But once Republicans regained a majority in both Houses and Trump became president, they successfully repealed the individual mandate, effective January 1, 2019.

THE PUBLIC OPTION Although Congress did not include a "public option" in the ACA, it struggled with the issue.

The ACA provides that each state will establish an "insurance exchange" where individuals and employers can choose between the various health plans offered in that state. The idea behind the "public option" was that one of those plans should be a government-sponsored health plan; that is, a plan in which the government would act much like insurance companies act, and directly pay medical providers for services rendered. Proponents of a "public option" saw it as a way to provide competition to private insurance plans that otherwise might raise premiums unreasonably.

The insurance industry strongly opposed the idea, claiming it would create unfair competition for private insurers.

During the markup in the Finance Committee, I voted for an amendment to add a "public option," but the amendment failed. In 2020, Joe Biden campaigned for president on a promise to support enacting a public option.

THE SENATE HELP COMMITTEE

The HELP Committee has broad jurisdiction over health issues, but lacks the jurisdiction to raise revenue. In the Senate, the Finance Committee has exclusive jurisdiction to change the tax code, and since any major health care reform would require not only changes in health care policy but also increased revenue, both committees had important roles to play.

In June 2009 the Senate HELP (Health, Education, Labor and Pensions) Committee began its markup of legislation in the Caucus Room of the Russell Building. That room has a special significance in the history of the Senate, since it has been the venue for high-profile hearings on such issues as the sinking of the *Titanic* and Watergate.

In the HELP Committee, we began with a handicap: our chair, Ted Kennedy, was not well enough to take charge of preparing a bill for consideration by the committee. Ted had suffered a seizure in May 2008 and was spending most of his time in Massachusetts. He asked his good friend and the next ranking Democrat on the committee, Chris Dodd of Connecticut, to take charge of the development and the marking up of the legislation.

On June 17, the committee began its markup. At the request of Senators Kennedy and Dodd, the expert and dedicated Democratic staff of the committee had put together a bill we could use to begin our deliberations. A "markup" of legislation involves the chair presenting the committee with a proposed bill and then having one or more "markup sessions" in which committee members debate and vote on amendments. Here, the markup continued for thirteen days. During that time, Chris Dodd made repeated and serious efforts to encourage input and involvement by Republican senators. He made a particular effort to encourage involvement by Wyoming senator Mike Enzi, the committee's ranking Republican. Those efforts led nowhere.

Although very few Republican members of Congress, in either the House or Senate, wanted to come out in opposition to reform, they would not support the type of major reform being advocated by the president and congressional Democrats. In the 111th Congress, the HELP Committee was the first in either the House or Senate to complete work on a health care reform bill. At the end of the markup, we voted to report the bill to the full Senate on a party-line vote. Even though we could not win over a single Republican, we Democrats on the committee still considered it a significant accomplishment that we reported a bill.

THE SENATE FINANCE COMMITTEE

Before the HELP Committee had completed developing its proposed bill, the Finance Committee was hard at work on its own version of a reform bill.

Early in 2009, the Finance Committee had conducted hearings on what health care reform should include. At the end of that process, chair Max Baucus determined that the best chance of getting bipartisan support for a bill was to ask a small group of senators from the committee, both Democrats and Republicans, to try to come to a preliminary agreement. The press dubbed this group the "Gang of Six." Max Baucus, Kent Conrad, and I were the Democrats; Chuck Grassley, Mike Enzi, and Olympia Snowe, the Republicans. Our Gang of Six meetings, held in Max's office conference room on the fifth floor of the Hart Building, began in the spring of 2009 and continued into September.

Besides the six of us, staff from the Finance Committee and personal staff for each senator also attended the meetings. Since health care reform was a major issue dominating headlines, there were always several reporters staking out the Baucus office as we arrived and left. We had all agreed the discussions that occurred in our meetings should not be made public, but, as with most such agreements in our nation's capital, this one was often ignored. In order to avoid a barrage of press questions, I made it my practice to exit the Baucus office through the back entrance. This provided a direct route back to my office two floors above.

The discussions were serious efforts to understand the consequences, both intended and unintended, of the various reform proposals senators wanted included in the bill. We discussed many issues, but one I expressed concern about was whether health care coverage was going to be affordable for many under the ACA. If we were going to include an individual mandate requiring people to get coverage, how could we ensure people could afford the cost of that coverage, together with any co-pays and deductibles? This discussion got us into the details of the various plans we intended to include in the bill (i.e., the gold, silver, bronze, and "young invincible" plans).

At one point early in the process, President Obama invited us to meet with him in the Oval Office. The president greeted us all warmly and, after we had settled on the couches in the Oval Office, he stated that he understood very well how difficult it would be to get bipartisan agreement on a bill. He stated that, despite the difficulty, he hoped we would give it our best effort for the good of the country. At one point he turned to the three Republicans and said, in very measured tones, "I know how hard it is for you to agree to anything I might support in this area. It is particularly hard since nearly half the members of your party don't consider me to be a US citizen." At that time, several prominent Republicans, including Donald J. Trump, publicly questioned the existence and legitimacy of the president's Hawaiian birth certificate.

The only discordant note in the meeting was a statement by Senator Grassley, which I had heard him make several times before. He said he wanted to see bipartisan legislation enacted, but that his definition of "bipartisan" was not fifty-eight Democrats and three Republicans. I assumed from that statement that unless we could persuade several more Republican senators to join, Chuck was not willing to vote for a bill. Mitch McConnell's effort to keep a united Republican caucus in opposition to health care reform seemed to be working.

That summer, Max organized another memorable meeting by conference call, this time to hear from a representative group of Democratic and Republican governors. We wanted to hear the governors' views on the proposed Medicaid expansion.

Once the governors were on the line, Max described what we were considering: the federal government would pay 100 percent of the cost of newly eligible Medicaid enrollees for the first three years (2014, 2015, and 2016); after that the federal share would decline to 90 percent by 2020 and for subsequent years. Under the existing Medicaid program, the federal government was only covering on average 57 percent of the cost of Medicaid beneficiaries. Nine of the ten governors on the call reacted favorably to the proposed policy. The one exception was Haley Barbour, governor of Mississippi. Barbour stated he would not support the proposal to expand Medicaid coverage, regardless of the cost-sharing arrangement between the federal government and the states. He stated that Mississippi could not afford to spend any more on Medicaid. This seemed ironic since Mississippi had more to gain from the Medicaid expansion than any other state in the union. The demographics of New Mexico made us second in line, behind Mississippi, to benefit from the expansion.

The meetings of this Gang of Six continued longer than I, or perhaps any of us, had expected. Once the HELP Committee completed its markup in mid-July, there was great pressure from the White House, and from other senators, for the Gang of Six to end these discussions, and for the Finance Committee to mark up a bill. With the August recess approaching, the window of opportunity was closing for our committee to complete its work.

President Obama and his chief of staff, Rahm Emanuel, were eager to see these discussions succeed, but also to see them conclude. All members of the group received frequent calls from Rahm about our progress. These calls usually came while we were meeting together in Max's conference room.

I remember receiving one such call and excusing myself from the room. Rahm started with his usual straightforward approach, "Jeff, you guys need to get these meetings over with. Chuck Grassley says you are the one holding things up because you keep asking questions." I responded, "Rahm, I am not the only one asking questions. Besides, the questions I'm asking are ones we ought to have answers to before we try to pass a bill."

From the rest of the call, I gathered I had not persuaded him.

Right-wing attacks on health care reform were many and varied, and they continued unabated. We expected some attacks that were grounded in reality. For example, the decision to include tax increases in the bill ensured that some would oppose it. The alternative would have been simply to add the future cost of the legislation to the deficit and long-term debt of the country. That did not strike me, or anyone else involved in the reform effort, as a responsible course of action.

The specific tax increases that drew the most vocal opposition in congressional debates were the tax penalty on individuals who did not get coverage, and the tax penalty on employers of fifty or more full-time employees who failed to provide adequate health insurance coverage. Two other tax increases applied to all taxpayers with incomes of over $200,000 per individual, and $250,000 per couple: an increase of the payroll tax by 0.9 percent, and an increase in the tax on net investment income of 3.8 percent. I believe the opposition to these tax increases on high-income individuals was a primary reason for the persistent efforts to repeal the ACA after its enactment.

But other attacks on the legislation were neither expected nor grounded in reality. One example was former governor and vice-presidential candidate Sarah Palin's charge that the legislation set up "death panels," which would decide whether to provide life-sustaining care. On August 7, 2009, she posted the following statement on her Facebook page:

> Government health care will not reduce the cost; it will simply refuse to pay the cost. And who will suffer the most when they ration care? The sick, the elderly, and the disabled, of course. The America I know and love is not one in which my parents or my baby with Down Syndrome will have to stand in front of Obama's "death panel" so his bureaucrats can decide, based on a subjective judgment of the "level of productivity in society," whether they are worthy of health care. Such a system is downright evil.[4]

The provision she was complaining about was a provision in the House bill (HR 3200) intended to permit payment to physicians for providing counseling, if requested by a Medicare patient, about living wills and end-of-life options. Much of the right-wing media amplified Palin's total distortion of what was in the bill. The provision allowing for reimbursement for counseling of this type seemed to me to be sound public policy, but the public concern generated by Palin's attack caused Congress to delete it from the bill. Commentators have pointed out that in fact the closest thing the United States had to "death panels" already existed: private insurance carriers denying coverage for medically necessary treatments.

Because of the "death panel" charges and others, public support for reform continued to decline. That decline became obvious during the August recess.

I returned to New Mexico for most of the recess. My schedule that month included the usual office hours, travels around the state, and meetings with constituents. I also scheduled three town halls on health care reform. As I saw it, this would allow me to explain what was being considered in Congress and to get feedback from as many constituents as possible.

The first town hall was at the convention center in Clovis, New Mexico. I began by explaining the general outline of the health care bill we were trying to pass in the Senate and then opened the meeting for questions and comments from the audience. What followed was a series of impassioned speeches denouncing the proposed health care reform as a big government takeover of the health care system. Many of those at the meeting had come well prepared, with speeches attacking various aspects of the bill. Several raised the "death panel" complaint voiced by Palin. I did my best to point out that there was nothing in the bill that established "death panels," but many in the audience believed Palin instead of me. After each speech condemning the reform effort, there was loud applause by the crowd. If there were people at the meeting who favored efforts to reform the health care laws, they kept quiet. If they had spoken up, they would have been met with loud boos—just as I was.

The day after the raucous meeting in Clovis, I held another town hall in my hometown of Silver City. We met in the large lecture room in the Bess-Forward Global Center at Western New Mexico University. This location has special meaning for me because the university built it with funds donated by Lennie Merle Bess-Forward, who taught me English in the seventh grade at the Training School, three blocks down the street. She was a wonderful human being and an excellent and devoted teacher.

After the Clovis meeting, I was not sure what to expect.

I started by giving the same explanation I had given in Clovis about what we were trying to accomplish in the Senate with health care reform. A period for questions and comments followed, during which we heard from both opponents and proponents of reform. Even though some opposed health care reform, there did not seem to be the same animosity, either toward the reform or toward me, that I had seen in Clovis. About an hour and a half into the meeting, I noticed my family's longtime friend, former Republican state representative Murray Ryan, standing up and getting ready to leave the auditorium. I interrupted the question-and-answer period to thank Murray for coming to the meeting and for his great public service to our state. He very graciously said, "I am glad that I came. I don't know all the details about the reform you are considering, but I do think we need to be doing something, and I'm glad you are back in Washington working on it for us." Murray's statement allowed us to end the meeting on a high note.

My final town hall that week was in the Reserve High School gymnasium. Reserve is the county seat of Catron County, which has a well-deserved reputation for opposing government authority in most areas. One example of that philosophical bent was the resolution passed by the county commission some years ago urging that all homeowners in the county keep at least one firearm in their house.

At this town hall, the crowd was small (only thirty), but since Reserve has fewer than 300 residents, not that small by Reserve standards. When we got to the question-and-comment period, there were some who saw a great need to get on with the reform effort, but there were others strongly opposed.

One woman recounted the horrors she had experienced in trying to establish that their family's insurance policy covered her daughter's extensive health problems. She favored reform, and the sooner, the better.

A respected longtime Republican rancher, who was also chair of the county commission, spoke in opposition to the proposed reform. He pointed out that he and his family had never had health insurance and that when they needed health care, they went to town and paid for it. To him, enacting a requirement that he purchase insurance would be an overreach by the federal government. Two things were clear from what he said: he had the resources to pay for the health care he and his family had needed, and their need for health care had not been major. His explanation of his personal situation persuaded me that his opposition to reform was heartfelt and genuine. Unfortunately, many Americans did not have either his family's resources or their history of good health.

During this August recess, most senators did what I did, and held town halls on health care reform in their home states. There was particular interest in the town halls held by Chuck Grassley, the senior senator from Iowa. Chuck was the ranking Republican on the Finance Committee and part of our Gang of Six. At one of these meetings he added to the public concern when asked about "death panels." He said: "And I don't have any problem with things like living wills. But they ought to be done within the family. We should not have a government program that determines if you're going to pull the plug on Grandma."[5]

Chuck's statement was a powerful sign that the attacks on the reform effort were having an impact. Instead of correcting the questioner's misunderstanding about the bill, and stating that no "death panels" were being set up, his response seemed to imply that "death panels" were under consideration. Chuck's statement also showed that our efforts in the Gang of Six to craft a bipartisan bill had failed.

Ted Kennedy died of brain cancer on August 25, as we were approaching the end of the August recess. Thirteen months earlier he had suffered a seizure at Hyannis Port. The day before that seizure I had visited with him in the Senate gym, where he had both his Portuguese water dogs with him. His death was a significant loss to the country and to the Senate. He had a genuine passion for the causes he championed, and during his almost forty-seven years in the Senate, no one had worked harder to increase access to health care for all Americans.

Governor Deval Patrick appointed Ted's longtime friend and political ally Paul Kirk to succeed him in the Senate. Paul stated publicly that he would not run for the seat in the upcoming special election. Democrats nominated Massachusetts attorney general Martha Coakley, but Republican state senator Scott Brown defeated her in the special election. Once he was sworn in in February, the shift of this Massachusetts Senate seat from Democrat to Republican eliminated our ability to muster the sixty votes necessary to stop filibusters. This presented a substantial challenge to getting a health care reform bill to President Obama for signature.

By the time the Senate returned from its annual August recess, all of us in the Gang of Six could see that the Finance Committee would not have a bipartisan bill to consider. This was a major disappointment for Senators Baucus and Conrad, and for me, but the forces opposed to bipartisan cooperation on this issue were too formidable to overcome. Senator Baucus, as chair of the committee, took the best course available to him, and put forward a "chairman's mark" as a starting document for the committee markup. It contained what we three Democrats had been trying to persuade one or more of the three Republicans to support.

On September 22, 2009, the Finance Committee began the markup of the chair's proposal. There were twenty-three senators on the committee: thirteen Democrats and ten Republicans. As the markup began, senators, both Democrats and Republicans, had filed 546 proposed amendments. Members did not expect votes on most of the filed amendments, because it was clear they couldn't pass or because the sponsor filed the amendment just to send a message about a particular issue. However, many amendments still required a vote. Since the Finance Committee had jurisdiction over Medicaid, some amendments related to the proposed Medicaid expansion, and since this was the committee with jurisdiction over taxes, there were also many tax-related amendments.

The committee completed its markup after several long days and late evening sessions. The process ended, to the relief of all, at 2:00 a.m. Friday morning, October 2. All Democrats plus one Republican, Senator Olympia Snowe from Maine, voted to report the bill to the full Senate. Senator Snowe's "aye" vote raised the possibility that there might be some Republican support for the bill when it reached the Senate floor.

That was not to be the case.

ENACTING A FINAL BILL

Once the two Senate committees had acted, responsibility shifted to Majority Leader Harry Reid to prepare a combined bill (i.e., merge the two bills into a single piece of legislation that could get the support of enough senators to overcome the filibuster that awaited it).

In late November, Senator Reid presented his merged and revised legislation for consideration on the Senate floor. He did so after negotiating with several Democratic senators so that, when the Senate voted on cloture, they would support going forward. A manager's package, containing the various revisions Reid had made to accommodate individual senators, was proposed as an amendment on December 19. After overcoming many procedural hurdles, the Senate passed the legislation on Christmas Eve. We achieved the necessary sixty votes with all fifty-eight Democratic senators and the two independents.

All Republican senators voted "no."

The normal course would have been for the House to enact its proposal and then for a conference committee to resolve differences between the Senate and House bills. However, the death of Ted Kennedy and Scott Brown's election to replace him substantially complicated things. Brown was sworn in on February 4. During the special election campaign he had stated that if a final bill came to the Senate floor, he would vote "no," with the rest of the Republican senators. That meant we lacked the sixty votes necessary to overcome a filibuster. In the Senate, we no longer had enough votes to pass any version of the ACA if the House returned it to us. The House would have to pass, and send to the president, the bill passed by the Senate on Christmas Eve.

To get House Democrats to agree to this course of action, Pelosi and Reid agreed on a plan to allow an additional package of revisions to be enacted by both the House and the Senate using the procedural device called "reconciliation." Immediately after the House passed the Senate-passed ACA, both the House and Senate would pass another package of provisions that could be passed with a simple majority, and could not be filibustered in the Senate. President Obama would then have two bills to sign, with the second modifying the first.

On March 25, 2010, he signed both bills, in the required order, and the ACA became the law of the land.

At the time the ACA became law, some criticized President Obama, Speaker Pelosi, and Majority Leader Reid for failing to enact a bipartisan bill. From my vantage point, it seemed clear we did not have the option of enacting a bipartisan bill. In both Senate committees, we had made every effort to win Republican support. Senator McConnell, as the Republican leader, worked tirelessly to keep Republican senators from supporting any major health care reform bill. His efforts succeeded.

POST-ENACTMENT OPPOSITION

Opponents of the ACA did not see enactment of the law as a reason to lessen their opposition. Instead, attacks on the law took on new life. Those attacks came in four venues: the Congress, the courts, the administration (after Trump's election in 2016), and the states.

THE CAMPAIGN IN CONGRESS TO "REPEAL AND REPLACE"   In the lead-up to enactment, the unrelenting attacks on "Obamacare" had persuaded a majority of Americans to oppose at least some aspects of the legislation. Republicans seized on this in the 2010 elections to rally opposition to the law. They recognized that many of their constituents did not favor outright repeal, so they advocated for "repeal and replace" instead. That became the slogan, repeated thousands of times by ACA opponents.

Carl Hulse of *The New York Times* spoke with Josh Holmes, the Mc-Connell staffer credited with coming up with the "repeal and replace" slogan. When Hulse asked what he had in mind when he said "replace," the staffer replied, "I don't do policy."[6]

That was the problem that became obvious as early as the markup sessions, when the ACA was working its way through Congress: opponents of the bill had nothing to propose as a replacement. They did not favor a single-payer system, and they did not favor expanding coverage absent such a system.

In the Congress that met in 2011 and 2012, House Republicans voted thirty-five times in favor of repealing, undoing, or gutting the ACA. In the next Congress, they voted an additional nineteen times for similar proposals.

The "repeal and replace" strategy could not succeed with Democrats in control of the Senate and the White House, so the next effort by congressional opponents in Congress came in 2013, when Republicans proposed to withhold funding for the operation of the entire federal government unless Democrats would agree to "defund" the ACA. This ill-conceived strategy resulted in much of the federal government shutting down from October 1 through 16 (see chapter 1). Several senators, most notably Ted Cruz of Texas and Mike Lee of Utah, encouraged House Republicans in this effort, as did the Tea Party and much of the right-wing media. After sixteen days, Speaker Boehner relented and agreed to allow a vote on a Senate-passed government funding plan (see chapter 1).

Donald J. Trump's election as president in 2016, together with Republican majorities in both houses of Congress, once again prompted new efforts to "repeal and replace" Obamacare. During the 2016 campaign,

Trump followed the script congressional Republicans had written. In most campaign speeches he would repeat that one of his first actions as president would be to "repeal and replace" Obamacare. There was no discussion about what the replacement might look like.

In 2017, feeling an understandable need to follow through on the "repeal and replace" commitment, Speaker Paul Ryan introduced the AHCA, the American Health Care Act. Those who supported the ACA attacked Ryan's proposal as a denial of health care coverage to millions of Americans. Conservatives who favored something closer to outright repeal also attacked it as "Obamacare lite." The Congressional Budget Office (CBO) added to the debate when it released its analysis of the proposal, showing that, if enacted, 24 million fewer Americans would have health care coverage by 2026. When Ryan could not persuade a majority of the House to pass the bill as proposed, he changed the bill and passed it through the House, 219 to 216. The CBO estimated that this new bill would only add 23 million to the number of uninsured by 2026.

In the Senate, Majority Leader Mitch McConnell also offered a proposal that purported to "repeal and replace" the ACA. He decided to call off the scheduled vote when fewer than fifty senators indicated support. The next proposal, offered by Rand Paul, was to repeal the ACA two years hence, and to develop a replacement for the act during that period. That proposal failed on a vote of 45 "ayes" and 55 "nays."

McConnell's last effort was an eight-page bill, dubbed a "skinny repeal," which would have eliminated the individual and employer mandates, and repealed the tax on medical devices. In a dramatic early morning session on July 28, that bill failed when all Democrats and three Republicans voted "no." Some saw this as John McCain's finest hour. Doctors had diagnosed McCain with terminal cancer, and although earlier he had supported efforts at repeal, he came to the Senate floor that day and cast the deciding vote against the bill.

In my view, if Republicans had succeeded in their efforts to repeal the law, without a credible alternative to put in its place, it would have proved to be a political mistake. By this time, most Americans opposed repeal. And by the time campaigns began for the 2018 midterm elections, Nancy Pelosi urged incumbent House Democrats to make their support for the

ACA a centerpiece in their campaigns. Republicans who had earlier campaigned in favor of repealing the law, avoided the issue.

The change in public sentiment, together with Democratic success in regaining a majority in the House, ended GOP legislative efforts both to "repeal and replace" and to "defund" the ACA.

THE COURTS WEIGH IN After the ACA became law in 2010, the state of Florida, the National Federation of Independent Businesses (NFIB), and several others sued to challenge its constitutionality. The key provision they challenged was the individual mandate. In *NFIB v. Sebelius*, the Supreme Court rejected the challenge to the individual mandate (see discussion above), but it agreed with an attack on the ACA provisions that expanded Medicaid.

At the time Congress enacted the ACA, all fifty states plus the District of Columbia were participating in the Medicaid program. Under the ACA, Congress required states wishing to continue participating in Medicaid to extend coverage to eligible persons with incomes under 138 percent of the poverty level.

Justice John Roberts, speaking for himself and six other members of the court, concluded that imposing this requirement was onerous on the states, and therefore exceeded the constitutional authority of Congress.

This ruling by the court came as a complete surprise to me. I had sat through many meetings on the issues involved in writing health care legislation, with members of both the HELP Committee and the Finance Committee, and we were well-staffed with competent legal counsel. During those meetings, it never occurred to me, or to anyone else present as far as I know, that Congress did not have authority to require states to expand the group of individuals covered by Medicaid, as a condition of remaining in the Medicaid program.

In Justice Ginsburg's dissenting opinion, she made the point that I assumed was obvious:

> The spending power conferred by the Constitution, the Court has never doubted, permits Congress to define the contours of programs financed with federal funds. [Citations omitted.] And to expand

coverage, Congress could have recalled the existing legislation, and replaced it with a new law, making Medicaid as embracive of the poor as Congress chose.

The question posed by the 2010 Medicaid expansion, then, is essentially this: To cover a notably larger population, must Congress take the repeal/reenact route, or may it achieve the same result by amending existing law? The answer should be that Congress may expand by amendment the classes of needy persons entitled to Medicaid benefits. A ritualistic requirement that Congress repeal and reenact spending legislation in order to enlarge the population served by a federally funded program would advance no constitutional principle and would scarcely serve the interests of federalism. To the contrary, such a requirement would rigidify Congress' efforts to empower States by partnering with them in the implementation of federal programs.[7]

Justice Ginsburg went on to argue—

Given past expansions, plus express statutory warning that Congress may change the requirements participating States must meet, there can be no tenable claim that the ACA fails for lack of notice. Moreover, States have no entitlement to receive any Medicaid funds; they enjoy only the opportunity to accept funds on Congress' terms . . . Congress is simply requiring States to do what States have long been required to do to receive Medicaid funding: comply with the conditions Congress prescribes for participation.[8]

Seven members of the Supreme Court disagreed with Justice Ginsburg's analysis. The court's ruling on this part of the ACA meant that each state could expand its Medicaid program or continue with no expansion of benefits. The result is that in 2022 there are still twelve states that have not expanded Medicaid coverage, and several million Americans—whom Congress intended to cover through the ACA—who have no health care coverage.

"LET IT IMPLODE": TRUMP'S EFFORT TO SABOTAGE THE ACA Having failed to repeal the ACA, and having failed in the effort to have the entire law declared unconstitutional, President Trump tweeted out his strategy for the future: "Let ObamaCare implode."[9]

He pursued that effort, to let the law "implode," on several fronts. One was to discontinue payments to insurers that allowed those insurers to lower co-pays and deductibles for people receiving coverage through insurance exchanges. The courts restored those payments. Another effort was to decrease resources to inform people of the opportunity to apply for coverage through insurance exchanges. A third strategy of the Trump administration was to assist states in their efforts to limit the number of people eligible for Medicaid benefits.

EFFORTS IN THE STATES TO LIMIT MEDICAID EXPANSION When Trump became president, thirty-one states had opted to take advantage of the funds being offered in the Affordable Care Act and expand Medicaid coverage. In some states that had not expanded Medicaid, advocates in favor of increased coverage proposed ballot measures to accomplish what the governors and legislators had refused to do. Fifty-three percent of Utah voters supported a ballot initiative to expand Medicaid coverage. Sixty-one percent of Idaho voters endorsed the expansion called for in the ACA.

In both states, Republican governors and legislators, having failed to prevent expansion, set about to try limiting that expansion. GOP legislators in Utah proposed legislation to limit Medicaid coverage to only those with incomes below 100 percent of the poverty level (rather than the 138 percent prescribed in the ACA). Idaho legislators enacted similar restrictions on those entitled to Medicaid coverage. There is a question, which either the courts or Congress will decide, on whether states can receive funds under the ACA for these partial expansions of Medicaid. The Trump administration argued that they can.

There also has been an effort in these same states, and several others, to limit the number of people covered by Medicaid by imposing work requirements on participants. At least one federal district court judge has ruled that states cannot impose such work requirements since it is contrary to the purposes of Medicaid and the ACA. Appellate courts have not yet ruled on the issue.

Under the Biden administration, these state efforts to deny coverage are meeting federal resistance.

Issues Not Yet Resolved

A majority of Americans now support most of the reforms included in the ACA. It has moved the country toward a more accessible and affordable health care system. If that majority continues to grow, I hope we will soon see an end to efforts to sabotage the law. When that occurs, and when Congress can, once again, make progress in reforming our health care system, I hope it will give priority to two issues: health care workforce development, and reducing health care costs and cost growth.

HEALTH CARE WORKFORCE DEVELOPMENT

One of the enormous challenges the country faces is how to train or attract enough health care workers. The pandemic has underscored this problem. Even after the pandemic, the demand for physicians, nurses, and others in the health care profession will only increase because of our aging population and because of the greater number of people getting access to health care under the ACA.

At the time the ACA was being drafted, it seemed clear to me that the country was giving too little attention to the need to train physicians and other health care professionals. I proposed establishing a National Health Care Workforce Commission to assess our workforce needs and make recommendations to Congress and the administration on how to address the problem.

We included language establishing that commission in the ACA. During the year following enactment, President Obama appointed a distinguished group of professionals as members. However, Congress has never appropriated the small ($3 million) amount needed for staffing and commission meetings. Each year, Republican opposition to funding anything related to the ACA has been an obstacle to proceeding with this important work.

This is not a problem that will go away. It is shortsighted for the United States to continue spending well over $1 trillion of taxpayer money each year for health care services with no serious effort to understand or plan for the nation's health care workforce needs.

As the name "The Affordable Care Act" makes clear, Congress was eager to do all it could to rein in the cost of health care services. Experts who testified in congressional hearings all agreed on "the need to bend the cost curve." The cost of health care services had been growing much faster than the cost of other goods and services for the two decades prior to enactment of the law.

In the ACA, Congress made several good-faith efforts to address the problem of excessive health care costs. Health insurance exchanges established in the bill were designed so that people could compare the offerings from insurance companies and realize cost savings by doing so. By expanding coverage, both to people getting insurance through exchanges and to new Medicaid recipients, Congress intended to reduce the amount of "free health care" hospitals and other health care providers have to provide, and this would reduce the "cost shift" that puts constant upward pressure on the premiums paid by those with private insurance. Congress also enacted the "medical cost ratio" requirement to limit the amount insurance companies could charge over the cost of health care services. And the ACA tried to reduce the growth in health care costs by encouraging health care providers to join accountable care organizations (ACOs), the belief being that these types of organizations could better coordinate a patient's health care services and improve the quality of those services and reduce costs.

These provisions were well intended, but they have not done enough. Health care costs as a percentage of GDP in the United States should not be twice what citizens pay in most other developed countries (see the chart on the next page).

Congress needs to take up the issue again and determine what more it can do.

If a future Congress makes a serious effort to confront the excessive growth in health care costs, that effort should include provisions to reduce the costs of prescription drugs. To do so, Congress should allow and direct the Department of Health and Human Services (HHS) to negotiate with pharmaceutical companies for more reasonable pricing of prescription drugs. This recommendation, and others, is part of a report issued by the

HEALTH CARE SPENDING AS A PERCENTAGE OF GDP, 1980–2019

Legend: — US (16.8%) ⋯ SWIZ (11.3%) -- GER (11.7%) ▬ FRA (11.1%) ≡ SWE (10.9%) — CAN (10.8%) ⋯ NOR (10.5%) -- UK (10.2%) — NETH (10.2%) ⋯ AUS (9.4%) ∿ NZ (9.1%)

PERCENT OF GDP

Notes: Current expenditures on health. Based on System of Health Accounts methodology, with some differences between country methodologies. GDP refers to gross domestic product. 2019 dates are provisional or estimated for Australia, Canada, and New Zealand.

Source: Eric C. Schneider et al., *Mirror, Mirror 2021: Reflecting Poorly: Health Care in the U.S. Compared to Other High-Income Countries* (Commonwealth Fund, Aug. 2021). https://doi.org/10.26099/01DV-H208. Data derived from OECD Health Data, July 2021.

National Academies of Science, Engineering and Medicine (NASEM) in 2017.[10] I was privileged to join others in drafting that report. If Congress can ever resist Big Pharma's lobbying, it should adopt these recommendations.

AN UNSOLVED MYSTERY

Looking back on the ACA saga, I must confess I still don't understand the reasons for the virulent and persistent opposition.

A principal reason offered was that Republicans opposed expanding the reach and authority of the federal government. I can understand that, but it does not seem to me a sufficient reason to explain the strength and persistence of the opponents. The influence of special interests, primarily interests involved in the health insurance industry, undoubtedly reinforced this ideological motivation. Also, many of their wealthy political supporters opposed the law because of their strong objection to the tax increases it included. As mentioned earlier, I am sure some Republican members opposed the reform because they did not want to give President Obama a significant legislative victory prior to his reelection campaign.

As Republicans in Congress opposed passage of the bill, opposition to Obamacare became enshrined as orthodoxy for Republican candidates. The more they campaigned against it and voted to "repeal and replace" it, the more their political base opposed the law. That pressure from their political base caused members of Congress to harden their own opposition. Something akin to a negative feedback loop developed, and even those few Republicans in Congress who might have been willing to support reform, or lessen their opposition to the law once enacted, were not willing to break with their party on an issue where the party position was so entrenched. The sad fact is that for many Republicans, Obamacare was seen as a symbol of the Obama presidency. They did not support Obama as their president, so they opposed Obamacare.

Even this set of explanations seems inadequate. I hope students of American government and politics can provide additional insights on this mystery.

9 Improve Elementary and Secondary Education

IN AUGUST 1983, the National Commission on Excellence in Education issued its report, which was called "A Nation at Risk."[1] Terrell Bell, President Reagan's secretary of education, had appointed eighteen experts to serve on the commission. The report documented the deficient academic performance by students in schools throughout the country. It also highlighted that US students were not measuring up to students in other countries on tests of academic subjects. On the nineteen tests the commission reviewed, American students were never first or second, and compared with other industrialized nations, were last on seven of those tests.

The crucial question—one that did not get enough discussion in the report—was: "What is the federal government's responsibility for improving education?" That large question has been at the heart of our national debates about education in recent decades. It leads to several more specific questions:

- Should there be national goals to improve education?
- Should there be national standards that we expect students and schools to meet?
- If so, how should we set those standards?
- How do we assess whether students and schools are meeting the standards?
- What incentives or penalties should the federal government employ if a state, or school district, or school does not meet those standards?
- Should there be a common core of material we expect students to master, no matter which state or school district they live in?

The federal government has traditionally deferred to the states on issues related to education. That changed somewhat with enactment of the Elementary and Secondary Education Act of 1965 (ESEA), part of President Lyndon Johnson's Great Society. The primary thrust of that act was to target federal funds to schools with a predominance of students from poor families. It did not tell states or local school districts how to educate children.

Since first enacting the ESEA, Congress has reauthorized it several times. In the reauthorizations that occurred before the end of the last century, the role of the federal government remained largely unchanged (i.e., to provide federal funds, but leave decisions about education to states and local school boards). In 2001, that changed when Congress passed the No Child Left Behind Act (NCLB). It increased the federal government's involvement in trying to improve education. In 2015, Congress backed away from that involvement with enactment of the Every Student Succeeds Act (ESSA).

My disappointing conclusion is that during the last thirty-five years, our efforts to improve K–12 education in the country have moved us two steps forward, and then one-and-a-half steps back. The difficulty of the undertaking explains part of this. It is no simple task to overcome inertia in the over 130,000 elementary and secondary schools in the country that are working to educate over 50 million students. In addition, we continue to be undecided about the proper role for the federal government in education.

In recent decades, ideological opposition to an activist federal government and our refusal to embrace an active federal role have impeded our ability to provide a world-class education to US students. That continues today.

Setting National Education Goals

The 1983 "A Nation at Risk" report failed to get much attention from President Reagan, but his successor, President George H. W. Bush, convened the nation's first National Education Summit in Charlottesville, Virginia.

President Bush and all fifty governors attended that summit in September 1989. The purpose was to agree upon and commit to a set of national education goals. The six they agreed on were both general and ambitious:

Goal 1: By the year 2000, all children will start school ready to learn.
Goal 2: By the year 2000, the high school graduation rate will increase to at least 90 percent.

Goal 3: By the year 2000, American students will leave grades 4, 8, and 12 having demonstrated competency in challenging subject matter, including English, mathematics, science, history, and geography, and every school in America will ensure that all students learn to use their minds well, so they may be prepared for responsible citizenship, further learning, and productive employment in our modern economy.

Goal 4: By the year 2000, US students will be first in the world in mathematics and science achievement.

Goal 5: By the year 2000, every adult American will be literate and will possess the skills necessary to compete in a global economy and exercise the rights and responsibilities of citizenship.

Goal 6: By the year 2000, every school in America will be free of drugs and violence and will offer a disciplined learning environment conducive to learning.

In 1990, as a follow-up to the Charlottesville meeting, President Bush and the governors issued a joint statement, later followed by legislation, establishing the National Education Goals Panel. The panel consisted of fourteen members, with Governor Roy Romer of Colorado as chair. I was honored to be chosen as one of the two senators on the panel, along with Thad Cochran of Mississippi.

Although the goals panel had no authority to require action, the idea of having such a panel seemed to me to be a way to keep a focus on the national goals. As we began our first meeting, we all seemed optimistic about what we could accomplish. Unfortunately, the achievement we hoped for never materialized.

As a further follow-up to the Charlottesville summit, President Bush installed a new secretary of education, former governor and former president of the University of Tennessee Lamar Alexander. He faced the hard job of trying to enact legislation to achieve the agreed-upon national goals.

The Bush administration entitled its legislative proposal "America 2000." It proposed to establish programs funded by the federal government to help states and school districts achieve the national goals. One proposed program would have provided grants to establish 535 New American Schools (one for each congressional district plus 100 more). The idea was for these schools to try out and demonstrate reform strategies that other schools in the country could then adopt. Another proposal was to require report cards on all the nation's public schools.

When introduced, America 2000 had significant support in Congress. In the Senate Ted Kennedy, then chair of the Labor and Human Resources Committee, and Claiborne Pell, the long-serving head of the Subcommittee on Education, were prime sponsors. Business leaders and prominent education leaders also supported the effort. One such leader was Al Shanker, head of the American Federation of Teachers. His stature and lifelong commitment to improving education added weight to the effort.

Despite this strong initial support, the legislation encountered major opposition in both the House and the Senate. Opposition came mainly from Republican members concerned about an expanded federal government role in education. Some Democrats also had serious concerns, particularly about a proposal in the bill to provide federal funding for private school vouchers. And, as expected, the idea of the federal government imposing requirements for testing of students proved controversial.

Legislative action on the bill came to a head and then stalled in the last months leading up to the 1992 election. Eventually it became clear to President Bush, Lamar Alexander, and most others involved in the effort, that enactment of far-reaching education legislation would have to wait for President Bush's second term.

That second term never came.

The Push for National Standards

When I arrived in the Senate, the most recognized effort to promote high national standards for US high school students was the College Board's Advanced Placement (AP) courses.

The College Board first made Advanced Placement courses available nationally for use at the high school level in 1955. The idea was to provide challenging academic coursework and to achieve three major objectives: first, raise academic standards more generally in high schools; second, reduce the later cost of higher education by allowing students to obtain college credit through AP courses; and third, allow for valid comparisons about student proficiency, regardless of where the student went to school, by having an accepted set of national materials and tests.

The availability of AP instruction has varied significantly from state to state, and high school to high school. There has never been a requirement that high schools offer these courses, and many have chosen not to offer them. Despite this, the number and variety of AP courses, and the number of students taking the courses, has steadily increased since they were first introduced. The federal government has had a program to help increase AP course offerings, by helping to train teachers, and also by helping students to pay the cost of the testing once they completed a course. During my time in the Senate, I, along with several other senators, tried to increase funding levels for this federal effort, with modest success.

George W. Bush's election as president moved national standards, and the federal government's proper role in elementary and secondary education, to the front burner. As governor of Texas, Bush had made improving education a top priority. In 2001, as president, he made enactment of the No Child Left Behind Act (NCLB) his first major domestic legislative initiative. This effort at setting national education standards was the most ambitious in our nation's history.

Many saw NCLB as the culmination of an effort to require states to adhere to high educational standards at all grade levels and to measure and report progress in meeting those standards. The name for the new reauthorizing legislation was the slogan used by the Children's Defense Fund, a nonprofit founded by Marian Wright Edelman in 1973. The administration's proposal required that each state develop a plan for improving education, together with an expectation for "Adequate Yearly Progress" (AYP) toward achieving the reforms. It mandated that states administer standardized tests each year, and publish annual report cards for each school, specifying the demographic characteristics of the students and setting forth student achievement data. It also required states to take corrective action for schools that failed to achieve AYP. The corrective action ranged from developing an improvement plan to restructuring the entire school.

President Bush signed NCLB on January 8, 2002. At the time he signed it, there were great hopes that states, working with the federal government, could move K–12 education to a higher achievement level. The legislation prompted states and local school districts to adopt many useful reforms, but it is beyond dispute that the legislation fell short of meeting its goals. Many state officials, education leaders, teachers, parents, and students resisted the new requirements in the act. In 2015, Congress backed away from many of the requirements in the law and passed the Every Student Succeeds Act (ESSA), which was much less intrusive on the prerogatives of states and local school districts.

The Common Core

Recognizing the entrenched resistance to an increased federal role in education, those supporting NCLB had tried to avoid setting national standards by providing that each state could set its own expectations for improvement.

That left education leaders at the state and local level with the difficult task of determining what standards to set. In order that each state would not have to grapple with this problem on its own, an effort was started to come up with a "common core": a set of standards for what students in each grade, kindergarten through high school, should know and be expected to do. The National Governor's Association (NGA) and the Council of Chief State School Officers (CCSSO) worked with teachers' organizations (National Education Association, National Federation of Teachers, National Council of Teachers of Mathematics, National Council of Teachers of English, and others) to develop these Common Core State Standards.

The first reaction of many conservatives, which continues today in some quarters, was to denounce this effort as another attempt by Washington to dictate national standards. For the first few years after work on the Common Core began, many who had opposed NCLB remained opposed or at least skeptical of the new initiative. However, since there was very little evidence of Washington controlling the process, vocal opposition eventually diminished. By 2020, forty-one states plus the District of Columbia had adopted the Common Core.

Some of the controversy has subsided, but it is still an open question whether the development and adoption of the Common Core has done much to improve student performance. It is easier to adopt standards than it is to make the necessary changes so that teachers and students can measure up to those standards.

Retreat to Local Control

CONGRESSIONAL ACTION AFTER NCLB

Like most legislation, NCLB included an expiration date—in this case, 2007. If Congress does not reauthorize a law by the date set, it expires, but the programs and activities set out in the law usually continue, as long as Congress appropriates funds. That had been the practice over the history of reauthorizations of the Elementary and Secondary Education Act. Often, Congress's failure to reauthorize legislation in a timely fashion resulted from its inability to get its work done. In the case of NCLB, the delay in reauthorizing the law resulted from the controversy about its requirements.

With Republicans controlling Congress, in 2015, seven years after NCLB had expired, the law was finally replaced. The name chosen for this new version of the ESEA was the Every Student Succeeds Act (ESSA).

Although it enjoyed bipartisan support and a Democratic president signed it, ESSA represented a retreat in federal efforts to improve elementary and secondary education. One analyst described it as follows:

> The new act, the ESSA, moves education in a direction that was unthinkable just a few short years ago: no definite equity provisions, no demands for specific student achievement, and no enforcement mechanism to prompt states consistently to pursue equity or achievement.[2]

The ESSA kept much of the intent of the NCLB Act, but it largely eliminated the carrots and sticks available for the federal government to encourage improved performance.

THE TRUMP ADMINISTRATION POSITION

In government, one way to deal with an issue is to announce that it is someone else's problem. That was the approach the Trump administration took with elementary and secondary education.

During his campaign for president, Trump aligned himself with those who have long sought to diminish the federal government's role. During each presidential election since Congress established the Department of Education in 1979, Republican candidates have called for eliminating the department. Donald Trump was no exception. As a candidate, he promised to eliminate the department and also the "Common Core." Since the "Common Core" was not a federal mandate, this second promise is one he could not fulfill.

In April 2017, President Trump issued a largely symbolic executive order intended to underscore his desire to eliminate federal involvement in elementary and secondary education. It made clear that under his administration, the federal government would not require any minimum standards to be met by states or local districts.

Congress's enactment of the ESSA and the Trump administration's assertion of its commitment to local control reduced the prospects of the federal government playing a significant role in improving the nation's schools. It is my hope and belief this will change in the new Biden administration. Without a significant federal effort, we will continue with a patchwork of educational quality and deficiency from community to community, and state to state. Massachusetts will do just fine. That state has a long tradition of commitment to quality education. Some other states will also do well. But many states that suffer from high rates of poverty will continue without the commitment or the resources needed to improve their schools. And the 2020–2021 pandemic added a whole new set of challenges for our nation's schools and teachers.

Three Priority Areas

When improving elementary and secondary education once again becomes a national priority, I would urge a greater effort in three areas. First, reduce the dropout rate in our nation's high schools. Second, provide incentives for states to require a two-hundred-day school year. Third, enact a new federal initiative to improve proficiency in math and the sciences.

The dropout rate is a problem that varies greatly from state to state and from district to district. The second and third issues, expanding learning time and improving math and science proficiency, are both areas where the federal government should provide help.

REDUCING THE DROPOUT RATE

The second of the national education goals adopted in 1989 was that by 2000 the "high school graduation rate will increase to at least 90 percent." It is now 2022, and in most states that goal has not been met. A realistic assessment of the situation revealed how challenging that goal is.

Some states like Massachusetts and Utah have dropout rates in the single digits. However, in my home state of New Mexico, getting students to remain in high school until graduation remains a challenge. The dropout problem we face in New Mexico in 2022 is much the same as it was when I graduated from high school in 1961 in Silver City, New Mexico. When my classmates and I began high school, we had over one hundred students in our freshman class. Four years later, sixty-two seniors graduated.

In the summer of 2004, I devoted a week of the August congressional recess to traveling New Mexico meeting with school administrators, teachers, and students about the dropout problem. The purpose was to better understand what was causing the problem and what solutions might work.

The most memorable comment I heard that week was from the school superintendent in Clovis, New Mexico. When I asked what was being done in Clovis to reduce the number of kids who dropped out before graduation, he said,

> The strategy we have adopted is to emphasize attendance. Most kids don't just wake up one day and decide to quit school. Long before that, they get in the habit of just not attending school every day. So we try to emphasize to students, and particularly to their parents, that, absent a genuine health problem, they need to be at school every day.

EXPAND STUDENT LEARNING TIME:
THE TWO-HUNDRED-DAY SCHOOL YEAR

US students attend school fewer days each year than do students in most industrialized countries. They also receive fewer hours of instruction than students elsewhere. It is not realistic to believe they will significantly improve their standing relative to others in the industrialized world unless they spend more time learning.

Adding additional learning time to the school year is not a panacea for all the problems faced by US schools, but in my view it is an essential step. Given the decentralized, and locally controlled, nature of US schools, it is also one of the most difficult reforms to accomplish. Most of those involved in the educational system (teachers, students, and school administrators) oppose increasing the number of school days, or the hours of schooling required each day, and it is not hard to understand why. Teaching school is hard work, and teachers expect, and should expect, more pay if their work time increases. Since most funding for education comes from states and local governments, this increased cost may well mean increased taxes, and most elected officials oppose that.

If this situation is to change, the federal government will have to make a significant commitment to help states expand the learning time available in public schools. A first step would be to gain a national consensus on the need for a two-hundred-day school year. A second step would be for the federal government to offer to supplement—with appropriate funding—the efforts of states that agree to expand learning time to meet this goal.

ADEQUATELY FUND AN INITIATIVE TO IMPROVE PROFICIENCY IN MATH AND SCIENCE

The strongest argument for federal government involvement in elementary and secondary education is the need for US students to do better in math and the sciences. If one accepts the premise that our economic prosperity depends on the United States remaining a world leader in science and technology (see chapter 5), then it is not an option for the federal government to just ignore our students' poor performance in math and science compared with our economic competitors.

The Program for International Student Assessment (PISA), administered by the Organization for Economic Cooperation and Development (OECD), is the international test for comparing student proficiency. The most recent assessment shows US high school students ranking thirty-first among students in the thirty-five OECD industrial nations.

Student performance in the United States has been measured over time by the National Assessment of Educational Progress (NAEP). And according to that test, there has been little improvement for US students in math or the sciences in recent decades.

For this to change, the federal government should authorize and fund a long-term initiative to improve training for math and science teachers. The nonprofit National Math and Science Initiative has developed the model for what we should do, but for the initiative to help nationwide, there will have to be a dramatic increase in federal government funding for the effort.

10 Manage and Preserve Public Lands

I FIRST MET BRUCE BABBITT when he and my wife, Anne, practiced law together for a few months in late 1968 through early 1969. Anne and I had moved to Santa Fe after we graduated from Stanford Law School in 1968. I had joined the Army Reserve and that fall the Army ordered me to report for basic training at Fort Dix, New Jersey. While I was away, Anne lived in Phoenix with her parents and worked at Brown and Bain, the law firm where Bruce was a partner. Bruce later ran for attorney general of Arizona and began his distinguished career in public service. He went on to become governor, and in 1993 President Clinton appointed him secretary of the interior, where he served with distinction for eight years.

I have always admired Bruce's record of public service, so on a trip back to New Mexico and my hometown of Silver City for the Fourth of July celebration in the mid-1990s, it surprised me to see a stuffed dummy hanging in effigy with a sign saying "Babbitt" around its neck. The dummy was in Gough Park, where the Fourth of July parade always begins and ends. Those responsible for hanging the secretary of the interior in effigy were protesting the Clinton administration's public land policies. In retrospect, I should not have been so surprised.

The Core of the Dispute

Most disagreements involving public lands have their roots in the larger controversy about the proper role of government and general opposition to an active and involved government. Efforts to protect public lands come in several forms: legislation, executive orders, regulation, or agency management practices. Those who oppose these efforts often do so for ideological reasons. They favor private ownership of land, water, and other natural resources, rather than public ownership. Many also have an economic self-interest in that they benefit from the use of those lands and resources for their private gain.

The basic disagreement is the same. On the one side are those who favor preservation and protection of public lands. These include most members of the public. People described as "liberals" or "environmentalists" often lead these efforts. Native American tribes also share the view that we should preserve public lands for future generations. On the other side are those who consider themselves "conservatives," including companies and individuals engaged in economic activities on the public lands (grazing, mineral extraction, oil and gas production, and timber harvesting). Many of these groups and individuals believe the federal government owns too much land. They favor transfers of public land to the private sector. Short of that, they believe the federal government should reduce regulations and restrictions on private use of public lands.

This basic disagreement arises in many contexts. Here are a few examples:

- How much livestock grazing should we permit on public lands?
- What is the right level of protection for particular public lands? That is, are the lands in question deserving of protection as wilderness, as national monuments, or as conservation areas?
- How much effort should we make to protect wildlife and wildlife habitat (often through enforcement of the Endangered Species Act)?
- What restrictions should we impose on mining of coal and hard rock minerals, and should those who mine have to pay a royalty?
- What restrictions should apply to the drilling and production of oil and gas on public lands?
- When should the government grant access across public lands for transportation or energy infrastructure projects (oil and gas pipelines, electric transmission lines, etc.)?
- What is the proper level of regulation for offshore drilling for oil and gas, to avoid tragedies such as the 2010 BP oil spill?
- How should the government regulate offshore wind farms?
- How should the government regulate methane emissions from wells on public lands?

Often opposition to federal policies for managing public lands is dressed up as a principled stand for "states' rights." In most cases, the dispute is about the actual policy in question, not about which level of government is adopting or implementing the policy.

The Sagebrush Rebellion

The term "Sagebrush Rebellion" came into usage in the late 1970s to describe efforts by those resisting Bureau of Land Management and Forest Service management practices on public lands. I came to the Senate when the "Sagebrush Rebellion" was well under way. Most disputes involved grazing, but the term was used to describe a much larger set of controversies.

Ronald Reagan, while still a candidate, gave the rebellion a boost during a 1980 campaign speech in Salt Lake City. At a campaign rally, he told the crowd, "I happen to be one of those who cheers and supports the Sagebrush Rebellion. Count me in as a rebel."

Once sworn in, President Reagan made good on his Salt Lake City statement by appointing James Watt as secretary of the interior. Reagan had promised to ease restrictions on the use of public lands, and his supporters saw Watt as the ideal choice for a cabinet secretary committed to that policy. Prior to Watt's appointment, he had directed the Rocky Mountain Legal Foundation in Denver, a nonprofit that describes itself as "dedicated to individual liberty, the right to own and use property, limited and ethical government, and the free enterprise system." As secretary of the interior, Watt met the expectations of President Reagan and made himself the public face of the Sagebrush Rebellion.

Watt's term as secretary was controversial, to say the least. He announced his resignation in the fall of 1983 after addressing the US Chamber of Commerce and mocking affirmative action. In describing a coal leasing panel he had recently appointed, he said, "I have a black, a woman, two Jews and a cripple. And we have talent."

Basic Facts and How We Got Here

To understand what is at stake in these and other public land disputes, it is useful to have some essential facts.

Today the public owns, and the federal government manages, much of the American West: 573,498,120 acres in the eleven contiguous western states and Alaska. The departments and agencies with the greatest responsibility over public lands are the Department of the Interior (the Bureau of Land Management, the National Park Service, and the Fish and Wildlife Service), the Department of Agriculture (Forest Service), and the Department of Defense.

Significant federal ownership of public land began when the Founders established the nation's capital in Washington, DC, in 1790. Prior to that, the national government had operated out of leased and borrowed space in lower Manhattan and Philadelphia.

In the nineteenth century, the national government greatly expanded its land holdings. Some more notable actions were:

- President Thomas Jefferson's Louisiana Purchase;
- The Northwest Ordinances;
- Expanded territory resulting from the war with Mexico, recognized in the Treaty of Guadalupe Hidalgo;
- The Gadsden purchase; and
- Acquisition of Alaska (Seward's Folly).

As the nation expanded westward, Congress enacted measures to dispose of large portions of the public domain. Among those were transfers of land to railroads as a subsidy for expanding rail lines, grants of land to states under the Morrill Land-Grant Act to support land-grant colleges, and grants of land to those willing to homestead.

A large body of laws and regulations administered by several federal agencies governs what remains as public lands or "public domain." To find a pattern in these laws, one can think of the "multiple use land policy" articulated in FLPMA (The Federal Land Policy Management Act) as the "default." But if "multiple use" is the general rule for how we manage public lands, the exceptions to the rule—in the form of other more restrictive laws and regulations—often overwhelm the rule itself. By these exceptions, I am referring to such laws as:

- The Antiquities Act (which allows the president to establish national monuments);

- The Wilderness Act (which limits usage of public lands designated as wilderness); and
- The Endangered Species Act (which provides authority to protect habitat for listed species).

Each of these laws has the effect of imposing higher levels of protection on particular lands.

Besides enacting laws of general applicability to different categories of public land, there is also a long history of Congress enacting land bills designating particular tracts of land for particular types of management and preservation. And just as the public has a low opinion of the Congress overall but likes their own congressional representative, often members of Congress who oppose increased restrictions on the use of public land will join their constituents in supporting increased restrictions on lands in their home states or congressional districts.

The Omnibus Public Land Act of 2009

One highlight of my time in the Senate came when we enacted the Omnibus Public Land Management Act of 2009. The bill was first introduced in the 110th Congress and then reintroduced in the 111th Congress in modified form. After substantial procedural maneuvering, it became law on March 30, 2009.

During the time I chaired the Energy and Natural Resources Committee, and in most Congresses, that committee reported a great many bills to the full Senate for consideration. During each Congress, each senator, with few exceptions, would propose bills affecting the public lands in his or her state. Some of these bills involved nothing more than making a boundary change or transferring a few acres of federal land to a community for some local public purpose. But some bills involved setting aside large tracts of public land for management as monuments or as wilderness, or establishing a new national park.

By 2008, our committee had reported well over 150 public land bills. These bills were pending on the Senate calendar, but their consideration was being blocked by the threat of filibuster. By this time in the Senate, even the threat of filibuster was enough to dissuade the majority leader from bringing up a bill. In the case of the 150 public land bills, Senator Tom Coburn (R-OK) was the senator threatening to filibuster. The rationale given for the threat to filibuster was that the federal government had too much involvement with federal lands already, and many of these land bills could cause additional federal expenditures.

We solved the problem by developing an omnibus federal lands bill containing 159 individual public land bills. Since the omnibus bill contained legislation sponsored both by Republican and Democratic senators, we were hoping it could receive enough bipartisan support to pass. In fact, that happened.

One of the most important provisions we included in the 2009 act was language to establish the National Conservation Lands. In the minds of most people, the US Park Service is the agency with the mandate to conserve our public lands and manage national monuments. In 2000, Secretary of the Interior Bruce Babbitt acted to clarify that the Bureau of Land Management also had conservation as one of its primary missions. He signed an administrative order establishing the National Landscape Conservation System (now known as National Conservation Lands). Eight years after Babbitt's action, president of the Trust for Historic Preservation Dick Moe and president of the Wilderness Society Bill Meadows urged me to introduce legislation in the Senate establishing National Conservation Lands as a permanent part of the Department of the Interior. I was glad to do so, and even gladder when it became law as part of the 2009 act.

Today, in 2021, the Bureau of Land Management manages some 33 million acres as National Conservation Lands. This represents about 13 percent of the 258 million acres under their jurisdiction.

President Obama and the Antiquities Act

After the 2010 election, and the Republican takeover of the House, the Obama administration embraced a strategy of looking for opportunities where the president could move forward with his agenda for public lands without action by Congress. The Antiquities Act, signed into law by President Teddy Roosevelt, gives the president authority to designate national monuments when he believes doing so will help protect significant natural, cultural, and scientific features on federal lands. Environmental groups and the president's advisors saw this authority as a tool they could use to make progress.

During his two terms in the White House, President Obama designated twenty-eight national monuments. Two of those monuments are located in New Mexico: the Rio Grande del Norte and the Organ Mountains-Desert Peaks. I had proposed legislation to accomplish the same thing during my last years in the Senate. After I left, I applauded President Obama's use of his authority under the Antiquities Act to do what Congress should have done earlier.

Revenue from Federal Lands

Besides disputes about how to manage federal land, there is also a long history of disputes about how much revenue the government should get from federal lands and how to share and use that revenue.

Oil and gas production on federal lands is big business. In fiscal year 2010, 36 percent of US oil production came from federal lands, and the federal government owned 24 percent of US crude oil reserves.

With onshore production in the contiguous forty-eight states, the federal royalty is 12.5 percent. That means producers pay the federal government a 12.5 percent royalty on sales of oil and gas taken from public lands. Until 2007, that same 12.5 percent applied also to production offshore, in the outer continental shelf (the two-hundred-mile ocean front claimed by the federal government). In 2007, the secretary of the interior used his authority to raise the royalty on offshore production to 18.75 percent.

I have a distinct memory of President George W. Bush discussing the federal royalty rate during a trip he made to New Mexico in June 2006. The occasion was the president's visit to the Federal Law Enforcement Training Center (FLETC) in Artesia, New Mexico, a facility operated by the US Customs and Border Protection Agency to train Border Patrol agents and other federal law enforcement officials. Since they could not accommodate Air Force One at the Artesia airport, the president flew to the Roswell airport instead, some thirty miles north of Artesia. When he arrived, Senator Domenici, Congressman Steve Pearce, and I joined him on the helicopter flight from the Roswell airport to Artesia. During that flight, the president raised the issue of federal royalty rates for oil and gas production on federal land. I'm not sure what prompted him to bring up the topic—it may have been the pumping oil wells we were flying over. At any rate, he stated, in unequivocal terms, that he thought the federal royalty rate of 12.5 percent was too low. His point was that the royalty paid to private landholders in Texas, Louisiana, and most other places was 20 percent or more and that most states charged a higher royalty rate for production on state-owned lands. In his view, US taxpayers were being shortchanged with the royalty charged for production on federal land. I stated my agreement with the president, but did not detect a great deal of enthusiasm from my Republican colleagues on the helicopter. As I write these words, the royalty rate paid to the US taxpayer for onshore production in the contiguous states remains at the 12.5 percent it was in 2006.

One other detail about royalties from oil and gas production that has always seemed misguided to me relates to the language of the federal oil and gas lease itself. The standard lease used by the federal government and states requires companies to pay royalties only on oil and gas that is "severed and sold" by the company, not on the oil and gas "produced." Because of this, the federal government gets no royalty on oil and gas produced on public lands unless it goes to market and is sold. That means the government gets nothing for the gas that is flared or vented. This has two obvious adverse effects: first, it denies the taxpayer compensation; and second, it provides a perverse incentive that contributes to the continued venting and flaring of gas that adds to the problem of global warming. Experts have long recognized that methane emissions are a much greater contributor to global warming, on a volume basis, than are CO_2 emissions.

Under President Obama, the BLM began an effort to tighten federal regulations to reduce GHG emissions resulting from oil and gas production on federal land, but the Trump administration did its best to end that federal effort. Fortunately, the Biden administration has followed through on the Obama administration's earlier efforts.

As with most of the labyrinth of federal laws and regulations, the devil is in the details when it comes to sharing revenues from oil and gas production on federal lands. In forty-nine states, the federal government and the states share that revenue equally. Alaska is a special case: it receives a 90 percent share.

Prior to 2006, royalties from production in the outer continental shelf came to the federal treasury, because the federal government owned the land and it was not within any state's boundaries. In that year, Congress enacted the Gulf of Mexico Energy Security Act (GOMESA), ceding 37 percent of the royalty from oil and gas production in much of the outer continental shelf in the Gulf of Mexico to four coastal states: Alabama, Mississippi, Louisiana, and Texas. I opposed the legislation. President Truman resisted a similar effort during his time as president. Lands covered by the outer continental shelf are a national resource and the revenue they produce should benefit the residents of all states.

Case Studies in Trying to Bridge the Divide: Two Successes, One Failure

Each dispute about the uses of public land is different. Sometimes we can bridge the divide between competing camps. At other times, that is not possible.

Here are three examples of efforts to reconcile conflicting interests. In two cases we succeeded. In one, I failed.

THE VALLES CALDERA

The Valles Caldera National Preserve is a unit of the National Park System that includes 89,900 acres in the heart of the Jemez Mountains, just west of Los Alamos, New Mexico. A caldera is a bowl-like hollow in the earth, formed by the collapse of a volcanic dome and its magma chamber. In the Valles Caldera there are seven major grassland valleys, interspersed between a central resurgent dome and other small forested volcanic domes, all within the larger thirteen-mile-wide caldera. The caldera was created by the last major volcanic eruption in the Southwest, 1.2 million years ago.

After 1848, when New Mexico became a US territory, the first recognized owners of the land were the heirs of Luis Maria Cabeza de Baca. In 1860, Congress allowed Baca's heirs to select alternative lands in return for giving up all claim to their grandfather's 1821 grant on the Gallinas River in San Miguel County. The grandfather had received the earlier grant before New Mexico was part of the United States, and under the Treaty of Guadalupe Hidalgo, the US government had pledged to honor such grants. This resulted in the heirs being recognized as the rightful owners of what is now the Valles Caldera. It remained in private ownership from that date until 2000.

There was some interest in Congress for acquiring the caldera as early as 1888, inspired by the writings of Adolph Bandelier and Charles Lummis. In 1900, archaeologist Edgar Lee Hewett, who worked to create the Bandelier National Monument, lobbied to include the Valles Caldera and create the "Pajarito National Park." There was also another unsuccessful attempt in 1938.

In 1961, the Bond family, who then owned the ranch, became interested in selling it, and the next year Senator Clinton Anderson began a serious effort to bring the caldera into public ownership. He introduced "A Bill to Provide for the Establishment of Valles Caldera National Park in the State of New Mexico" into the Senate. Despite Anderson's efforts, the bill failed to become law; the reasons included concern about the cost of acquiring the land, and a dispute about the legal rights to log timber on the property.

In 1963 Patrick Dunigan purchased the property.

I was fortunate to be in the Senate as a member of the New Mexico congressional delegation when we had a new opportunity to acquire the caldera for preservation and public use. In 1997, Dunigan's sons and heirs, Andy, Mike, and Brian Dunigan, came to visit each of us in the New Mexico congressional delegation to advise us they had decided to sell the property. Their strong preference was for the government to buy it, but if that was not possible, they planned to offer it to others.

Despite my enthusiasm for the proposal, there would be hurdles to overcome. Bill Clinton was president, and Democrats controlled the House of Representatives, but Republicans controlled the Senate. During my time on the Senate Energy and Natural Resources Committee (sixteen years by then), I had had many occasions to witness the vehement opposition of my Republican colleagues to additional land acquisition by the federal government. The days of Teddy Roosevelt were long past. Paying the Dunigan family their asking price of $101 million to purchase the private ranch would also not be an easy sell.

When it became clear that everyone in our delegation did not share my enthusiasm for moving ahead with a government purchase of the property, I decided in September 1997 to introduce legislation to have the Forest

Service acquire and manage the property. By introducing the legislation, I hoped the issue would become much more visible to the public, and that the public would begin to voice its support. I decided to propose the Forest Service as the managing agency, rather than Park Service, based on two considerations: first, the Forest Service owned the land surrounding the property and this might reduce the cost of managing the new acquisition; and second, based on my observation of other debates in the Congress on land acquisitions, I believed there would be less opposition to Forest Service management than there would be to adding the property as a unit of the National Park System. My principal aim was to bring the property into public ownership and prevent it from being sold off to developers.

President Clinton and Secretary of the Interior Bruce Babbitt supported the effort, and their support was essential to our ultimate success. In the budget he submitted to Congress in February 1998, the president requested funding for the acquisition. He also took the occasion of a trip to Los Alamos that same month to announce his support.

Besides administration support, public support also proved decisive. I am persuaded that absent that public support the effort might well have stalled. That is what happened when Senator Anderson was pursuing his bill in the early 1960s.

The obvious piece of unfinished business was to gain the support of Senator Domenici, who served on the Senate Appropriations Committee and, in a Republican-controlled Senate, would have a major say on whether Congress provided the funds. Pete had made it clear to me he would not support a straight purchase of the ranch. Instead, he would support government acquisition of the property only if we followed a model used for acquisition of The Presidio in San Francisco. Under this model, although the government would own the land, it would not be part of any federal department. Instead, an independent board, appointed by the president, would have the job of managing the property. With the Valles Caldera, a crucial part of the model, in Pete's view, was that the government would manage the property as a working ranch, to allow it to be self-sufficient and thus avoid the need for annual appropriations.

I believed, and I expressed my views to those involved, that the concept of a self-sustaining working ranch did not make good sense for the Valles Caldera. What was working well for The Presidio in San Francisco would not work well in the heart of the Jemez Mountains in rural New Mexico. But this "working ranch" idea was the only formulation Pete would support, so my staff and I went to work with his staff to draft legislation to implement this idea. Pete advised President Clinton that this was the management model he would support, and we introduced a bill to accomplish this in October 1998, in both houses of Congress. After much pulling and hauling (well documented by Bill DeBuys in *Valles Caldera, A Vision for New Mexico's National Preserve*), Congress appropriated the required funds and enacted the legislation establishing the Valles Caldera Trust. President Clinton signed the legislation at Camp David on July 24, 2000.

The enacted law provided for public ownership of the land, but it also contained several other important provisions. One such provision related to property the Santa Clara Pueblo Indians sought to gain from the Dunigan holdings. That land formed part of the headwaters for the Santa Clara Creek, that flowed through Santa Clara Pueblo to the Rio Grande south of Espanola. The Santa Clara Pueblo Indians and their leaders deserve great credit for persisting and succeeding in their efforts to have that portion of the ranch added to their lands. Pueblo Indian leaders also expressed their concern that transferring ownership of the larger ranch not affect their ability to use the property for religious ceremonies. In the legislation we made provisions to ensure that those protections were in place for all tribes and pueblos with an ancestral connection to the caldera.

Another provision dealt with the very real possibility that the working ranch model for management of the property would prove unworkable. This provision stated that if the property did not become self-sufficient within an eighteen-year period, the Board of the Trust would submit to Congress its recommendation on whether the trust should continue or be terminated. If terminated, the property would become part of the national forest that surrounded it. I believed we needed something like this, as a "fallback."

After ten years, long before the eighteen-year deadline, it was obvious the land management model Congress had adopted was not working well. The board members, the directors, and the staff who had worked to get the preserve established and operating, had done their very best to manage the property as Congress had directed; however, all their good efforts could not overcome the design flaws in the management structure.

There were three fundamental problems. First, the property could not generate enough revenue to cover the cost of maintenance and operation of the preserve. Second, since the legislation had established the preserve as an independent entity, separate from any federal department or agency, there was no champion within the administration for an annual budget for the preserve (there were several years when the administration's budget had requested no funds for the preserve, and the Congress had had to add funds in the appropriations process). Third, because of inadequate funding, the managers of the preserve could not provide the public access that many of us had expected and hoped for when the federal government acquired the property. Despite all of this, those in charge of the trust made significant investments in science and education programs and ecological restoration projects. These accomplishments remain positive, long-lasting legacies of the trust experiment.

While the continued management of the preserve under a "working ranch model" made little sense, it also was clear that the National Park Service was the federal agency with both the experience and the mandate to manage property such as this. Some in the Forest Service resisted the effort to move the property from the Department of Agriculture to the Department of the Interior, but with Democrats controlling the House and Senate, and with President Obama now in office, that move seemed possible. To achieve that aim, I introduced, with Senator Tom Udall as my cosponsor, the Valles Caldera National Preserve Management Act in May 2010.

There is "a time for every purpose," and the remaining months of the 111th Congress and the 112th Congress did not prove to be the time for enacting our proposed bill. David Brooks, the excellent and long-serving public lands expert on the Energy and Natural Resources Committee staff, and I made several efforts to agree with Senator Murkowski and other Senate Republicans on a package of public land bills that would include the Valles Caldera. I regret that we failed in that effort.

In 2013, after I had left the Senate, Senators Tom Udall and Martin Heinrich (who had succeeded me both in the Senate and on the Senate Energy Committee) introduced a changed version of the earlier bill. In 2014, Congress included it in a package of public land bills added to the annual Defense Authorization Act. Senators Udall and Heinrich deserve great credit for persisting, and succeeding, in passing the bill. David Brooks, still with the Senate Energy and Natural Resources Committee, was essential to that process.

With President Obama's signature on December 19, 2014, the Valles Caldera National Preserve became part of the National Park System.

It was a good day for New Mexico and for the country.

The next year, when the Park Service took over management of the Valles Caldera National Preserve, they chose Jorge Silva-Bañuelos as its first superintendent. Jorge had been a key person on my staff working for Park Service management of the property and, at the time the transfer to the Park Service occurred, was serving as the last executive director of the trust.

The director of the National Park Service could not have made a better choice.

THE COLLABORATIVE FOREST RESTORATION PROGRAM (CFRP) AND THE COLLABORATIVE FOREST LANDSCAPE RESTORATION PROGRAM (CFLRP)

In recent decades, most public land management issues have involved conflicts and controversies about the use of those lands. In contrast, two little-known programs, one that has application only in New Mexico (the Collaborative Forest Restoration Program [CFRP]) and one with national application (the Collaborative Forest Landscape Restoration Program [CFLRP]), have tried to sidestep those conflicts and bring people together to work on restoration of forest lands.

The CFRP was designed to address the high density of trees and undergrowth in New Mexico's forests. These densely grown forests largely resulted from fire suppression practices used by the Forest Service over many decades. The program provides cost-shared grants to accomplish forest restoration projects, with the purposes of reducing stand density, increasing forest biological functions, increasing watershed production, and developing viable economic uses for small diameter trees. The CFRP also helps achieve the important goal of reducing the threat of severe wildfires.

In 1999 I introduced the legislation to establish the program. In 2000 it became law.[1] It authorized $5 million each year for the Forest Service to use in New Mexico to make cost-shared grants for experimental forest restoration projects. The impetus for the proposal came from the work of Walter Dunn, a US Forest Service employee, who was spending a year working in my Senate office as a fellow. Walter not only developed the proposal to establish the CFRP, but also returned to New Mexico to work on its implementation once the legislation had passed.

In the first fifteen years of its operation, the program invested $60 million in over two hundred projects. These projects have created local jobs and accomplished needed forest restoration work on over 33,000 acres. In addition, the CFRP has increased cooperation among the groups and interests concerned about the use and restoration of forest lands. In the 10-Year Report to Congress, the Forest Service emphasized its belief that the program has decreased litigation, enhanced trust between partners, and led to better decision-making.[2]

Building on the success of the CFRP, in 2008 I introduced legislation to establish the Collaborative Forest Landscape Restoration Program (CFLRP). The CFLRP was designed to accomplish restoration work on much larger tracts of Forest Service land throughout the country. The program borrowed from lessons learned in the implementation of the CFRP, and was enacted in the Forest Landscape Restoration Act that was included in the 2009 Omnibus Public Lands Act.

In its report to Congress ten years after the beginning of the CFLRP, the Forest Service stated it had used the program to work on twenty-three projects that involved collaborative restoration work on 5.7 million acres. One clear benefit, in addition to the jobs created, was that it reduced the threat of severe wildfires in the restored areas.

Those who seek to get economic benefit from the use of public lands and those committed to preserving those lands for future generations can have genuine disagreements, but they also have a long-term shared objective of maintaining healthy and productive forest lands. The CFRP in New Mexico and the CFLRP nationwide are examples of how well-designed and implemented programs can help bring these stakeholders together to achieve this shared goal. With the increased threat of catastrophic forest fires resulting from global warming, the need for such programs is greater than ever. I hope future Congresses maintain and expand them.

THE MIMBRES

A third example of an effort to preserve public lands and resources involved the Mimbres culture of southwest New Mexico. Much to my regret, that effort failed.

The Mimbres people lived in small groupings in the valleys of southwest New Mexico between about 900 and 1100 A.D. We remember them today for the distinctive and sophisticated artwork they left on bowls and other ceramics.

I grew up in Silver City, near the sites where the Mimbres people lived and created their art. I remember several Saturdays during my high school years when I took part in field trips organized by the Grant County Archaeological Society to work on excavation of Mimbres sites. When I came to the Senate, it occurred to me that there might be an opportunity to help preserve this cultural legacy. With that purpose in mind, in 1988 I introduced legislation calling on the secretary of the interior to "analyze the significance of the Mimbres culture, and to identify sites appropriate for understanding and interpretation." The bill passed, and the Park Service completed its study in 1991.

The study recommended creating a national monument to recognize the Mimbres culture, and to protect and interpret the cultural resource properties for the benefit of present and future generations. As part of the study, the Park Service evaluated twenty-two of the largest and most significant sites in the Mimbres Valley and surrounding areas. It recommended the national monument comprise four sites. It further recommended that, in order to prevent further looting of sites by pot hunters, a Mimbres Archaeological Site Protection System should be established to coordinate the protection of other Mimbres cultural properties.

In July 1991, based on the recommendations in the National Park Service report, I introduced the Mimbres Culture National Monument Establishment Act, with Senator Domenici as a cosponsor. Besides establishing the national monument, the act also proposed establishing a visitors' center in Silver City with exhibits to help people understand and appreciate Mimbres culture and art. I believed that involving the National Park Service and establishing a visitors' center would lead to better protection of Mimbres sites and also bring tourists to southwest New Mexico.

Even before I introduced the bill, opponents of the proposed monument organized. Some, including the New Mexico Farm and Livestock Bureau, opposed the bill because of their view that the federal government should not be purchasing additional private land in the West. A few opposed it because of fears that the federal government might threaten their own private property. And some residents near the proposed monument sites expressed opposition based on concerns about increased traffic in the area.

In December 1990, both the Silver City Town Council and the Grant County Commission adopted resolutions to support the proposal, but in September 1992, the county commission reversed their position and opposed the bill. Several local landowners calling themselves People for the Preservation of Private Lands rallied opposition with false claims that the legislation threatened rights of private property owners up and down the Mimbres Valley.

To provide information about the proposal and answer questions from its critics, I scheduled a town hall-type meeting in the Mimbres Valley on August 16, 1992. The meeting was a full house. It was obvious from the questions and statements that opponents of the legislation were adamant in their opposition. One woman in the front row had taken responsibility for capturing on video each statement I made, hoping that opponents could seize upon some misstatement.

The bill had passed unanimously in the Senate in 1991. In the fall of 1992, about six weeks after the meeting in the Mimbres Valley, it came up for a vote in the House and was defeated. Opponents had worked hard to rally opposition. Joe Skeen, the congressman representing that part of our state, lobbied his colleagues heavily against the bill.

In retrospect, I see two reasons the legislation failed. First, I underestimated the intensity of the opposition, and, second, we did not generate a critical mass of public support for the project in the local area. There were many who thought it would be a good thing to do, but few had taken a genuine interest in seeing the legislation passed. The intensity of the opposition far exceeded the intensity of the support.

The effort to establish the national monument did lead to one positive result. A local landowner transferred the Mattocks Ruin, one of the sites designated for inclusion in the national monument, to a foundation to establish the Mimbres Culture Heritage Site. The foundation's purpose with the Mattocks site was what we had envisioned for the larger national monument: preserving the site and allowing the public to visit and learn about the Mimbres people. I've been impressed by the efforts the foundation has made with very limited resources.

LESSON FROM THE THREE CASE STUDIES

The interests of the public and the interests of those who wish to use public lands for a private purpose often conflict. This gives rise to genuine disputes. Politicians can either take on the difficult task of trying to find common ground and bridge the divide, or they can add to the disagreement by championing one point of view and denouncing those who disagree. It's not always possible to reach consensus, but for a senator from the West, trying to do so is a pretty good definition of leadership.

11 Avoid Unnecessary Wars

THERE IS A TRADITION for retiring senators to give a farewell speech on the Senate floor. On December 13, 2012, I gave such a speech. My purpose was to review the previous thirty years to assess where we had made progress as a nation and where we had fallen short or even lost ground.

On foreign policy, my view was then and remains—

> as regards our Nation's security from foreign aggression, the end of the cold war and the collapse of the Soviet Union were the most positive developments that we have seen in the last 30 years.
>
> In contrast, the decision to invade Iraq was the biggest national security blunder. That disastrous decision cost our nation dearly in servicemen and women killed and injured and in resources that should have been used to strengthen our economy here at home.
>
> (Excerpt from Farewell Speech to the Senate, attached as appendix.)

A *Bunch of "Unknown Unknowns"*

On September 12, 2002, President George W. Bush addressed the United Nations and urged them to join with the United States in enforcing UN sanctions against Iraq. We now know he was speaking in code. His genuine request, which became clear in the next few months, was for other nations to join the United States in a military action to oust Saddam Hussein from power.

Before President Bush made his plea to the United Nations, he had already decided to seek congressional support for the planned invasion. The polls showed that a majority of the American public supported invading Iraq because of the repeated administration alarms about the threat posed by Saddam Hussein's "weapons of mass destruction." So, Bush's plan was to ask Congress to pass a joint resolution that authorized the president to use the armed forces of the United States "as he determines to be necessary and appropriate" in order to "defend the national security of the United States against the continuing threat posed by Iraq. . . ."[1]

While the president's decision to ask Congress for authorization to use military force seemed straightforward enough, his timing of the request seemed highly suspect. The administration was planning to invade Iraq the next spring: 2003. But Congress was being asked to go on record favoring the invasion in the last days leading up to the 2002 midterm election. There were two obvious effects of this—both favorable from the perspective of the Bush administration. First, bringing the issue to a head in Congress at this time would help ensure that people went to the polls in November with a heightened concern for national security, which would likely benefit Republican candidates at election time. Second, scheduling the vote prior to the election would set the stage for attack ads against Democratic senators and representatives who dared to vote "no." I wrote in my notebook, "Many suspect that the decision to ramp up demands for military action NOW has more to do with Karl Rove's political strategy than with any change in the level of threat from Iraq."

Once a vote on the resolution was scheduled in early October, the administration pursued an "all hands on deck" effort to lobby the Congress. A first target for the effort was the Senate Armed Services Committee.

The Democratic Steering Committee makes committee assignments for Democratic senators, and when I took the oath of office in 1983, in addition to my assignment to the Energy and Natural Resources Committee (see chapter 6), I was assigned to the Senate Armed Services Committee. Just as assigning me to the Energy Committee made sense, this assignment also made sense. There is a large military presence in New Mexico: three Air Force bases, White Sands Missile Range run by the Army, and two Department of Energy laboratories whose primary mission is maintaining our nuclear deterrent.

By the fall of 2002, I had served on the committee for nearly twenty years and had traveled across the Potomac to the Pentagon for briefings and ceremonies many times. This time, in September 2002, Secretary of Defense Rumsfeld had invited the twenty members of the Armed Services Committee to attend a breakfast and briefing on the Iraq situation.

The Pentagon had arranged for transportation in three vans they had brought to the northeast corner of the Russell Building. When I arrived at the vans about 7:30 that Tuesday morning, I sat down in one beside my friend Senator Max Cleland from Georgia. Max had joined the committee nearly six years earlier, in 1997, after being elected senator from Georgia to fill the open seat resulting from Sam Nunn's decision not to seek reelection. He was a logical choice for assignment to the Armed Services Committee because of the strong military presence in Georgia and because of his personal history. As an Army captain in the Vietnam War, he had received both a Silver Star and a Bronze Star for valorous action in combat. He had also been severely injured in Vietnam when a hand grenade belonging to a fellow soldier had exploded. Max lost both legs and his right forearm in the accident, and was permanently confined to a wheelchair.

That morning as we headed to the Pentagon, Max was in a heated reelection campaign back in his home state of Georgia. Karl Rove, the rest of the Bush political apparatus, and the Republican Senate Campaign Committee were doing their best to defeat him.

When the vans arrived at the Pentagon, they ushered us into an elevator to take us to the third-floor conference room where Secretary Rumsfeld and several uniformed officers stood ready to greet us.

The breakfast and briefing went according to protocol. While breakfast was served by uniformed military servers, Secretary Rumsfeld made his presentation. To illustrate his points, he put up a series of satellite images of installations on the ground in Iraq. His key message was that the threat to the United States and its allies from "weapons of mass destruction" was real. President Bush had delivered that same message to the UN the previous week.

After we had all eaten our scrambled eggs and bacon and the presentation concluded, the secretary invited questions. I asked no questions, but several senators did. The thrust of the questions was, "What evidence do we have that these 'weapons of mass destruction' actually exist? How certain are we that the threat is real?"

Secretary Rumsfeld seemed to sidestep the questions, but he reiterated his well-rehearsed explanation of the overall situation. It was an explanation I later heard him repeat several times:

There are known knowns. These are things we know we know. There are known unknowns. That is to say, there are things that we know we don't know. But there are also unknown unknowns. There are things we don't know we don't know.[2]

With both the breakfast and briefing finished, the secretary thanked us all for coming. As we filed out to board the elevators that would take us back to the vans, we all shook hands and thanked him as well. Everyone was polite, but everyone also was aware of the strong disagreements about what had been discussed.

On our way back to Capitol Hill, once again Max and I sat together. For the first few minutes, no one in the van said anything. It was as though we were trying to digest what we had just heard. But as we crossed the Potomac and started back up Constitution Avenue toward the Capitol, Max leaned over toward me and said in a low voice, "Can you believe this? We're getting ready to invade a country half way around the world, based on a bunch of 'unknown unknowns.'"

Lead-up to the Vote

The 9/11 terrorist attack on the World Trade Center was the spark that ignited the first serious discussions in the Bush administration about invading Iraq. This may seem odd, since there was no evidence that Saddam Hussein and his regime had prior knowledge or involvement in the 9/11 attacks. Despite that, the administration seized on the 9/11 attacks to justify removing Saddam Hussein from power. Many in the George W. Bush administration believed that President George H. W. Bush should have removed Saddam when he had the chance in the first Iraq war. Now they saw another chance.

In his 2002 State of the Union address, later dubbed the "axis of evil" speech, President Bush signaled his intention to shift the concern from just terrorist organizations, to state actors, and to highlight the threat America faced from "weapons of mass destruction." As he stated it, "Our second goal is to prevent regimes that sponsor terror from threatening America and our friends and allies with weapons of mass destruction." After mentioning North Korea, Iran, and Iraq, he said,

States like these, and their terrorist allies, constitute an Axis of Evil, arming to threaten the peace of the world. By seeking weapons of mass destruction, these regimes pose a grave and growing danger. They could provide these arms to terrorists, giving them the means to match their hatred. They could attack our allies or attempt to blackmail the United States. In any of these cases, the price of indifference would be catastrophic.[3]

Five months later, by the summer of 2002, President Bush had decided to remove Saddam. We now know this because of the Downing Street Memo, dated July 23, 2002—an internal British government document that surfaced three years after the invasion—recounting the discussion at a meeting Prime Minister Tony Blair had with the key leaders in his government. The memo summarized the conclusions the head of MI6 (the British equivalent of the CIA) had reached based on his recent trips to Washington. Bush, Cheney, and Rumsfeld saw military action as inevitable. They would justify that military action by citing the threat of terrorism and WMD. The Downing Street memo stated, "The intelligence and facts were being fixed around the policy."[4]

Based on this information from MI6, the British defense secretary advised Prime Minister Blair that if he wanted UK military involvement, "he would have to decide this early."

The Downing Street Memo also made the interesting point that the Bush administration's timeline for action was tied, in some unspecified way, to the upcoming congressional elections. What became clear as the summer and fall progressed was that the Bush administration was ramping up its campaign to sell the country and the Congress on the need to invade. Vice President Cheney, Secretary of Defense Rumsfeld, National Security Advisor Condoleezza Rice, and President Bush himself sought opportunities to sound the alarm and persuade the country and Congress that Saddam and his regime posed a real and immediate threat to the United States.

In an October 7 speech in Cincinnati, Bush did his best to argue that Saddam was operating arm-in-arm with Al Qaeda. He said:

We know that Iraq and al Qaeda terrorist network share a common enemy—the United States of America. We know that Iraq and al Qaeda have had high-level contacts that go back a decade. Some al Qaeda leaders who fled Afghanistan went to Iraq. These include one very senior al Qaeda leader who received medical treatment in Baghdad this year, and who has been associated with planning for chemical and biological attacks. We've learned that Iraq has trained al Qaeda members in bomb-making and poisons and deadly gases.[5]

We now know that this argument about a close working relationship between Saddam and al Qaeda was without foundation. In that same speech the president raised concerns that Iraq could be able to produce a nuclear weapon "in less than a year," and use such a weapon to "threaten America." At the time the president was making these arguments, he had access to the relevant intelligence, and members of Congress did not. That made it impossible to dispute his claims.

On October 2, the Republican and Democratic leaders in both the House and the Senate introduced the Iraq resolution (Joint Congressional Resolution to Authorize the Use of United States Armed Forces Against Iraq). With both party leaders in both houses of Congress supporting the resolution, there was no doubt it would pass. Five days after it was introduced, the president gave his best arguments for it in the speech in Cincinnati. Polling showed the administration's aggressive campaign to sell the idea of military action in Iraq was succeeding, and that most Americans supported giving the president the requested authority. Given the high level of public support in early October, the president had every reason to want the congressional resolution voted on before the election.

On Thursday afternoon, October 10, the House passed the joint resolution 296 to 133. All but 2 Republican House members voted "aye," and 82 Democrats joined them. That same Thursday, the final vote was to happen in the Senate, and many members, myself included, felt the need to make statements on the Senate floor. Those statements delayed the final vote until early Friday morning.

Most of the time, roll call votes in the Senate are routine—with no great excitement or drama. The clerk calls the roll of all senators, and then the vote remains open for fifteen or more minutes, during which time each senator wishing to vote can come to the floor and do so. Often after voting, a senator will leave the floor before the clerk announces the final vote count to return to his or her office, or to meet with constituents, or to return phone calls.

For this vote on the Iraq resolution, the majority and minority leaders (Trent Lott and Tom Daschle) followed the rare procedure of asking all senators to be present at their desks and seated during the entire roll call vote. When the clerk called each senator's name, in alphabetical order, that senator would stand and state his or her vote. With few exceptions, all senators remained at their desks until the clerk had tallied the vote and the presiding officer announced the result. At 12:50 a.m., Friday, October 11, Vice President Cheney announced that the resolution had passed by a vote of 77 "ayes" to 23 "nays."[6]

The administration timed the vote on the Iraq resolution to bring maximum pressure on members of Congress up for reelection in early November. Some, from conservative states, did not want to vote "no" and risk giving their political opponents an issue to attack them on in the last weeks of the campaign.

To his regret, Max Cleland was one of those who voted for the resolution. It seemed to him and most observers as something he had to do if he wanted to remain in the Senate.

In his 2002 campaign, Max was challenged by Representative Saxby Chambliss (R-GA). While Max had been severely wounded in the Vietnam War, Chambliss had avoided military service. Despite Max's exemplary military service, in the campaign Chambliss questioned his commitment to homeland security and implied that Max did not adequately support the war on terror. To make his point he ran a thirty-second attack ad showing images of Max along with images of Osama bin Laden and Saddam Hussein. Senator McCain, in an interview with the *Washington Post*, said, "I've never seen anything like that ad. Putting pictures of Saddam Hussein and Osama bin Laden next to a man who left three limbs on the battlefield—it's worse than disgraceful; it's reprehensible."[7]

Despite his vote for the resolution, Max lost the election 46 percent to 53 percent. He later called that vote to authorize the invasion the worst vote he had cast.

It was easier for those of us who did not represent a southern state, and were not on the ballot that year, to vote "no."

Several of us in the Senate had spoken out against going to war in Iraq, but to my mind, Senator Byrd deserves special recognition for his efforts. Senator Byrd was eighty-six, but there was no one in either house of Congress who spoke more forcefully against the Bush administration's planned invasion of Iraq. I remember that more than a year later, I was visiting Senator Byrd in his office in the capitol on an unrelated issue. As I was leaving, he pointed to the framed Senate clerk's vote tally on the Iraq resolution, which he had hanging next to the door. He said, "Jeff, you're on that list. I keep it there to remind me who joined in opposing the Iraq War."

Lead-up to the Invasion

In the period after the Iraq resolution passed and before the invasion, the administration did its best to persuade the country that its aim was to find and eliminate weapons of mass destruction, and that, if that could be accomplished, a US-led invasion of Iraq was not inevitable. Now that we know the facts, it is clear that their real aim was to remove Saddam Hussein from power. Potential terrorist attacks and the threat from weapons of mass destruction were the arguments used by the administration, but as stated in the Downing Street Memo, "Bush wanted to remove Saddam, through military action, justified by the conjunction of terrorism and WMD." Regardless of what weapons Iraq did, or did not, possess, and regardless of what access Iraq permitted to inspectors to discover those weapons, President Bush's one non-negotiable demand was the removal of Saddam from power.

On March 7, Zbigniew Brzezinski (President Carter's national security advisor), Senator John Warner (R-VA), and I discussed these issues with Jim Lehrer on the PBS NewsHour. The discussion showed that all four of us, to some extent, accepted the administration's assurances that it might be possible to avoid an invasion. Seven months after the Downing Street Memo had been written, there we were, acting as though an invasion might be avoided. At one point in the discussion, Senator Warner stated, "Don't give up on the diplomatic process yet. They're working very hard on it."[8]

On March 13, I gave my last Senate speech arguing against an invasion. The main point I made was that, if our aim was to protect America and our allies from weapons of mass destruction, there were still alternatives to war that we should pursue. I stated, "A decision to wage war at this time, absent the support of our traditional allies, contradicts the foreign policy on which this Nation has been grounded for many decades."

On March 19, 2003, President Bush announced he had ordered US troops to invade:

> My fellow citizens, at this hour, American and coalition forces are in the early stages of military operations to disarm Iraq, to free its people and to defend the world from grave danger.[9]

After "Shock and Awe"

The US invasion of Iraq began with fighter jets attacking key Iraqi military installations. In an unfortunate show of hubris, the Pentagon had labeled the combat "Operation Shock and Awe." Within three weeks Saddam's army was defeated. Jubilant Iraqis knocked over Saddam's statue in Firdos Square.

After that, the bad news began.

First, widespread looting erupted in Baghdad. Rumsfeld dismissed its importance: "Freedom's untidy, and free people are free to make mistakes and commit crimes and do bad things. They're also free to live their lives and do wonderful things."[10]

To reestablish authority, the Pentagon flew in Ahmed Chalabi. Chalabi had been a founder of a group that called itself the Iraqi National Congress (INC). In fact, it was an umbrella organization for groups opposed to Saddam Hussein's regime. The INC had been a major proponent of the war and a major source of the false intelligence used to justify the war.

The Pentagon had hoped Chalabi could emerge as the new leader of Iraq, but it soon became clear that few in Iraq had ever heard of him and fewer still wanted him as their leader.

Next, Rumsfeld sent Paul Bremer III to Baghdad as head of the Coalition Provisional Authority. Bremer is credited with a large role in two disastrous decisions: first, the decision to remove all members of the Baath Party from positions of authority, and second, the decision to dismantle Saddam's army. The result was several hundred thousand men, on the streets, with guns, and without jobs.

On Sunday, May 11, 2003, the *Albuquerque Journal* quoted me saying that much of the intelligence Bush had used to justify the war had been "defective or manipulated," and that the intelligence had "been disproved."[11] President Bush and his wife, Laura, were in Santa Fe that weekend, and the press asked Ari Fleischer, the president's press secretary, to respond to my comments. He issued the following statement:

> It's only three weeks since major combat ended and already Senator Bingaman has begun to wobble. Iraq had 12 years to hide weapons of mass destruction, but it's taken Sen. Bingaman only three weeks to give up the search.
>
> What does the senator think Saddam Hussein used the mobile bio weapons lab for?[12]

In October 2004, the CIA concluded that Saddam did not possess stockpiles of illicit weapons at the time of the US invasion in March 2003 and had not begun any program to produce them.[13] I can only conclude from Fleischer's 2003 statement that by the time President Bush ordered US troops to invade Iraq, the president and his close advisors believed their own rhetoric.

Meanwhile, back in Iraq, the Sunni insurgency continued to gain strength, and it became clear that the Bush administration had no plan to defeat it.

My firsthand encounter with the mess we had gotten ourselves into occurred in March 2004, on a Senate Armed Services Committee trip to the region with Senators Carl Levin, Jay Rockefeller, Jack Reed, and Frank Lautenberg.

In Baghdad the security situation was terrible. The extensive security precautions provided for us by Blackwater (the private security firm hired by the Pentagon to protect visiting VIPs) particularly struck me. On a short excursion outside the green zone (which our military considered relatively safe), across a portion of the red zone (which they considered anything but safe), I noted—

- Each of us in the convoy wore an armor-plated vest
- The armor-plated SUVs we rode in had electronic equipment on

board to deactivate IEDs (improvised explosive devices), that had become a common hazard for troops
- Ahead of our convoy were two Humvees with turrets mounted with machine guns
- When our vehicles had to stop, Blackwater guards with automatic weapons would surround the vehicles to be sure no one could come near
- At all times we were in the red zone, a helicopter with snipers aboard followed us overhead

The whole scene was far different from Vice President Dick Cheney's March 2003 prediction: "My belief is we will in fact be greeted as liberators."[14]

Casualties and Consequences

The Department of Defense lists 4,424 US personnel as casualties of the war and 31,952 as wounded in action.

The estimates of Iraqi military and civilian casualties are much less certain, but also much higher. The organization Iraq Body Count estimates that the war has been responsible for 288,000 "total violent deaths including combatants."[15]

There is no doubt that the US invasion of Iraq ushered in, and contributed to, a protracted period of violence and political turmoil in Iraq and the Middle East. The consequences of our decision to invade are still being felt.

Conclusions and Lessons

- America is a nation of patriots, and most Americans are willing to support military action when told by the president it is required to confront a grave threat.
- The military-industrial complex, which President Eisenhower warned about, is alive and well. In most cases, it is ready to support the use of military power to achieve foreign policy objectives. This was certainly the case with the invasion of Iraq.

- In making the case for the use of military power, the president has two great advantages. First, he has the bully pulpit that insures maximum public attention to his statements and arguments. Second, he has a near monopoly on access to the intelligence needed to justify or oppose the use of force. Not only does he have access to intelligence that his opponents are denied, but also he can use that intelligence selectively to support his chosen course of action. In this case, as MI6 advised Prime Minister Blair, "the intelligence and facts were being fixed around the policy."
- Members of Congress are inclined to support the views of their constituents, so if a president can generate strong public support for a proposed military action, that support will generate support in Congress as well. This is particularly true when members are in the heat of reelection campaigns.
- No president should decide to commit US combat forces without a detailed and realistic plan for "what comes next." In the case of Iraq, no such plan existed.

PART III

How Congress
Can Do Better

Suggestions for Congress

CONGRESS MUST ACT to counter the destructive effects of the four tactics I described in chapter 1. Fortunately, there are ways each can be dealt with. Here are some suggestions:

Maintain a Functioning Congress and Government

Congress has a responsibility to fund the operations of government. The president shares that responsibility, and neither the president nor members of Congress should threaten to shut down the government. When there is disagreement on policy issues, the activities to fund, or the level of funding, the only acceptable course should be to maintain current funding levels until compromise is possible.

To achieve this, I favor replacing the governing norm that has now broken down with legislation to provide that when a funding bill expires, there is an automatic continuation of funding at then-existing levels, until Congress enacts a new funding bill. Several bills have been introduced that would accomplish this.[1] Any of these bills would be an improvement on the status quo. Unfortunately, as I write this, none has been brought before the Senate for a vote.

If Congress cannot enact legislation such as this, the second-best solution is to refuse to reward the party that chooses to shut down the government. The party wishing to see the government funded should refuse to negotiate on whatever issue is in dispute, until government funding is restored.

That is what Nancy Pelosi and Chuck Schumer did in the 2018 shutdown.

Eliminate Threats to Default on the Debt

When budget deficits require the secretary of the Treasury to borrow, he or she should have that authority. The debt ceiling, and Congress's frequent need to increase or suspend it, has created an opportunity for political posturing and extortion that Republican congressional leaders in particular have exploited.

The periodic need to raise the debt ceiling, and the repeated threats to default, are problems that can be fixed. A simple majority of the House and Senate has the power to repeal the law that establishes the debt ceiling. To do so, the Senate would need to change its rules and precedents to eliminate the right to filibuster. Given the demagoguery and public confusion about the debt ceiling, getting the votes to repeal the law probably is not doable. Here are five more realistic options to consider:

1. In the Senate, rules and precedents could be changed to provide that votes related to the debt limit may not be filibustered.
2. The debt ceiling could be raised by including a provision in a reconciliation bill. This was the course advocated by Senator McConnell in the 2021 debt ceiling crisis. It would give Republican senators the strongest argument that they had no part in bringing about the increase. Since all Republican senators can be expected to vote against any Democratic reconciliation bill, and since reconciliation bills cannot be filibustered, senators voting "no" could accurately claim they were powerless to prevent the increase.
3. Adopt something like the "McConnell Mechanism" used in the Budget Act of 2011. Under that procedure, when an increase in the debt ceiling is required, the president makes a formal request to Congress for additional borrowing authority. That request is approved automatically after fifteen calendar days, unless both houses of Congress pass, and the president signs, a resolution of disapproval. The president would have the right to veto any such resolution, and a two-thirds vote in both houses would be required to override that veto.[2]
4. Use a reconciliation bill to raise the ceiling to such a level that it is not an issue requiring votes by Congress for the next decade or more. This is the solution adopted in Denmark, the only other major economy with a statutory debt ceiling.
5. Some have proposed that the president use his authority under the Fourteenth Amendment ("the public debt of the United States,

authorized by law," shall "not be questioned") to direct the Treasury secretary to take whatever steps are necessary to honor the federal government's obligations. This approach has the disadvantage that it would face a legal challenge, and it is not clear what position the courts would take.[3]

If none of these options is successful, this president and future presidents should still refuse to negotiate with Congress for debt ceiling increases, just as President Obama refused to in 2013.

Faced with that refusal, I hope Congress would do as it did in 2013 and choose not to default. If Congress chooses otherwise, the only remedy is with the voters.

In the Senate, Eliminate the Filibuster and Grant the Majority Leader the Power to "Move the Previous Question"

Senate rules should be changed to eliminate the requirement for sixty votes to end debate on a bill, but doing so will not totally solve the problem of obstruction.

To prevent the type of repeated obstruction McConnell engaged in when Harry Reid was the majority leader, it is also necessary to give the majority leader the right to "move the previous question." As long as the only way to end debate is to "invoke cloture," even if only fifty-one votes is required, the minority has a powerful tool to delay and impede the proper functioning of the Senate. The only way to head off more obstruction in the Senate is to grant the majority leader, after a reasonable time for debate, the right to put a question to a final vote.

In the Senate, Adopt a Rule Requiring the Judiciary Committee and Senate to Act on a President's Nominee for the Supreme Court

A majority of the Senate can change Senate rules, but there is still value in having rules for how the Senate and its committees are expected to operate.

To return to a procedure where a president of either party can expect a hearing on his or her nominee to fill a Supreme Court vacancy, I support enacting a Senate rule requiring the Judiciary Committee and the Senate to consider and vote on a nominee for the Supreme Court, in cases where the nomination is delivered to the Senate prior to September 1 of the president's final year in office. After that date, the president could still send a nomination to the Senate, and the Senate could act on it, but there would be no rule requiring the Senate to do so.

IN ADDITION TO THE CHALLENGES faced by Congress, each senator and representative has his or her own set of challenges. The future of Congress depends on members personally confronting and overcoming the five impediments discussed in chapter 2: pressure to toe the party line, pressure to vote the way the polls dictate, pressure from ideological bias, pressure from special interests, and pressure from the media. Only by doing so will they be able to find common goals with members of the other party, deliberate, and then compromise on how to achieve those common goals.

Here are my suggestions to members of Congress to help them better serve the public interest.

Focus on Worthy Goals for the Country

One bit of tongue-in-cheek advice you hear as a newly elected member of Congress is, "Vote against everything that's going to pass, and for everything that's going to fail, then they can never blame you for what happens." That may be the safest course politically, but it is not what voters sent you to Congress for.

Either at the time you run, or soon after your election, decide what you want to accomplish for the good of the country. What are the big issues that deserve your concentrated attention? Here I have discussed eight significant challenges faced by the Congress and the country during the years I served in the Senate. The issues you choose may be the same or different, but it is important that you decide what you believe the nation's agenda should be.

It is not enough for a member of Congress just to respond to the agenda set by the president. I recall sitting at lunch one day with Senator Byrd and several others. One senator asked, "Senator Byrd, you are the longest-serving senator; how many presidents have you served under?" Byrd replied, "I have not served *under* any president, but I have served *with* eleven of them."

Deliberate

Don't just assume you know the answer.

Academics who study the workings of government are fond of referring to the Senate as "the world's greatest deliberative body." If true, this is a damning condemnation of the world's other legislative bodies.

"Deliberating" can mean at least two very different things. It can mean focusing on an issue, learning about an issue, and deciding which policy to adopt. Or it can mean trying to agree on how to package the various legislative solutions to somewhat related problems (i.e., trying to make a "deal" on the legislative package to bring up for consideration).

In my experience, Congress spends far too little time deciding on the right policy solutions, and too much time on the question of how to package various proposals.

The first part of deliberating (i.e., deciding on the right policy solutions) is not easy. The issues are many, there is never enough time to learn all you would like to know, and many of the most knowledgeable experts are paid by a special interest to champion a particular position.

If you, the newly elected member of Congress, have confidence that you know the solutions to the nation's many and complex problems, the task of "deliberating" is even more difficult. No one comes to Congress with sufficient knowledge and understanding to address intelligently the range of complex and constantly changing issues. We need people in Congress willing and able to learn on the job.

Most members of Congress do not define their job as "deliberating." Instead, they see their first responsibility as championing the positions their constituents elected them to champion. If a Republican candidate for Congress campaigns on a platform of repealing the Affordable Care Act, that candidate does not expect to arrive in Congress and "deliberate" on whether "repeal" is the right public policy. This is a natural result of the election process. During a campaign, voters want to know where a candidate stands. By election night candidates have taken strong positions on most issues, even if their knowledge on many is superficial.

Most decisions on issues in Congress do not result from deliberation. Members decide on what to do based on who proves most effective at gaining leverage to influence the outcome, and they gain leverage through various time-honored tactics. Some are a normal part of the process. An example is "logrolling," which is vote trading by legislative members to obtain passage of legislative proposals of interest to each member.

But the use of leverage can also be less benign. For example, to gain leverage on the administration, a senator can take advantage of the rules and traditions of the Senate to prevent, or at least delay, confirmation of an acceptable nominee for an administration position. It is not rare for a member to use this tactic to force administration support for a project important in his or her state.

The second aspect of "deliberating," trying to reach a "deal" on which proposals to package together for consideration on the House or Senate floor, presents its own set of problems.

For example, take Congress' efforts to reform the nation's immigration laws. The last major reform of our immigration laws occurred in 1996. During the twenty-five years since then, many efforts at reform have failed. There are several large, distinct objectives that motivate the effort to reform immigration laws: border security, modernization of our laws regarding legal immigration, and the status and ultimate disposition of those who have entered or remained in the country without legal authority. Subsumed under each of these large objectives are many more specific questions. Should we build a wall on our southern border with Mexico? Should immigration be based primarily on family kinship? What should be done with unaccompanied minors attempting to enter the country? Should Congress grant legal status to Dreamers? What should we do about adult undocumented residents who have lived in the United States without documentation for a decade or more? Which sectors of the economy should be included in any temporary worker program, and how large should such a program be? In future years, how much legal immigration should we permit?

Each question is part of the larger issue of "immigration reform." On some questions, such as whether to continue the legal status for Dreamers, a majority in Congress may be able to agree. But some in Congress will not consider that reform unless it is combined with their pet proposals for a long list of other immigration-related problems. And a majority of Congress opposes these other solutions. Instead of agreeing to move ahead and enact reforms supported by the majority, members of Congress continue to negotiate for more "leverage." The wrangling continues over what else they must include in order to get a "deal."

Insisting that legislation enjoying majority support be combined with legislation that lacks that support is a recipe for inaction. It results in legislative packages too large and too controversial to enact. The larger the number of controversial proposals included in a package, the more opportunity there is to defeat it.

Sometimes packaging together many issues and pieces of legislation helps create the critical mass of support needed for passage. That works well when none of the individual provisions is controversial; it does not work where the issues involved are highly contentious.

A partial solution is for congressional leaders to bring up smaller packages of legislation for consideration. Leaving this issue unaddressed, and continuing the trend toward larger and larger packages of legislation, is self-reinforcing. The larger the packages become, the more difficult it is to pass them. The more difficult it is to pass them, the greater the incentive for members to vote against any package that does not address the member's particular issue, or that contains something members consider objectionable.

Overcome the Five Impediments

PRESSURE TO TOE THE PARTY LINE

Each senator and representative is expected to support his or her party's position on most issues. That is an understandable consequence of party affiliation.

But on issues you consider most important to the nation, be willing to join with members from both parties to do the right thing.

In one of his final acts in the Senate, John McCain chose to break with his party and vote against repeal of the ACA. To my mind, that vote added substantially to his political legacy.

PRESSURE TO VOTE THE WAY THE POLLS DICTATE

"Pandering" is pleasing other people by doing or saying what they want you to do or say. On serious policy issues it is sometimes necessary to tell people what they don't want to hear or vote in ways they do not support.

One advantage of serving in Congress is you have better access than the public to accurate information about the issues. But that better access brings with it increased responsibility. On important issues, if you believe the facts are not as the public has been led to believe, your responsibility is to point that out. Speaking the truth when it contradicts conventional wisdom is not a way to gain popularity, but it is essential if a democracy is to remain healthy.

IDEOLOGY: THE BURDEN OF POLITICAL PHILOSOPHY

Ideology has a rightful place in politics, but it must be tempered by reality. Sometimes the need to achieve a result requires ideology to give way to practical considerations. When Congress was confronted with the threat of a collapsing financial system in 2008, adherence to ideology led some members to oppose government action. Fortunately, a majority in both the House and Senate were willing to put ideology aside and act.

PRESSURE FROM SPECIAL INTERESTS

The public interest can, and often does, conflict with the interests of particular companies or groups that lobby Congress. When such conflicts arise, each member must decide whether to support the special interest, or side with the public. That decision is not always easy. It can be particularly difficult when the special interest has a major presence in your state or district. During his time in the Senate, Scoop Jackson was often referred to as the senator from Boeing, but given the importance of Boeing to the people and economy of Washington State, he can be forgiven for not seeing a major conflict between the public interest and Boeing's interests. When LBJ was in the Senate, he was well known as a stalwart for Texas oil and gas interests, but in LBJ's defense, it is hard to overstate the importance of the oil and gas industry to the Texas economy during those years.

Supporting the position of a special interest that has a major economic presence in your state can sometimes be justified; at other times, it cannot.

But there are many instances where you will have to decide whether to support a special interest based not on their economic impact in your state, but on their support for you in the last campaign or in future campaigns. In such cases, the interest of the public should win out.

THE MEDIA

To serve the public interest each member needs to guard against becoming the "darling," and consequently the captive, of those segments of the media that promote the polarization of the electorate.

Many in the media have come to emphasize advocacy over reporting. They have become a major factor driving increased polarization. To accomplish their advocacy they seek out, and give a platform to, those politicians who share their views. The more outspoken and unyielding the politician is in support of those views, the more coverage they can count on.

All members need to decide the extent to which they want their efforts to reinforce the polarization.

Find Members from the Other Party Who Share your Goals and Use the Committee Process to Develop Legislation and Gain Momentum

Early in your efforts to develop and enact legislation, seek out members of the other party to work with you. Bipartisan support for a measure sends a strong signal to party leaders that the issue cannot be dismissed as an exercise in politics as usual.

As discussed in chapter 8, both Chris Dodd in the HELP Committee and Max Baucus in the Finance Committee made major efforts to gain the support of Republican members. The effort failed, and the ACA became law without Republican support in Congress. This was the exception that proved the rule. Almost always some level of bipartisan support has been essential for enacting major legislation.

Where bipartisan support for a set of goals is possible, determine what you can agree on to achieve the goals, and use the committee process to expand on and refine that agreement.

Even in the polarized environment Congress faces today, committees are usually the place where policy agreements have the best chance of developing and gaining momentum.

As discussed in chapter 6, with the 2005 and 2007 energy bills, Pete Domenici and I agreed to a set of provisions to present to the full Energy Committee. That began an extended process of accepting and rejecting amendments. Eventually the committee reported bills to the full Senate with broad bipartisan support. Those bills, after being combined with other energy-related bills from other committees, were further amended on the Senate floor, and then passed with a majority of votes from Democrats and Republicans.

Without an initial agreement on goals, those efforts would have failed. Also, without the extensive work done both in committees and on the Senate floor, we would not have gained the support needed for enactment.

Be Open to Compromise to Achieve Incremental Progress Toward Worthy Goals

Compromise is another essential element in a properly functioning Congress. But while most people concede that compromise is important to the functioning of Congress, there are powerful reasons it is difficult to achieve. First, members themselves often disagree on the issues. Second, their constituents have strongly held views. If you get elected by constituents who embrace extreme views, it is difficult for you to compromise. The problem is compounded when you are elected by pandering to those extreme views.

Interest groups also often try to discourage compromise. Each group does its best, during a campaign, to extract from you a commitment on the issues it considers most important. In recent years, many groups have insisted the candidate even sign a written "pledge" on their most important issue or issues. This can be the NRA demanding candidates pledge to protect the right to bear arms, the Americans for Tax Reform requiring a signed pledge not to raise taxes, or any other interest group making its favorite demands. The effect of all such "pledges" is to limit your flexibility to support a compromise.

Media outlets targeted at particular segments of the public also make it more difficult for members to compromise.

Congress cannot resolve all issues by negotiated compromise. But on most issues, in a properly functioning democracy, elected officials need to be open to the possibility of compromise. When we think of politicians with political courage, we usually think of those who refuse to compromise. But in this period of extreme polarization in our nation's politics, it often takes more courage to compromise than it does to stand your ground.

Jeff Bingaman's Farewell Speech to the Senate

IN 1981, in his first inaugural address, President Reagan said, "Government is not the solution to our problem; government is the problem."

I came to the Senate two years later in 1983 with the firm belief that in most cases his statement was wrong.

I believed then and I believe now that the federal government can be a constructive force for good; in protecting and maintaining the civil liberties of all Americans, in maintaining and strengthening our economy, in protecting our environment and in helping Americans live productive and fulfilling lives.

As I look back over the last 30 years, many of the arguments that have consumed our time here in the Senate, whether on questions of spending or taxes or regulation or fiscal policy, have divided between those who saw government as the problem and those who believed that it could and should be a constructive force for helping the American people deal with problems. I consider myself, furthermore, in the second camp—firmly in the second camp.

In each of the major areas of national concern I'd like to be able to report progress for the country, since I arrived in the Senate. Unfortunately, the record of progress is not so clear. In many areas we have made progress, but there are also instances where we have lost more ground than we have gained. And as issues continue to be reconsidered, I'm reminded of the well-known statement that "success is never permanent in Washington."

As regards our Nation's security from foreign aggression, the end of the cold war and the collapse of the Soviet Union were clearly the most positive developments that we have seen in the last 30 years.

If the end of the cold war was the most positive national security development that I've witnessed since coming to the Senate, the invasion of Iraq to bring about regime change in that country was the biggest national security blunder. That blunder cost our nation dearly in servicemen and women killed and injured and in resources that should have been used to strengthen our economy here at home. Last month I was stopped by a woman in northern New Mexico who thanked me for my service in the Senate and particularly for my vote against granting President Bush authority to take our country into that war.

The nation's fiscal policy is very much the focus of the Senate's attention in these final weeks of the 112th congress. And on this issue, again, we have made one step forward during the time I've been in the Senate but, unfortunately, we've taken two steps back.

I arrived in the Senate in January of 1983—a period of large deficits compared to anything the country had experienced for several decades. And those large deficits grew and persisted through the Reagan presidency.

In 1990, the democratically controlled congress and President George H. W. Bush made a significant step towards reining in the deficits with the Reconciliation Act of 1990. That law created the statutory PAYGO requirement. It also increased marginal rates for the wealthiest Americans, and I was proud to support the measure.

In 1993, another major step was taken when, at the urging of President Clinton, Congress enacted the Omnibus Budget Reconciliation Act of that year, 1993. Again, that measure both raised taxes and constrained spending. It was denounced by many here in the Senate as sure to throw the economy into recession.

In fact, just the opposite occurred, and the economy prospered. As a result of these policy changes and the strong economy of the 1990s, we enjoyed a period of balanced budgets and even surpluses in 1998, 1999, 2000 and 2001.

Unfortunately, those surpluses were not to continue. President George W. Bush urged Congress to cut taxes and Congress was all too willing to oblige. And though I didn't support the 2001 or 2003 tax cuts, they were passed.

At about the same time that we were cutting taxes more than we could afford, we were also going to war in Afghanistan and in Iraq, and adding a new drug benefit to Medicare. No provision was made to raise revenue or cut spending elsewhere to pay for any of these mammoth undertakings. And of course the cost of health care, both the cost to government and to families and businesses to purchase private insurance, continued to grow at too rapid a pace.

The result was a return to large deficits and, of course, those large deficits grew substantially larger because of the recession that began in December of 2007.

Today we're trying to strengthen our economy while at the same time trying to reduce projected deficits. That long-term deficit reduction will once again require higher taxes and also new constraints on spending, and I hope that even in these final days of this 112th Congress we can reach agreement to proceed.

In the long-standing fight to provide Americans with access to affordable health care, we have seen significant progress.

In 1997 we enacted the Children's Health Insurance Program, which resulted in nearly 8 million American children obtaining access to health care.

And of course, in 2010, we adopted the Patient Protection and Affordable Care Act. This unfairly maligned legislation has the promise of moving us much closer to the goal of universal health care, and I am proud to have worked with my colleagues in the Senate in writing that legislation and seeing it enacted.

Now that the election is behind us, I hope the efforts to repeal that legislation is at an end. I hope the two parties can find ways to improve the legislation with a particular focus on better controlling the growth in the cost of health care.

In addressing the various energy challenges facing the country, again, there's progress to report.

In 2005 and 2007, Congress enacted major energy bills. Those bills moved us toward a better and more comprehensive national energy policy. Those bills promoted an adequate and more diverse supply of energy. They increased the efficiency and effectiveness of how we use energy in our economy. They promoted strong market reforms and consumer protections for electricity, and they struck a balance between meeting our energy goals and lessening environmental impacts of energy, including overall greenhouse gas emissions. As a result of that balanced approach, we have arrested what had been an increasing dependence on foreign oil, coupled with technological advances that have opened new sources of supply. We're headed to greater levels of energy independence than we had thought possible, even as recently as seven years ago.

The bipartisan consensus that allowed us to enact those bills has, unfortunately, eluded us in the current Congress. I hope that in future Congresses there will reemerge a recognition that climate change is a reality, that our policies to meet our energy needs must also deal responsibly with environmental issues, including the damage caused by greenhouse gas emissions.

As regards our nation's policy on education, the good news is that we seem to have moved past the period where the Republican nominee for President announces a commitment to eliminating the federal Department of Education.

President Clinton deserves great credit for making the support particularly of higher education a priority of his presidency. President George W. Bush deserves credit for making a serious effort to preserve and improve elementary-secondary education.

Although that effort has not succeeded, as many of us who supported it had hoped, I remain persuaded that the federal government needs to persist in trying to play a constructive role in improving education in this country.

The states and local school districts deserve credit for developing and adopting the common core standards. I hope that future congresses will strongly support the steps and the funding needed to upgrade student performance by implementing those standards. President Obama and his administration have demonstrated their strong commitment to this goal.

In addition to these areas of concern that I've mentioned, we have seen some progress in maintaining and advancing the science and engineering in this country. We successfully found ways to better integrate the strengths of our defense laboratories through technology transfer and partnering. We've also seen some important increases in funding for research, particularly in support of the life sciences. And that growth has stagnated in recent years. It needs to continue and be replenished. But as we continue that support, we must also recognize the need to do more to support research and development in the physical sciences and in engineering.

One significant advance I was proud to support was the establishment of ARPA-E, the Advanced Research Projects Agency-Energy in the Department of Energy. That effort to identify and fund breakthrough science and engineering initiatives to meet our energy challenges holds great promise for our nation and for the entire world.

We've also seen progress in providing increased protection for public lands. One particular bill in that area was the Omnibus Public Lands Bill that was passed in 2009. It added wilderness protection to over 2 million acres, it designates 1,100 miles of wild and scenic rivers, added more than 2,800 miles to the national trail system, and I was proud to be part of the effort to enact that legislation.

Finally, I'll make a few comments on the way that we in the Congress conduct our own business. Any fair assessment has to conclude that in this area we have lost ground in the last two decades. Public opinion of the performance of Congress is at an all-time low, and it is not hard to see why. I'll mention three obvious ways in which the functioning of Congress has worsened.

First is the willingness of some in Congress to shut down the government. In 1995 we saw the leadership of the House of Representatives demonstrate that they considered refusing to fund the government as an acceptable bargaining ploy in their efforts to prevail in disputes with President Clinton and Democrats on spending issues.

Since 1995, that threat to withhold appropriations has been made several more times, and as we saw then, shutting down the government is harmful, wasteful to Americans. I hope this irresponsible threat will soon be viewed as unacceptable.

A second way the malfunctioning of Congress became clear is when in August of 2011—just less than 18 months ago—the Republican leadership in Congress determined that another tool at their disposal was the ability to refuse to increase the debt ceiling. By doing so, they could deny the Secretary of the Treasury the authority to borrow money to meet the obligations that the government had already undertaken. To my knowledge, this was the first time the Congressional leadership of one of our major parties had stated their willingness to see our nation default on its debt.

This threat to force a default on the obligations of the federal government resulted in the sequester of government spending, which is scheduled to begin January 1. It also resulted in a downgrading of U.S. debt by one of the leading credit rating agencies.

We now hear renewed threats to use the so-called "leverage" as a way to demand cuts in Medicare and in social security. Once again, I believe this is an irresponsible action. I hope Congress will get beyond it.

But of course a third way in which the functioning of the Senate—not the full Congress, but the Senate—has worsened is the abuse of Senate rules allowing unlimited debate or filibusters. As the Senate currently operates, the threat of filibuster is used routinely to obstruct the Senate from doing its business, even when the issue before the Senate is relatively uncontroversial. Many times following a delay caused by obstruction, an overwhelming number of Senators will vote for the legislation or the nomination, which the Senate has been delayed in considering.

I strongly encourage my colleagues to make the necessary changes in Senate rules to limit the ability of one or a few Senators to obstruct the Senate from doing its regular business. My colleague, Senator Udall, is here on the floor with me. He's been a leader in this effort to get these rules changed, and I commend him for that.

So the record of our progress both as a country and as a congress over the last 30 years has been mixed. There's progress to report. I've mentioned some of that. There are also many missteps and failures that we need to acknowledge.

My conclusion remains that many of our challenges as a nation can only be met with the help of a strong and effective national government. There are times when the actions of the government are more a problem than a solution, but there are many more occasions where enlightened action by the government is important and even essential.

I consider it an honor and a privilege to have represented the people of New Mexico in the Senate for the last 30 years. I thank the people of my state for their confidence in electing me and supporting me during the time I have served here. I thank the very capable and committed men and women who have worked on my staff both in Washington and in New Mexico during these 30 years.

And I thank all my colleagues here in the Senate for their friendship and help to me during this period.

Of course I thank my wife, Anne and our son John and his wife Marlene for their support that allowed me to serve in the Senate.

To all my friends and colleagues who will be here in the next Congress and in future Congresses, I hope you can find the common ground necessary for our country to effectively move forward and meet its challenges. The endeavor is a worthy one, and I wish you every success.

Congressional Record, 112th Cong., 2nd sess. (2012), S8022-S8024, https://www.congress.gov/congressional-record/2012/12/13/senate-section/article/s8022-1?s=2&r=.

Notes

Chapter One

1. Steven Levitsky and Daniel Ziblatt, *How Democracies Die: What History Reveals about Our Future* (New York: The Crown Publishing Group, 2018).

2. *Congressional Record*, 104th Cong., 1st sess. (1995), S18937-S18939.

3. Trump Twitter Archive, July 29, 2018, https://www.thetrumparchive.com/?dates=%5B%222018-07-27%22%2C%222018-07-31%22%5D.

4. Trump Twitter Archive, July 31, 2018, https://www.thetrumparchive.com/?dates=%5B%222018-07-27%22%2C%222018-08-01%22%5D&results=1.

5. Sheryl Gay Stolberg, "G.O.P. Faces Another Midterm Threat as Trump Plays the Shutdown Card," *New York Times*, July 29, 2018, https://www.nytimes.com/2018/07/29/us/politics/trump-shutdown-republicans-midterms.html.

6. Peter Kasperowicz, "Trump: I Am Proud to Shut Down the Government for Border Security," *Washington Examiner*, December 11, 2018, https://video.search.yahoo.com/search/video?fr=mcafee&ei=UTF-8&p=proud+to+shut+down+the+government+for+border+security&type=E211US1249G91369#id=3&vid=a07a6dce23815fef4efb3a977e8c6220&action=view.

7. "Newt Gingrich: Lessons Learned from Past Government Shutdowns," *NPR*, January 14, 2019, https://www.npr.org/2019/01/14/685062279/newt-gingrich-lessons-learned-from-past-government-shutdowns.

8. "Alexander Says Shutting Down the Government Should Never Be a Bargaining Chip," *The Chattanoogan*, January 20, 2018, https://www.chattanoogan.com/2018/1/20/361946/Alexander-Says-Shutting-Down-The.aspx.

9. David A. Fahrenthold, Lori Montgomery, and Paul Kane, "In Debt Deal, the Triumph of the Old Washington," *Washington Post*, August 3, 2011.

10. "Full Transcript: President Obama's Sept. 16 Speech on the Economy and the Navy Yard Shooting," *Washington Post*, September 16, 2013, https://www.washingtonpost.com/politics/transcript-president-obamas-sept-16-speech-on-the-economy/2013/09/16/c63b2c30-1ee4-11e3-b7d1-7153ad47b549_story.html.

11. Tony Romm and Mike DeBonis, "House Adopts Bill Opening Door for Lawmakers to Raise Debt Ceiling, after Democrats, Republicans, Strike Deal," *Washington Post*, December 7, 2021, https://www.washingtonpost.com/us-policy/2021/12/07/democrats-republicans-debt-ceiling-deal/.

12. Adam Jentleson, *Kill Switch: The Rise of the Modern Senate* (W.W. Norton and Co., 2021), 208.

13. Jason Silverstein, "Here's What Mitch McConnell Said about Not Filing [*sic*] a Supreme Court Vacancy in an Election Year," *CBS News*, September 19, 2020, https://www.cbsnews.com/news/mitch-mcconnell-supreme-court-vacancy-election-year-senate/.

Chapter Two

1. S. 1766–110th Congress: "Low Carbon Economy Act of 2007," www.Gov Track.us.2007, October 15, 2021, https://www.govtrack.us/congress/bills/110/s1766.

2. *Congressional Record*, 106th Cong., 2nd sess. (2000), S1872.

3. "Resolution Regarding the Republican Party Platform," gop.com, August 24, 2020, https://prod-static.gop.com/media/Resolution_Platform_2020.pdf.

4. Abraham Lincoln, Fragments on Government, *Abraham Lincoln Speeches and Writings 1832–1858* (New York: The Library of America, 1980), 301.

5. Ronald Reagan Presidential Library & Museum, "Inaugural Address 1981," January 20, 1981, https://www.reaganlibrary.gov/archives/speech/inaugural-address-1981.

6. William J. Clinton, "Address before a Joint Session of the Congress on the State of the Union," January 23, 1996, The American Presidency Project, https://www.presidency.ucsb.edu/documents/address-before-joint-session-the-congress-the-state-the-union-10.

7. Amy Fried and Douglas B. Harris, *At War with Government: How Conservatives Weaponized Distrust from Goldwater to Trump* (New York: Columbia University Press, 2021).

8. Mara Liasson, "Conservative Advocate," *Morning Edition*, NPR, May 25, 2001, https://www.npr.org/templates/story/story.php?storyId=1123439.

9. Isaiah Berlin, *The Proper Study of Mankind: An Anthology of Essays* (New York: Farrar, Straus and Giroux. 1997), 240.

10. "Senator Rand Paul Rips Collective at Energy and Natural Resources Committee Hearing," YouTube, April 12, 2011, https://video.search.yahoo.com/search/video?fr=mcafee&ei=UTF-8&p=senator+Paul+rails+against+the+collective&type=E211US1249G0#id=2&vid=8f59173e3323fb3b35558b67dbaoa7e9&action=click.

11. "Senator Rand Paul Rips Collective at Energy and Natural Resources Committee Hearing," YouTube, April 12, 2011, https://video.search.yahoo.com/search/video?fr=mcafee&ei=UTF-8&p=senator+Paul+rails+against+the+collective&type=E211US1249G0#id=31&vid=8f59173e3323fb3b35558b67dbaoa7e9&action=click.

Chapter Three

1. "The Financial Crisis Inquiry Report, Final Report of the National Commission on the Causes of the Financial and Economic Crisis in the United States," Government Printing Office, January 2011, https://www.govinfo.gov/content/pkg/GPO-FCIC/pdf/GPO-FCIC.pdf.

2. Yoni Blumberg, "How a Late Night Phone Call from Warren Buffett in 2008 May Have Helped Save the US Economy," CNBC.com, December 11, 2018, updated December 12, 2018, https://www.cnbc.com/2018/12/11/how-warren-buffett-helped-save-the-economy-during-the-financial-crisis.html.

3. Ben S. Bernanke, *The Courage to Act: A Memoir of a Crisis and Its Aftermath* (New York: W.W. Norton and Company, 2015), 334.

4. Ron Paul, "The Bailout Surge," The Tenth Amendment Center, November 28, 2008, http://www.tenthamendmentcenter.com/2008/11/28/the-bailout-surge/.

5. Mitt Romney, "Let Detroit Go Bankrupt," *New York Times*, November 18, 2008, https://www.nytimes.com/2008/11/19/opinion/19romney.html.

6. Steven Rattner was chief Washington economic correspondent for the *New York Times* before his investment banking career with Lehman Brothers, Morgan Stanley and Lazard. He later left Lazard with thirty partners to found the Quadrangle Group, which grew to manage more than $6 billion in private equity, distressed securities, and hedge funds.

7. *Congressional Record*, 111th Cong., 1st sess. (2009), S2294.

8. The Republicans voting for the bill were Olympia Snowe and Susan Collins from Maine, and Arlen Specter from Pennsylvania.

Chapter Four

1. *Congressional Record*, 103rd Cong., 1st sess. (1993), S7645.

2. *Congressional Record*, 103rd Cong., 1st sess. (1993), S7852.

3. Testimony of Chairman Alan Greenspan, before the Committee on the Budget, US Senate, The Federal Reserve Board, January 25, 2001, https://www.federalreserve.gov/boarddocs/testimony/2001/20010125/default.htm.

4. Americans for Tax Reform (website), Federal Taxpayer Protection Pledge, accessed March 4, 2022, https://www.atr.org/wp-content/uploads/2014/02/2020PledgeFederal.pdf.

5. This Day in Quotes, "Nothing Is Certain except Death and Taxes," November 13, 2010, http://www.thisdayinquotes.com/2010/11/nothing-is-certain-except-death-and.html?m=1/.

6. Paul Krugman, "Learn to Stop Worrying and Love Debt," *New York Times*, December 3, 2020, https://www.nytimes.com/2020/12/03/opinion/biden-republicans-debt.html.

Chapter Five

1. The National Academies of Sciences, Engineering, Medicine, "Rising above the Gathering Storm: Energizing and Employing America for a Brighter Economic Future," The National Academies Press, 2007.

2. American Association for the Advancement of Science, "Historical Trends in Federal R&D," October 14, 2021, aaas.org/programs/r-d-budget-and-policy/historical-trends-federal-rd.

3. Uri Dadush, *Industrial Policy: A Guide for the Perplexed*, OCP Policy Center, January 2016, 1.

4. Francis Fukuyama, *The End of History and the Last Man* (New York: Free Press, 1992), 125.

5. "Trump: You Don't Have a Country without Steel," CNN, accessed March 4, 2022, https://edition.cnn.com/videos/politics/2018/03/01/trump-aluminum-steel-tariffs-sot.cnn.

6. Christian Gomez, "Trump Reviving Deep State Ex-Im Bank?," *The New American*, June 2018, https://thenewamerican.com/trump-reviving-deep-state-exim-bank/.

Chapter Six

1. Senate Committee on Energy and Natural Resources, *Greenhouse Effect and Global Climate Change*, 100th Cong., 1st sess., June 23, 1988, 39.

2. Senate Committee on Energy and Natural Resources, *Greenhouse Effect and Global Climate Change*, 100th Cong., 1st sess., June 23, 1988, 40.

3. "The President's News Conference in Rio de Janeiro," The American Presidency Project, accessed March 4, 2022, https://www.presidency.ucsb.edu/documents/the-presidents-news-conference-rio-de-janeiro.

4. A. C. Thompson, "Timeline: The Science and Politics of Global Warming," PBS, Frontline, April 24, 2007, http://www.pbs.org/wgbh/pages/frontline/hotpolitics/etc/cron.html.

5. *Congressional Record*, 108th Cong., 1st sess. (2003), S15155.

6. *Congressional Record*, 108th Cong., 1st sess. (2003), S15328.

7. Office of Nuclear Energy, "Blue Ribbon Commission on America's Nuclear Future Report to the Secretary of Energy," January 26, 2012, energy.gov/ne/downloads/blue-ribbon-commission-americas-nuclear-future-report-secretary-energy.

Chapter Seven

1. DARPA had a stellar record of accomplishment. It had provided the funding and direction to develop the internet, initially ARPANET. It also deserves credit

for developing Transit, a predecessor to the Global Positioning System (GPS), and research into the artificial intelligence fields of speech recognition and signal processing.

2. Department of Energy Loan Programs Office (website), About Us Home, accessed March 4, 2022, https://www.energy.gov/lpo/about-us-home.

3. Department of Energy Loan Programs Office (website), Portfolio, accessed March 4, 2022, https://www.energy.gov/lpo/portfolio.

4. The White House, "Remarks of President Barack Obama—Address to Joint Session of Congress," February 24, 2009, https://obamawhitehouse.archives.gov /the-press-office/remarks-president-barack-obama-address-joint-session-congress.

5. Republicans voting for the bill were Murkowski (R-AK), Brownback (R-KS), Sessions (R-AL), and Corker (R-TN). Democrats voting against the bill were Landrieu (D-LA) and Menendez (D-NJ).

6. Zoya Teirstein, "Meet the CEPP, the Biggest Federal Climate Policy You've Never Heard Of," grist.org, September 29, 2021, https://grist.org/politics/meet-the -cepp-the-biggest-federal-climate-policy-youve-never-heard-of/.

7. Chris Mooney and Brady Dennis, "On Climate Change, Scott Pruitt Causes an Uproar—and Contradicts the EPA's Own Website," *Washington Post*, March 9, 2017, https://www.washingtonpost.com/news/energy-environment/wp/2017/03/09 /on-climate-change-scott-pruitt-contradicts-the-epas-own-website/.

Chapter Eight

1. Joseph Connor, "Howls of 'Socialism' Killed Truman Health Insurance," *HistoryNet*, October 2019, https://www.historynet.com/howls-of-socialism-killed -truman-health-insurance.htm.

2. C. Stephen Redhead et al., "ACA: A Brief Overview of the Law, Implementation, and Legal Challenges," *CRS Report for Congress R41664*, Congressional Research Service, Library of Congress, Washington, DC (July 3, 2012), 1, https:// fas.org/sgp/crs/misc/R41664.pdf.

3. *Nat'l Fed'n of Indep. Bus. v. Sebelius* 567 U.S. 519, 607-608 (2012) (Ginsburg, J., dissenting).

4. Glenn Kessler, "Sarah Palin, 'Death Panels' and 'Obamacare,'" *Washington Post*, June 17, 2012, https://www.washingtonpost.com/blogs/fact-checker/post /sarah-palin-death-panels-and-obamacare/2012/06/27/gJQAysUP7V_blog.html.

5. See Angie Drobnic Holan, "PolitiFact's Lie of the Year: 'Death Panels,'" PolitiFact, December 18, 2009, http://www.politifact.com/truth-o-meter/article /2009/dec/18/politifact-lie-year-death-panels/.

6. Carl Hulse, "'Repeal and Replace': Words Still Hanging Over G.O.P.'s Health Care Strategy," *New York Times*, January 15, 2017, https://www.nytimes

.com/2017/01/15/us/politics/affordable-care-act-republicans-health-care.html
?searchResultPosition=1.

7. *Nat'l Fed'n of Indep. Bus. v. Sebelius*, 567 U.S. 519, 624 (2012) (Ginsburg, J., dissenting).

8. *Nat'l Fed'n of Indep. Bus. v. Sebelius*, 567 U.S. 519, 625-626 (2012) (Ginsburg, J., dissenting) .

9. Christiano Lima, "After Health Care Loss, Trump Tweets 'Let ObamaCare Implode,'" *Politico*, July 28, 2017, https://www.politico.com/story/2017/07/28/trump-tweets-let-obamacare-implode-241068.

10. National Academies of Science, Engineering, and Medicine, "Making Medicines Affordable: A National Imperative," November 30, 2017, https://www.nap.edu/read/24946/chapter/1.

Chapter Nine

1. The National Commission on Excellence in Education, "A Nation at Risk: The Imperative for Educational Reform," April 1983, https://edreform.com/wp-content/uploads/2013/02/A_Nation_At_Risk_1983.pdf.

2. Derek W. Black, "Abandoning the Federal Role in Education; the Every Student Succeeds Act," *Calif. Law Review*, vol. 105 (2017): 1309.

Chapter Ten

1. Title VI of the Secure Rural Schools and Community Self Determination Act of 2000, Public Law 106–393, 106th Congress.

2. "Collaborative Forest Landscape Restoration Program 10-Year Report to Congress," Forest Service, https://www.fs.fed.us/restoration/documents/cflrp/REF_Report-CollaborativeForestLandscapeRestoration-508.pdf.

Chapter Eleven

1. "Joint Resolution to Authorize the Use of United States Armed Forces against Iraq," georgewbush-whitehouse.archives.gov, October 2, 2002, https://georgewbush-whitehouse.archives.gov/news/releases/2002/10/20021002-2.html.

2. "Donald Rumsfeld Unknown Unknowns," youtube.com, accessed March 5, 2022, https://video.search.yahoo.com/search/video?fr=mcafee&p=Rumsfeld+speech+on+%22known+unknowns%22#id=1&vid=3da0ef8a1bc16e027c249276d8f742e5&action=click.

3. "President Delivers State of the Union Address," georgewbush-whitehouse.archives.gov, January 29, 2002, https://georgewbush-whitehouse.archives.gov/news/releases/2002/01/20020129-11.html.

4. *The Sunday Times,* "The Secret Downing Street Memo," May 1, 2005, https://web.archive.org/web/20110723222004/http://www.timesonline.co.uk/tol/news/uk/article387374.ece.

5. "President Bush Outlines Iraqi Threat," georgewbush-whitehouse.archives.gov, October 7, 2002, https://georgewbush-whitehouse.archives.gov/news/releases/2002/10/20021007-8.html.

6. Authorization for Use of Military Force against Iraq Resolution of 2002, Public Law 107–243.

7. Peter Carlson, "Political Veteran," *Washington Post,* July 3, 2003, https://www.washingtonpost.com/archive/lifestyle/2003/07/03/political-veteran/0c86b425-57eb-4c5e-ad7f-79680f8aa440/?itid=lk_inline_manual_37.

8. The NewsHour with Jim Lehrer, March 7, 2003, NewsHour Productions, American Archive of Public Broadcasting (WGBH and the Library of Congress), Boston, MA, and Washington, DC, https://americanarchive.org/catalog/cpb-aacip_507-mp4vh5d72x.

9. "George W. Bush Sends Troops to Iraq," history.com, March 19, 2003, https://www.history.com/speeches/george-w-bush-sends-troops-to-iraq.

10. Sean Loughlin, "Rumsfeld on Looting in Iraq: 'Stuff Happens,'" cnn.com, April 12, 2003, https://www.cnn.com/2003/US/04/11/sprj.irq.pentagon/.

11. Michael Coleman, "Evidence on Iraq Flawed," *Albuquerque Journal,* May 11, 2003.

12. Gary E. Salazar, "Bush Back on Tax-Cut Stump," *Albuquerque Journal,* May 12, 2003.

13. "The Comprehensive Report of the Special Advisor to the Director of Central Intelligence on Iraq's Weapons of Mass Destruction (Duelfer Report)," United States Government Publishing Office, last updated April 25, 2005, https://www.govinfo.gov/app/details/GPO-DUELFERREPORT/context.

14. "Transcript for Sept. 14," NBC News, September 14, 2003, https://www.nbcnews.com/id/wbna3080244.

15. Iraq Body Count (website), accessed March 5, 2022, iraqbodycount.org.

Chapter Twelve

1. See, for example, End Government Shutdown Act, S. 104 (116th) and S. 2593 (116th); Stop STUPIDITY Act, S. 198 (116th); and Prevent Government Shutdowns Act of 2021, S. 2727 (117th).

2. Act of August 2, 2011, Pub. L. No. 112–25, §301.

3. Mike Lofgren, "Ending the Debt-Ceiling Charade," *New York Times,* October 8, 2021.

Index

Page numbers in *italic text* indicate illustrations.

artificial intelligence, research and
development of, 69
assistance, government, 47-49, 66
*Assuring Affordable Health Care for All
Americans* (Heritage Foundation), 113
ATVM. *See* Advanced Technology
Vehicles Manufacturing Loan Program
At War with Government (Fried and
Harris), 32-33
Augustine, Norm, 96
auto industry, US, 47-49, 92
AYP. *See* Adequate Yearly Progress

Baath Party, Iraq, 179-80
Babbitt, Bruce, 153, 158, 163
Baca, Luis Maria Cabeza de, 161
bailout, government, auto industry and,
47-49
Balanced Budget Act (1997), 59, 115
ballot measures, ACA and, 137
bankruptcy, Lehman Brothers and, 44
Barbour, Haley, 125-26
Barton, Joe, 88
battery technology, research and
development for, 92
Baucus, Max, 87, 124, 194
BEA. *See* Budget Enforcement Act
Bell, Terrell, 142
Bennett, Bob, TARP and, 47
Bernanke, Ben, 44-45, 46
Bess-Forward Global Center, 128
bias: industrial policy, 66-67, 74; media
and, 39-40
Biden, Joe, 62, 110, 123
Big Pharma. *See* pharmaceutical industry
bill, funding, 9, 12, 185
Bingaman, Anne (wife), 27-28, 153
Bingaman, Jeff (senator). *See specific
topics*
Bingaman, John (son), 28
Bingaman, John (uncle), 27
bin Laden, Osama, 177

bipartisan effort, 63, 100-102, 113-14, 132,
158, 194-95; Appliance and Equipment
Standards Program as, 35-36; climate
change and, 27, 94, 200; EISA as,
89-90, 94; EPACT as, 86-88, 94;
Gang of Six as, 124-25, 130-31
Blackwater, 180-81
Blair, Tony, 175
BLM. *See* Bureau of Land Management
Blue Ribbon Commission Report (2012),
89
Bodman, Sam, 97
Boehner, John, 4, 60-61
Boeing, as special interest, 193
Boll Weevils, vii
bonds, US government, credit rating of, 4
border wall, between US and Mexico, 6,
11-13, 33
Boxer, Barbara, 102
BP oil spill (2010), 154
Bremer, Paul III, 179-80
Brooks, David, 165-66
Brown, Scott, 130
Brownback, Sam, 46
Brzezinski, Zbigniew, 178
Buddhism, Pali Canon, 25
budget, federal, 29, 55, 57-60
Budget Act (1974), 19, 94
Budget Act (2011), 186
Budget Control Act (2011), 3, 4, 17, 61-62
Budget Enforcement Act (BEA) (1990),
56-57, 198
Buffett, Warren, 28, 45
Bureau of Land Management (BLM),
155, 158
Bush, George H. W., xiii, 57, 80-81, 198;
education and, 143-45; Iraq and, 174
Bush, George W., 9, 29, 70, 82, 146, 200;
Democrat Congress and, 89; health
care and, 115; Iraq and, 30, 171-72,
174-76, 179, 182, 198; national debt and,
63; public lands and, 159-60; subprime

mortgage crisis and, 45–46; TARP and,
    50; tax cuts and, 59–60
Byrd, Robert C., 178, 189

CAFE. *See* Corporate Average Fuel
    Economy
California, CAFE standards in, 92
Campaign Committee, Republican
    Senate, 173
cap-and-trade proposals, 27, 98–104
Capitol, invasion of (2021), media defense
    in, 39
carbon tax, 81–82, 105
Carter, Jimmy, viii, 78–79
casualties, in Iraq war, 181
Caucus Room, Russell Building, 123
CBO. *See* Congressional Budget Office
CCSSO. *See* Council of Chief State
    School Officers
CEDA. *See* Clean Energy Development
    Administration
CES. *See* clean energy standard
CFLRP. *See* Collaborative Forest
    Landscape Restoration Program
CFRP. *See* Collaborative Forest
    Restoration Program
Chafee, John, 113, 114
Chalabi, Ahmed, 179
Chamber of Commerce, US, 113, 114, 155
Chambliss, Saxby, 177
Cheney, Dick, 30, 82–85, 181
Children's Defense Fund, 146
Children's Health Insurance Program
    (1997), 199
China, 72, 106
Chu, Steven, 96, 97
Citizens United case, 38
civil rights, Republican Party and, 28
Civil Rights Act (1964), vii
Clean Air and Clean Water Acts, vii–viii
Clean Energy Development
    Administration (CEDA), 101

Clean Energy Standard Act (2012), 104
clean energy standard (CES), cap-and-
    trade compared to, 104
Clean Power Plan, EPA, 81, 106, 107
Cleland, Max, 173–74, 177
Climate Action Partnership, US
    (USCAP), 99
climate change, 27, 77, 94, 95, 160,
    200; cap-and-trade and, 98–104;
    conservative ideology and, 33, 99,
    105–6; Energy Task Force and, 82–83;
    GHG and, 79–80, 109; Paris Climate
    Accords and, 106–7, 109–10; wildfires
    and, 166–67
Climate Change Conference, UN (2009),
    106
Climate Stewardship Act (2003), 98–99
Clinton, Bill, viii, 7, 32, 59, 198; deficit and,
    53, 57; education and, 200; health care
    and, 113–14; public lands and, 163–64
Clinton, Hillary, 113
Clovis, New Mexico, 128, 150–51
Coakley, Martha, 130
coal, 73, 77, 100, 154
Coalition Provisional Authority, 179–80
Coburn, Tom, 157
Cochran, Thad, 144
Cole, Tom, on government shutdown, 11
Collaborative Forest Landscape
    Restoration Program (CFLRP), 166–67
Collaborative Forest Restoration Program
    (CFRP), 166–67
College Board, AP courses and, 145–46
Commerce Committee, Senate, CAFE
    standards and, 92
commitment, politician, government
    shutdown as judge of, 13
committee process, bipartisan effort in,
    194–95
Common Core State Standards, for
    education, 147–48, 149, 200
compromise, in Congress, 40, 195–96

Congress, US, xiv, 26, 27, 52, 135–36, 192; Budget Office of, 9, 64, 115, 134; compromise in, 40, 195–96; Democrat controlled, vii, 89, 100, 112, 165, 198; difficult votes in, 29, 176–78; dysfunction of, xv, 3, 5; leverage in, 190–92, 202; negotiation tactics of, 4–8, 14–15, 17–20, 23–24, 185–86, 191, 201; public interest as mission of, 25, 189; Republican controlled, 84, 85, 86, 122, 133, 148; special interests and, xiv, 36–38, 190; subprime mortgage crisis and, 44–45

Congressional Budget Office (CBO), 9, 64, 115, 134

Congressional Office of Technology Assessment, 70

Congressional Research Service (CRS), ACA and, 118–19

conservatives, 33, 63, 94, 99, 105–6

Constitution, US, 30–31, 36–37, 122, 135–36, 187

consumer behavior, tax credit and, 81

continuing resolutions, for funding, 7, 8, 18, 61

contributions, political, special interests and, 38

Cornyn, John, 20

Corporate Average Fuel Economy (CAFE), 47–48, 78, 81, 91–92, 93, 106–7

cost: of government shutdown, 9; health care, 139, 140, 141, 198–99; nuclear energy, 89

Council of Chief State School Officers (CCSSO), 147

Covid pandemic, 36, 62, 71, 149

crisis: debt ceiling as manufactured, 3; economic, 62; oil, 77–79; subprime mortgage, 43, 43–45

CRS. See Congressional Research Service

Cruz, Ted, 19, 133

Cuban American lobby, 38

Customs and Border Protection Agency, US, 159

DACA. See Deferred Action for Childhood Arrivals

DARPA. See Defense Advanced Research Projects Agency

Daschle, Tom, 84

death panel, media and, 127, 128, 130

debt, 55, 63, 64; compared to debt ceiling, 17, 20; GDP relation to, 54, 55, 64

debt ceiling, 3, 15, 16, 19, 186; as negotiation tactic, 5, 6, 14–15, 17–20, 185–86, 201

DeBuys, Bill, 164

Declaration of National Emergency, border wall and, 12–13

Defense Advanced Research Projects Agency (DARPA), 96, 208n1

Defense Authorization Act, public lands and, 165–66

defense spending, Republican presidents and, 62

Deferred Action for Childhood Arrivals (DACA) (2012), 10, 12, 13

deficit, federal, 53, 55, 56–57, 60–63, 199; ARRA and, 51, 54; Deficit Reduction Act and, 57–58, 59

Deficit Reduction Act (1993), 57–58, 59

deliberation, in Senate, 20, 190–91

Democratic Party, 9–10, 31, 118; Congress controlled by, vii, 89, 100, 112, 165, 198; entitlement programs and, 59–60; Senate Campaign Committee (DSCC), 38; Steering Committee, 172

Democratic Senate Campaign Committee (DSCC), 38

Denmark, debt ceiling and, 186

Department of Agriculture, US, 155, 156, 162–63, 165, 166–67

Department of Defense, US, 66, 69, 70

Department of Education, US, 149, 200

Department of Energy, US (DOE), 34–35,

48, 69, 70-71, 78, 91; Loan Project
Office of, 97-98
Department of Energy Organization Act
(1977), 78
Department of Health and Human
Services, US (HHS), 120, 139
Department of Interior, US, 156, 158, 161,
165-66, 168
Department of Treasury, US, 44, 49
Dingell, John, 88
divided government, 26, 27
Dodd, Chris, 123, 194
DOE. *See* Department of Energy, US
Dole, Bob, viii, 58, 113, 114
Domenici, Pete, 84, 85-86, 195; Mimbres
and, 168; Valles Caldera and, 163-64
Downing Street Memo, 175, 178
Dr. Strangelove, or (film), 64
Dreamers. *See* Deferred Action for
Childhood Arrivals (DACA)
dropout rate, 149-50
drugs, prescription, costs of, 139, 141
DSCC. *See* Democratic Senate
Campaign Committee
Dunigan, Patrick, 162
Dunn, Walter, 167
dysfunction: of Congress, xiv-xv, 3, 5;
Senate, xiii

Earth Summit, IPCC, 80-81
economy, 58, 62; deficit impact on,
54-55, 57; fiscal policy effect on, 59-60;
industrial policy and, 74; science
and technology, 66, 67, 151; stimulus
package for, 49-51; subprime mortgage
crisis and, 43-45
Edelman, Marian Wright, 146
Edison, Thomas, 91
education, 67-68, 149-52, 165; Common
Core and, 147-48, 200; national goals
for, 143-45, 150. *See also* Elementary
and Secondary Education Act (ESEA)

(1965); Every Student Succeeds Act
(ESSA) (2015); No Child Left Behind
Act (NCLB)
EISA. *See* Energy Independence &
Security Act
Eisenhower, Dwight D., 67-68, 181-82
elections, xiii, 29, 82; Iraq invasion relation
to, 172, 175-78; policy stance and, 190;
special interests and, 37-38
electorate, polarization of, 194
electricity, energy efficiency and, 90-91
Elementary and Secondary Education Act
(ESEA) (1965), 142-43, 148
Emanuel, Rahm, 126
embargo, oil, 78
Emergency Stabilization Act (2008), 44
employer, health care and, 111-12, 117, 119,
121
The Endangered Species Act, 154, 157
Energy and Natural Resources
Committee, Senate, 34, 77, 83-85,
100-101; EISA and, 89-90; EPACT
and, 86-88; Omnibus Public Land
Management Act in, 157-58, 166-67,
201
energy consumption, 109
energy efficiency, electricity and, 90-91
Energy Independence & Security Act
(EISA) (2007), 47-48, 89-90, 92-94
Energy Policy Act (EPACT) (2005),
86-88, 93, 94; loan program of, 70-71,
96-97
Energy Policy and Conservation Act
(1975), 90
Energy Security Act (1979), 78
Energy Task Force, Bush-Cheney, 82-83,
84-85
entitlement programs, 59-60, 63, 112
Environmental Protection Agency (EPA),
vii-viii; Clean Power Plan of, 81, 106,
107
Enzi, Mike, 123

EPA. *See* Environmental Protection
  Agency
EPACT. *See* Energy Policy Act (2005)
Every Student Succeeds Act (ESSA)
  (2015), 68, 143, 147-48, 149
executive order, Trump and, 149
Exon, Jim, 16
Export-Import Bank, 74-75

fab. *See* semiconductor industry
Farm and Livestock Bureau, New Mexico,
  169
FDA. *See* Food and Drug Administration,
  US
FDR. *See* Roosevelt, Franklin Delano
Federal Energy Regulatory Commission
  (FERC), 73
Federal Land Policy Management Act
  (FLPMA), 156
Federal Law Enforcement Training
  Center (FLETC), 159
Federal Reserve, US, Great Recession
  and, 43-44
Feinstein, Dianne, 92
FERC. *See* Federal Energy Regulatory
  Commission
filibuster, ix, x, 6, 87, 187, 202; ACA and,
  130, 132; Bush-Cheney Energy Task
  Force and, 85-86; debt ceiling and, 16,
  17, 19, 186; presidential nominations
  and, 20-21; public lands and, 157-58
Finance Committee, Senate, 123-24, 130-31
First Amendment, US Constitution, 36-37
flag burning, public interest and, 30-31
Fleischer, Ari, 180
FLETC. *See* Federal Law Enforcement
  Training Center
FLPMA. *See* Federal Land Policy
  Management Act
Food and Drug Administration, US
  (FDA), tobacco industry and, 37
Ford, Gerald, viii

Forest Landscape Restoration Act (2009),
  167
Forest Service, 155, 166-67; Valles Caldera
  and, 162-63, 165
fossil fuels, 81, 93-94, 107, *108*; climate
  change and, 80, 105, 109. *See also*
  natural gas; oil
Founding Fathers, US, 23, 38-39, 156
Fourteenth Amendment, US
  Constitution, 187
Framework Convention on Climate
  Change, UN (UNFCCC), 80-81
Franklin, Benjamin, 63
Freedom Caucus, House of
  Representatives, 33
free market, 75; government bailouts
  and, 47-49; industrial policy and,
  66-67, 72
Frist, Bill, 84-86
Fukuyama, Francis, 72-73
funding: ACA, 138; bills for, 9, 12, 185;
  education, 146, 148, 151, 152

Gang of Six, 124, 125-26, 130-31
Garland, Merrick, 22
gasoline, 79; EISA and, 90; tax on, 58, 91
GDP. *See* gross domestic product
Geithner, Tim, 3-4, 44
General Motors (GM), 48
GHG. *See* greenhouse gas
Gingrich, Newt, viii-ix, 58-59;
  government shutdown and, 4-5,
  7-8, 13
Ginsburg, Ruth Bader, 122, 135-36
global warming. *See* climate change
goals, 189; national education, 143-45, 150
Goddard Institute for Space Studies,
  NASA, 79
Goldwater, Barry, vii
GOMESA. *See* Gulf of Mexico Energy
  Security Act
Gore, Al, 53

governing norms, 4, 25, 185; appropriations bill as, 6-7; debt ceiling as, 14, 16; Supreme Court nominees and, 22

Grant County Archaeological Society, 168

Grassley, Chuck, 22, 125, 129-30

Great Recession (2008-2009), 43, 43-44, 60

greenhouse gas (GHG), 77, 79-80, 91, 100, 109, 199-200

Greenspan, Alan, 46, 60

Grisham, Michelle Lujan, 28

gross domestic product (GDP), 54, 55, 56, 64, 68; health care costs and, 139, *140*

growth, economic, 58

Gulf of Mexico Energy Security Act (GOMESA) (2006), 161

Hansen, James, 79-80

Hatch, Orrin, 51, 114

health care, 111-14, 128-29, 138; cost of, 139, *140*, 141, 198-99; Obama and, 115-16, 125; undocumented immigrants and, 117, 118. *See also* Affordable Care Act (ACA) (2010); Medicaid; Medicare

health science, NIH and, 68-69

Heinrich, Martin, 165-66

HELP Committee, Senate, 117, 123-24

Heritage Foundation, 113, 121

Heston, Charlton, 37-38

Hewett, Edgar Lee, 162

HHS. *See* Department of Health and Human Services

Holmes, Josh, 133

Hospital Readmissions Reduction Program, 120-21

House of Representatives, US, 33, 87, 100; Rules Committee, 33-34; Senate compared to, 28-29; Solyndra hearings in, 97-98

Hulse, Carl, 133

Humphrey, Herbert, vii

Hussein, Saddam, 171, 174-78, 180

Idaho, 137

ideology, political, xiv, 33, 65, 76, 153-54, 193; anti-government, 36, 64, 141, 143; climate change and, 94, 99, 105-6; industrial policy and, 73-74; libertarian, 35-36; public interest and, 31-32

immigrants, undocumented, health care and, 117, 118

immigration laws, 191

impeachment, of Nixon, viii

impediments, to serving public interest, 25, 52, 65, 76

INC. *See* Iraqi National Congress

independent voters, 28

individual mandate, ACA, 33, 36, 121-22, 125, 129, 135

industrialized world, education in, 150-51

industries, emerging, 69-71, 72-73, 74

institutions, financial, subprime mortgages and, 43-45

insurance, health, 111-12, 117, 118-20, 123, 139

insurance industry, 120; as special interest, 38, 114, 141

Intel, semiconductor industry of, 65-66

interest, low, national debt and, 64

Intergovernmental Panel on Climate Change, UN (IPCC), 80

Iraq, war in, 174, 180, 181, 197-98; election relation to, 172, 175-78; House Rules Committee and, 33-34; Operation Shock and Awe, 179; public sentiment and, 30, 171, 175, 176, 182

Iraq Body Count (organization), 181

Iraqi National Congress (INC), 179

Israel, 38, 78

Jackson, Scoop, 193

Japan, semiconductor industry in, 65-66

Jeffords, Jim, 83

jobs, creation of, 65, 69, 71, 74

Johnson, Lyndon Baines (LBJ), 112, 142-43, 193

war and, 30, 171, 175, 176, 182; public
    lands and, 157, 163
public support, public interest compared
    to, 30
"put America first" ideology, 31

Rand, Ayn, 35-36
Rather, Dan, xiii
Rattner, Steven, 49, 207n6
Reagan, Ronald, viii, 32, 56, 155, 197
recession, 2008, 17, 116, 199
reconciliation bill, 19, 132, 186
reform, filibuster, x, 187, 202
Reid, Harry, 9, 90, 131; cap-and-trade
    proposals and, 102-3; filibuster and,
    20-21, 187
renewable energy, 95, 101, 103; EPACT
    loans for, 70-71, 96-98
repeal and replace, ACA, 133-35, 141
representation, two-party, 26, 27
Republican National Convention, 57
Republican Party, 9, 20, 28, 47, 145, 149;
    climate change and, 94, 99; Congress
    controlled by, 84, 85, 86, 122, 133, 148;
    Contract with America as platform
    for, 58-59; health care and, 113, 115;
    ideologies of, 31-32, 62, 141; New
    Mexico state, 53; Senate Campaign
    Committee, 173
research, and development, 68-69, 92, 111;
    ARPA-E and, 95-96, 200-201
Reserve, New Mexico, 129
revenue, from public lands, 159-61, 164-65
Rising above the Gathering Storm (NAS),
    66, 96
Roberts, John, 135
Rocky Mountain Legal Foundation, 155
Romer, Roy, 144
Romney, George, 49
Romney, Mitt, 49, 121
Roosevelt, Franklin Delano (FDR), 27,
    74, 75

Roosevelt, Teddy, 111, 158
Rove, Karl, 172, 173
Rubin, Bob, 57
Rumsfeld, Donald, 30, 172-74, 179
Ryan, Murray, 129
Ryan, Paul, 134

Sagebrush Rebellion, 155
Sanders, Bernie, 46
Sandia National Laboratory, 88
Santa Clara Pueblo Indians, 164
Scalia, Antonin, 22, 30, 122
SCHIP. See State Children's Health
    Insurance Program (1997)
Schmitt, Harrison "Jack," xiii
Schumer, Chuck, 11, 19-20, 185
science, and technology, 68-71, 151-52,
    200; national security and, 67, 75-76;
    semiconductor industry as, 65-66
Second Liberty Bonds Act (1917), 14
security, national, 68-69; Iraq and, 171-72,
    197-98; science and technology for,
    67, 75-76
Sellers, Peter, 64
Sematech, 65-66, 70
semiconductor industry, 65-66
Senate, US, xiii, 38; Armed Services
    Committee, 66, 172-74, 180-81;
    cap-and-trade proposals in,
    102-4; Commerce Committee, 92;
    deliberation in, 20, 190-91; Energy and
    Natural Resources Committee, 34, 77,
    83-85, 86-88, 89-90, 100-101, 157-58,
    166-67, 201; Finance Committee,
    123, 124, 130-31; HELP Committee,
    117, 123-24; House compared to,
    28-29; Judiciary Committee, 188;
    party line votes in, 83, 124; presidential
    nominations and, 5, 6; Republican
    Campaign Committee, 173; Supreme
    Court nominees refused by, 6, 22-23,
    187-88